# HOW TO
# THINK LIKE
# A ROMAN
# EMPEROR

OTHER TITLES BY DONALD ROBERTSON

*The Philosophy of Cognitive-Behavioural Therapy:*
*Stoic Philosophy as Rational and Cognitive Psychotherapy (2010)*

*The Practice of Cognitive-Behavioural Hypnotherapy:*
*A Manual for Evidence-Based Clinical Hypnosis (2012)*

*Build Your Resilience (2012)*

*Stoicism and the Art of Happiness (2013)*

Enroll in the free e-learning course:
learn.donaldrobertson.name/p/roman-emperor

# HOW TO
# THINK LIKE
# A ROMAN
# EMPEROR

## THE STOIC PHILOSOPHY OF
## MARCUS AURELIUS

## DONALD ROBERTSON

St. Martin's Press  New York

www.stmartins.com

The Library of Congress Cataloging-in-Publication Data is available upon request.

ISBN 978-1-250-19662-0 (hardcover)
ISBN 978-1-250-19663-7 (ebook)

Our books may be purchased in bulk for promotional, educational, or business use. Please contact your local bookseller or the Macmillan Corporate and Premium Sales Department at 1-800-221-7945, extension 5442, or by email at MacmillanSpecialMarkets@macmillan.com.

First Edition: April 2019

10   9   8   7   6   5   4   3   2   1

*For Poppy, little and wise*

# CONTENTS

Introduction                                                    *1*

1. The Dead Emperor                                            *17*
   ⟫ THE STORY OF STOICISM ⟪

2. The Most Truthful Child in Rome                             *45*
   ⟫ HOW TO SPEAK WISELY ⟪

3. Contemplating the Sage                                      *83*
   ⟫ HOW TO FOLLOW YOUR VALUES ⟪

4. The Choice of Hercules                                     *113*
   ⟫ HOW TO CONQUER DESIRE ⟪

5. Grasping the Nettle                                        *155*
   ⟫ HOW TO TOLERATE PAIN ⟪

6. The Inner Citadel and War of Many Nations                 *187*
   ⟫ HOW TO RELINQUISH FEAR ⟪

7. Temporary Madness                                         *217*
   ⟫ HOW TO CONQUER ANGER ⟪

8. Death and the View from Above                             *253*

Acknowledgments                                        *271*

Notes                                                 *273*

Bibliography                                          *279*

Index                                                 *283*

# HOW TO THINK LIKE A ROMAN EMPEROR

# INTRODUCTION

When I was thirteen years old, my father died. He'd developed lung cancer in his fifties, which left him bedridden for a year before it finally killed him. He was a humble and decent man, who encouraged me to think more deeply about life.

I was totally unprepared for his death, and I coped with it badly. I became angry and depressed. I'd stay out all night, playing cat and mouse with the local cops, breaking into buildings and waiting for them to arrive so I could run into gardens and dive over hedges and fences to lose them. I was always in trouble, either for skipping lessons at school, arguing with my teachers, or getting in fights with my classmates. As soon as my sixteenth birthday came around, I was marched briskly down to the headmaster's office and given two choices: either leave voluntarily or be expelled. So I left, and I was subsequently placed in a special program for troubled kids. I felt that my life was spiraling rapidly out of control. I'd been labeled a "write-off" by school and social services. I didn't really see any point trying to prove them wrong.

Each evening my father would come home from his work as a digger driver on building sites and collapse exhausted in an armchair, hands covered in grease and dirt. The job didn't pay well, and he hadn't two pennies to rub together, but he never complained. When he was a young man, his best friend had passed away, leaving my father a farm in his will, to everyone's surprise. He refused the bequest, returning the land to the other man's family. He used to say, "Money won't bring you happiness," and he really believed that. He showed me that there are more important things in life and that true wealth comes from being contented with whatever you have rather than desiring to have more and more.

After my father's funeral, my mother placed his old leather wallet on the dining room table and told me to take it. I opened it slowly; I think my hands were shaking but I'm not sure why. Inside there was nothing except a badly worn scrap of paper. It turned out to be a passage he'd torn from the Book of Exodus: "And God said unto Moses, I AM THAT I AM: and he said, Thus shalt thou say unto the children of Israel, I AM hath sent me unto you." I was desperate to understand what on earth those words could possibly have meant to him. My own philosophical journey began *precisely* at that moment, as I stood there perplexed, with that piece of paper in my hand.

When I learned many years later that Marcus Aurelius had lost his father at an early age, I wondered if he'd been left searching in the same way I had for a sense of direction. After my father's death, I was left with religious and philosophical questions that troubled me very deeply. I remember being terrified of dying. I would lie in bed at night unable to sleep, trying to solve the riddle of existence and find some consolation. It was as though I had an itch at the back of my brain that I needed to scratch but couldn't quite reach. I didn't know it at the time, but that sort of existential anxiety is a common experience that drives people to the study of philosophy. The philosopher Spinoza, for example, wrote:

> I thus perceived that I was in a state of great peril, and I compelled myself to seek with all my strength for a remedy, however uncertain it might be; as a sick man struggling with a deadly disease, when he sees that death will surely be upon him unless a remedy be found, is compelled to seek such a remedy with all his strength, inasmuch as his whole hope lies therein.[1]

I took the phrase "I am that I am" to refer to the pure awareness of existence itself, which at first seemed like something deeply mystical or metaphysical to me: "I am the consciousness of my own existence." It reminded me of the famous inscription from the Delphic Oracle's shrine: *Know Thyself.* That became one of my maxims. I grew quite obsessed with the pursuit of self-knowledge, through meditation and all forms of contemplative exercises.

I found out later that the passage my father carried with him all those years plays an important role in the rites of a Masonic chapter called the "Royal Arch." During initiation the candidate is asked, "Are you a Royal Arch Mason?" to which he replies, "I—AM—THAT—I—AM." Freemasonry has a long history in Scotland, going back at least four centuries, and it has deep roots in my hometown of Ayr. My father and many of my friends' fathers were members of the local lodge. Most Freemasons are Christians, but they employ nondenominational language, referring to God as "the Great Architect of the Universe." According to the legend presented in some of their texts, a set of spiritual teachings originating with the builders of King Solomon's temple was brought to the West by the philosopher Pythagoras and further disseminated by Plato and Euclid. This ancient wisdom was reputedly handed down through the centuries by medieval Masonic lodges. They used esoteric rituals, geometric symbols such as the square, and compasses to convey their spiritual doctrines. Freemasonry also celebrates the four cardinal virtues of Greek philosophy, which correspond symbolically with the four corners of the lodge: *Prudence*, *Justice*, *Fortitude*, and *Temperance*. (Wisdom, justice, courage, and moderation, if you prefer more modern terms.) My father took these ethical teachings seriously, and they shaped his character in a way that left a lasting impression on me. Freemasonry, at least for sincere practitioners like my father, didn't represent the bookish sort of philosophy taught in the ivory towers of universities, but rather something derived from a much older conception of Western philosophy as a spiritual *way of life*.

As it happened, I wasn't old enough to become a Freemason, and with my reputation around town I wouldn't have been invited to join anyway. So, with negligible formal education behind me, I began reading everything I could about philosophy and religion. I'm not sure I would have even been able to articulate exactly what I was looking for at that time, except that it would have to somehow combine my interests in philosophy, meditation, and psychotherapy. I needed a more rational, philosophical guide to life, but nothing seemed to fit the bill. Then I had the good fortune to encounter Socrates.

I had been studying the collection of ancient Gnostic texts discovered at Nag Hammadi in Egypt, which are inflected with Greek philosophy. This led me to begin reading the Platonic dialogues, which portray Socrates, the quintessential Greek philosopher, questioning his friends and other interlocutors about their deepest values. He tended to focus on the cardinal virtues of Greek philosophy, later adopted by Freemasons. Socrates didn't write any books on philosophy—we know about him only through the works of others, mainly dialogues written by two of his most famous students, Plato and Xenophon. According to legend, Socrates was the first person to apply the philosophical method to *ethical* questions. He particularly wanted to help others to live wisely, in accord with reason. For Socrates, philosophy was not only a moral guide but also a kind of *psychological therapy*. Doing philosophy, he said, can help us overcome our fear of death, improve our character, and even find a genuine sense of fulfillment.

The Socratic dialogues are often notoriously *inconclusive*. Indeed, Socrates's insistence that he knew that he knew nothing about certain matters, referred to as "Socratic irony," later inspired the tradition known as Greek Skepticism. Nevertheless, he appears to have communicated *positive* teachings to his students about the best way to live. The cornerstone of these is captured in a famous passage from Plato's *Apology*. Socrates faces the trumped-up charges of impiety and corrupting the youth, which would lead to his execution. Rather than apologize, though, or plead for mercy and parade his weeping wife and children before the jury as others did, he just carries on doing philosophy by questioning his accusers and lecturing the jury on ethics. At one point, he explains in plain language what it means to him to be a *philosopher*:

> For I go around doing nothing but persuading both young and old among you not to care for your body or your wealth in preference to or as strongly as for the best possible state of your soul, as I say to you: "Wealth does not bring about virtue, but virtue

makes wealth and everything else good for men, both individually and collectively."[2]

That's how he lived his life, and his students sought to emulate that example. We are to place more importance upon wisdom and virtue than anything else. A "philosopher," in Socrates's
sense, is therefore a person who lives according to these values:
someone who literally *loves wisdom*, the original meaning of the
word.

Looking back, I realize that I turned to Socrates and other
ancient philosophers to find a *philosophy of life* like the one my
father had found in Freemasonry. However, as mentioned earlier,
the surviving dialogues typically portray Socrates's method of
questioning rather than providing a detailed *practical* account of
the Socratic art of living wisely.

While the ancient philosophers didn't provide me with the
practical answers I was looking for back then, they did inspire
me to read further. My newfound sense of purpose also helped
me to get my life back on track: I stopped getting in trouble and
enrolled to study philosophy at university, in Aberdeen. I noticed,
though, that something wasn't right—the way we approached
the subject was too *academic* and *theoretical*. The more time I
spent in the basement of the library poring over books, the further away I seemed to be drifting from Socrates's original conception of philosophy as a way of life, something that could
improve our character and help us flourish. If ancient philosophers were veritable *warriors* of the mind, their modern counter-
parts had become more like *librarians* of the mind, more interested
in collating and organizing ideas than putting philosophy to work
on a daily basis as a psychological practice.

Upon graduating, I began studying and training in psychotherapy because learning to help others seemed to offer me a route to self-improvement that I could relate to my studies in philosophy. It was a time of transition for the therapy field: Freudian and Jungian psychoanalytic approaches were slowly giving way to cognitive-behavioral therapy (CBT), which has since become the dominant form of evidence-based practice in psychotherapy. CBT was closer to the philosophical practice I was looking for because it encourages us to apply reason to our emotions. However, it's something you typically do for a few months and then set aside. It certainly doesn't aim to provide us with a whole way of life.

Modern therapy is necessarily more modest in scope than the ancient Socratic art of living—most of us these days are looking for a quick solution to our mental health problems. Nevertheless, once I started working as a psychotherapist, it became evident to me that most of my clients who suffered from anxiety or depression benefited from the realization that their distress was due to their underlying *values*. Everyone knows that when we believe very strongly that something very bad has happened, we typically become upset as a result. Likewise, if we believe that something is very good and desirable, we become anxious when it's threatened or sad if it has already been lost. For example, in order to feel social anxiety, you have to believe that other people's negative opinions of you are *worth* getting upset about, that it's really bad if they dislike you and really important to win their approval. Even people who suffer from severe social anxiety disorder (social phobia) tend to feel "normal" when speaking to children or to their close friends about trivial matters, with a few exceptions. Nevertheless, they feel *highly* anxious when talking to people they think are very important about subjects they think are very important. If your fundamental worldview, by contrast, assumes that your status in the eyes of others is of *negligible* importance, then it follows that you should be beyond the reach of social anxiety.

Anyone, I reasoned, who could adopt a healthier and more rational set of core values, with greater indifference toward the things most of us worry about in life, should be able to become much more emotionally resilient. I just couldn't figure out how to combine the philosophy and values of Socrates with something like the therapeutic tools of CBT. Around that time, though, as I was training in counseling and psychotherapy, everything changed for me because I suddenly discovered *Stoicism*.

The potential value of Stoicism struck me immediately when I stumbled across the French scholar Pierre Hadot's *What Is Ancient Philosophy?* (1998) and *Philosophy as a Way of Life* (2004). As the latter title implies, Hadot explored in depth the idea that ancient Western philosophers did in fact approach philosophy as a way of life. My eyes were opened to a whole treasure trove of *spiritual practices*, tucked away in the literature of Greek and Roman philosophy, which were clearly designed to help people overcome emotional suffering and develop strength of character. Hadot discovered that contemplative practices became very common in the philosophical schools of the Hellenistic period, a few generations after the death of Socrates. The Stoic school in particular focused on the practical side of Socratic philosophy, not only through the development of virtues such as self-discipline and courage (what we might call emotional resilience) but also through extensive use of psychological exercises.

Something puzzled me, though. Hadot compared these philosophical practices to early Christian spiritual exercises. As a psychotherapist, I spotted immediately that most of the *philosophical* or *spiritual* exercises he identified could be compared to *psychological* exercises found in modern psychotherapy. It very soon became evident to me that Stoicism was, in fact, the school of ancient Western philosophy with the most explicitly therapeutic orientation and the largest armamentarium, or toolbox, of psychological techniques at its disposal. After scouring books on philosophy for over a decade, I realized that I'd been looking *everywhere* except in the right place. "The stone the builders rejected has become the cornerstone" (118th Psalm).

As I began to devour the literature on Stoicism, I noticed that the form of modern psychotherapy most akin to it was rational emotive behavior therapy (REBT), the main precursor to CBT, first developed by Albert Ellis in the 1950s. Ellis and Aaron T. Beck, the other main pioneer of CBT, had both cited Stoic philosophy as the inspiration for their respective approaches. For instance, Beck and his colleagues had written in *The Cognitive Therapy of Depression*, "The philosophical origins of cognitive therapy can be traced back to the Stoic philosophers."[3] Indeed, CBT and Stoicism have some fundamental psychological assumptions in common, particularly the "cognitive theory of emotion," which holds that our emotions are mainly determined by our beliefs. Anxiety largely consists of the belief, for example, that "something bad is going to happen," according to Beck. From shared premises, moreover, Stoicism and CBT were bound to arrive at similar conclusions about what sort of psychological techniques might be helpful to people suffering from anxiety, anger, depression, and other problems.

One Stoic technique particularly caught my attention. Although it's well attested in the ancient sources, there's very little mention of anything like the "view from above"—as Hadot called it—in modern psychotherapy or self-help literature. It involves picturing events as though seen from high overhead, as they might be seen by the gods atop Mount Olympus, perhaps. Broadening our perspective often induces a sense of emotional equanimity. As I practiced it myself, I noticed, as Hadot did, that it brings together a confluence of themes central to ancient philosophy in a single vision. I also found that it was easy to turn it into a guided meditation script. As I was now training psychotherapists myself and speaking at conferences, I was able to guide rooms full of experienced therapists and trainees, up to a hundred at a time, through my version of the exercise. I was pleasantly surprised to discover that they took to it instantly, and it became one of their favorite exercises. They would describe how they were able to remain exceptionally calm while contemplating their situation in life from a detached perspective. I began sharing my resources online via my personal blog.

In America, the marketer and entrepreneur Ryan Holiday embraced Stoicism in *The Obstacle Is the Way* (2014) and *The Daily Stoic* (2016, coauthored with Stephen Hanselman). In the UK, the illusionist and television celebrity Derren Brown later published a book called *Happy* (2017), which drew inspiration from the Stoics. These authors were reaching a whole new audience far beyond academia and introducing it to Stoicism as a form of self-help and a philosophy of life. The scientific skeptic and professor of philosophy Massimo Pigliucci published *How to Be a Stoic* in 2017. In the same year, Republican politician Pat McGeehan released *Stoicism and the Statehouse*. Stoicism was also being used in the military, as part of Colonel Thomas Jarrett's Warrior Resilience Training. The NFL executive and former New England Patriots coach Michael Lombardi embraced it, and the philosophy began to gain more and more adherents from the world of sports. Stoicism was clearly experiencing a resurgence in popularity, and this was just the tip of the iceberg. Online communities for Stoics were flourishing, attracting hundreds of thousands of members across the internet.

## TELLING THE STORY OF STOICISM

A few years ago, when my daughter Poppy was four, she began asking me to tell her stories. I didn't know any children's stories, so I told her what came to mind: Greek myths, stories about heroes and philosophers. One of her favorites was about the Greek general Xenophon. Late one night, as a young man, he was walking through an alleyway between two buildings near the Athenian marketplace. Suddenly a mysterious stranger, hidden in the shadows, blocked his path with a wooden staff. A voice inquired from the darkness, "Do you know where someone should go if he wants to buy *goods*?" Xenophon replied that they were right beside the *agora*, the finest marketplace in the world. There you could buy any goods your heart desired: jewelry, food, clothing, and so on. The stranger paused for a moment before asking another question: "Where, then, should one go in order to learn how to become a *good person*?" Xenophon was dumbstruck. He had no idea how to answer. The mysterious figure then lowered his staff, stepped out of the shadows, and introduced himself as Socrates. Socrates said that they should both try to discover how someone could become a good person, because that's surely more important than knowing where to buy all sorts of goods. So Xenophon went with Socrates and became one of his closest friends and followers.

I told Poppy that *most* people believe there are lots of good things—nice food, clothes, houses, money, etc.—and lots of bad things in life, but Socrates said perhaps they're all wrong. He wondered if there was only one good thing, and if it was inside of us rather than outside. Maybe it was something like wisdom or bravery. Poppy thought for a minute, then, to my surprise, she shook her head, saying, "That's not true, Daddy!" which made me smile. Then she said something else: "*Tell me that story again*," because she wanted to continue to think about it. She asked me how Socrates became so wise, and I told her the secret of his wisdom: he asked lots of questions about the most important things in life, and then he listened very carefully to the answers. So I kept telling stories, and she kept asking lots of questions. As I came to realize, these little anecdotes about Socrates did much more than just teach her things. They encouraged her to think for *herself* about what it means to live wisely.

One day, Poppy asked me to write down the stories I was telling her, so I did. I made them longer and more detailed, then I read them back to her. I shared some of them online, via my blog. Telling her these stories and discussing them with her made me realize that this was, in many ways, a better approach to teaching philosophy as a way of life. It allowed us to consider the example set by famous philosophers and whether or not they provide good role models. I began to think that a book that taught Stoic principles through real stories about its ancient practitioners might prove helpful not just to my little girl but to other people as well.

Next, I asked myself who was the best candidate to use as a Stoic role model, about whom I could tell stories that would bring the philosophy to life and put flesh on its bones. The obvious answer was Marcus Aurelius. We know very little about the lives of most ancient philosophers, but Marcus was a Roman emperor, so far more evidence survives about his life and character. One of the few surviving Stoic texts consists of his personal notes to himself about his contemplative practices, known today as *The Meditations*. Marcus begins *The Meditations* with a chapter written in a completely different style from the rest of the book: a catalogue of the virtues, the traits he most admired in his family and teachers. He lists about sixteen people in all. It seems he also believed the best way to begin studying Stoic philosophy was to look at living examples of the virtues. I think it makes sense to view Marcus's life as an example of Stoicism in the same way that he viewed the lives of his own Stoic teachers.

The following chapters are all based upon a careful reading of history. Although I've drawn on a wide range of sources, we learn about Marcus's life and character mainly from the Roman historical accounts in Cassius Dio, Herodian, and the *Historia Augusta*, as well as from Marcus's own words in *The Meditations*. Sometimes I've added minor details or pieces of dialogue to flesh out the story, but this is how, based on the available evidence, I imagine the events of Marcus's life to have unfolded.

The final chapter of this book is written in a different style, resembling a guided meditation. It's closely based on ideas presented in *The Meditations* of Marcus Aurelius, although I've paraphrased his words to turn them into a longer account that's deliberately intended to evoke mental imagery and a more elaborate contemplative experience. I've also included a few sayings and ideas derived from other Stoic authors. I gave it the form of an internal monologue or fantasy because I felt that was a good way to present the Stoic contemplation of death and the "view from above."

This entire book is designed to help you follow Marcus in acquiring Stoic strength of mind and eventually a more profound sense of fulfillment. You'll find that I've combined Stoicism with elements of CBT in many places, which as we've seen is only natural because CBT was inspired by Stoicism and they have some fundamental things in common. So you'll notice that I refer to modern therapeutic ideas like "cognitive distancing," which is the ability to distinguish our thoughts from external reality, and "functional analysis," which is evaluating the consequences of different courses of action. CBT is a short-term therapy, a *remedial* approach to mental health issues like anxiety and depression. Everyone knows that prevention is better than cure. Techniques and concepts from CBT have been adapted for use in resilience building, to reduce the risk of developing serious emotional problems in the future. However, I believe that for many people a combination of Stoic philosophy and CBT may be even more suited for use as a long-term *preventive* approach. When we take it on as a philosophy of life, with daily practice, we have the opportunity to learn greater emotional resilience, strength of character, and moral integrity. That's what this book is really about.

The Stoics can teach you how to find a sense of purpose in life, how to face adversity, how to conquer anger within yourself, moderate your desires, experience healthy sources of joy, endure pain and illness patiently and with dignity, exhibit courage in the face of your anxieties, cope with loss, and perhaps even confront your own mortality while remaining as unperturbed as Socrates. Marcus Aurelius faced colossal challenges during his reign as emperor of Rome. *The Meditations* provides a window into his soul, allowing us to see how he guided himself through it all. Indeed, I would invite you, as a reader, to put effort into reading this book in a special way, to try and place yourself in Marcus's shoes and look at life through his eyes, through the lens of his philosophy. Let's see if we can accompany him on the journey he made as he transformed himself, day by day, into a fully-fledged Stoic. Fate permitting, more people may be able to apply the wisdom of Stoicism to the real challenges and everyday problems of modern living. However, that change won't leap off the page. It only comes by making a firm decision, here and now, to begin putting ideas like these into practice. As Marcus wrote to himself,

> Waste no more time arguing about what a good man should be; just be one.[4]

# 1.

# THE DEAD EMPEROR

The year is 180 AD. As another long and difficult winter draws to a close on the northern frontier, the Roman emperor Marcus Aurelius lies dying in bed at his military camp in Vindobona (modern-day Vienna). Six days ago he was stricken with a fever, and the symptoms have been worsening rapidly. It's clear to his physicians that he is finally about to succumb to the great Antonine Plague (probably a strain of smallpox), which has been ravaging the empire for the past fourteen years. Marcus is nearly sixty and physically frail, and all the signs show he's unlikely to recover. However, to the physicians and courtiers present he seems strangely calm, almost indifferent. He has been preparing for this moment most of his life. The Stoic philosophy he follows has taught him to practice contemplating his own mortality calmly and rationally. To learn how to die, according to the Stoics, is to unlearn how to be a slave.

This philosophical attitude toward death didn't come naturally to Marcus. His father passed away when Marcus was only a few years old, leaving him a solemn child. When he reached seventeen, he was adopted by the Emperor Antoninus Pius as part of a long-term succession plan devised by his predecessor, Hadrian, who had foreseen the potential for wisdom and greatness in Marcus even as a small boy. Nevertheless, he had been most reluctant to leave his mother's home for the imperial palace. Antoninus summoned the finest teachers of rhetoric and philosophy to train Marcus in preparation for succeeding him as emperor. Among his tutors were experts on Platonism and Aristotelianism, but his main philosophical education was in Stoicism. These men became like family to him. When one of his most beloved tutors died, it's said that Marcus wept so violently that the palace servants tried to restrain him. They were worried that people would find his behavior unbecoming of a future ruler. However, Antoninus told them to leave Marcus alone: "Let him be only a man for once; for neither philosophy nor empire takes away natural feeling." Years later, after having lost several young children, Marcus was once again moved to tears in public while presiding over a legal case, when he heard an advocate say in the course of his argument: "Blessed are they who died in the plague."[1]

Marcus was a naturally loving and affectionate man, deeply affected by loss. Over the course of his life, he increasingly turned to the ancient precepts of Stoicism as a way of coping when those closest to him were taken. Now, as he lies dying, he reflects once again on those he has lost. A few years earlier, the Empress Faustina, his wife of thirty-five years, passed away. He'd lived long enough to see eight of their thirteen children die. Four of his eight daughters survived, but only *one* of his five sons, Commodus. Death was everywhere, though. During Marcus's reign, millions of Romans throughout the empire had been killed by war or disease. The two went hand in hand, as the legionary camps were particularly vulnerable to outbreaks of plague, especially during the long winter months. The air around him is still thick with the sweet smell of frankincense, which the Romans vainly hoped might help prevent the spread of the disease. For over a decade now, the scent of smoke and incense had been a reminder to Marcus that he was living under the shadow of death and that survival from one day to the next should never be taken for granted.

Infection with the plague wasn't always fatal. However, Marcus's celebrated court physician, Galen, had observed that victims inevitably die when their feces turn black, a sign of intestinal bleeding. Perhaps that's how Marcus's doctors know he is dying, or maybe they just realize how frail he's become with age. Throughout his adult life he had been prone to chronic chest and stomach pains and bouts of illness. His appetite had always been poor. Now he *voluntarily* rejects food and drink to hasten his own demise. Socrates used to say that death is like some prankster in a scary mask, dressed as a bogeyman to frighten small children. The wise man carefully removes the mask and, looking behind it, he finds nothing worth fearing. Because of this lifelong preparation, now that his death finally draws near, Marcus is no more afraid of it than when it seemed far away. He therefore asks his physicians to describe patiently and in detail what's happening inside his body, so that he may contemplate his own symptoms with the studied indifference of a natural philosopher. His voice is weak and the sores in his mouth and throat make it difficult for him to speak. Before long he grows tired and gestures for them to leave, wishing to continue his meditations in private.

Alone in his room, as he listens to the sound of his own wheezing, he doesn't feel much like an emperor anymore—just a feeble old man, sick and dying. He turns his head to one side and catches a glimpse of his reflection on the polished surface of the goddess Fortuna's golden statuette by his bedside. His Stoic tutors advised him to practice a mental exercise when he noticed his own image. It's a way of building emotional resilience by training yourself to come to terms with your own mortality. Focusing his eyes weakly on his reflection, he tries to imagine one of the long-dead Roman emperors who preceded him gazing back. First he pictures Antoninus, his adoptive father, and then his adoptive grandfather, the emperor Hadrian. He even imagines his reflection slowly assuming the features depicted in paintings and sculptures of Augustus, who founded the empire two centuries earlier. As he does so, Marcus silently asks himself, "Where are they now?" and whispers the answer: "*Nowhere* . . . or at least nowhere of which we can speak."[2]

He continues to meditate patiently, albeit drowsily, on the mortality of the emperors who preceded him. There's nothing left of any of them now but bones and dust. Their once illustrious lives have gradually become insignificant to subsequent generations, who have already half-forgotten them. Even their names sound old, evoking memories of another era. As a boy, the Emperor Hadrian had befriended Marcus, and the two used to go boar hunting together. Now there are young officers under Marcus's command for whom Hadrian is just a name in the history books, his real, living body long ago replaced by lifeless portraits and statues. Antoninus, Hadrian, Augustus—all equally dead and gone. Everyone from Alexander the Great right down to his lowly mule driver ends up lying under the same ground. King and pauper alike, the same fate ultimately awaits everyone . . .

This train of thought is rudely interrupted by a bout of coughing that brings up blood and tissue from the ulceration at the back of his throat. The pain and discomfort of his fever vie for his attention, but Marcus turns this into another part of the meditation: he tells himself that he's just another one of these dead men. Soon he'll be nothing more than a name alongside theirs in the history books, and one day even his name will be forgotten. This is how he contemplates his own mortality: using one of the many centuries-old Stoic exercises learned in his youth. Once we truly accept our own demise as an inescapable fact of life, it makes no more sense for us to wish for immortality than to long for bodies as hard as diamonds or to be able to soar on the wings of a bird. As long as we can grasp the truth firmly enough that certain misfortunes are inevitable, we no longer feel the need to worry about them. Nor do we yearn for things that we accept are impossible, as long as we can see with crystal clarity that it is futile to do so. As death is among the most certain things in life, to a man of wisdom it should be among the least feared.

Although Marcus first began training in philosophy when he was just a boy of about twelve, his practice intensified in his mid-twenties, when he dedicated himself wholeheartedly to becoming a Stoic. Since then he has rehearsed his Stoic exercises daily, trained his mind and body to obey reason, and progressively transformed himself, both as a man and a ruler, into something approaching the Stoic ideal. He has tried to develop his own wisdom and resilience systematically, modeling himself after the philosophers who shared their teachings with him and the other great men who won his admiration, foremost among them Antoninus. He studied the way they met different forms of adversity with calm dignity. He carefully observed how they lived in accord with reason and exhibited the cardinal virtues of *wisdom*, *justice*, *fortitude*, and *temperance*. They felt the pain of loss but did not succumb to it. Marcus has been bereaved so many times, has practiced his response to it so often, that he no longer weeps uncontrollably. He no longer cries "Why?" and "How could this happen?" or even entertains such thoughts. He has firmly grasped the truth that death is both a natural and inevitable part of life. Now that his time has come he welcomes it with a philosophical attitude. You might even say that he has learned to befriend death. He still sheds tears and mourns losses, but as a wise man does. He no longer adds to his natural grief by complaining and shaking his fist at the universe.

Since completing his journal of reflections on philosophy several years earlier, Marcus has been passing through the final stage of a lifelong spiritual journey. Now lying in pain and discomfort, nearing the end, he gently reminds himself that he has already died many times along the way. First of all, Marcus the child died as he entered the imperial palace as heir to the throne, assuming the title Caesar after Hadrian passed away. After Antoninus passed away, Marcus the young Caesar had to die when he took his place as emperor of Rome. Leaving Rome behind to take command of the northern legions during the Marcomannic Wars signaled another death: a transition to a life of warfare and a sojourn in a foreign land. Now, as an old man, he faces his death not for the first time but for the last. From the moment we're born we're constantly dying, not only with each stage of life but also one day at a time. Our bodies are no longer the ones to which our mothers gave birth, as Marcus put it. Nobody is the same person he was yesterday. Realizing this makes it easier to let go: we can no more hold on to life than grasp the waters of a rushing stream.

Now Marcus is growing drowsy and on the verge of drifting off, but he rouses himself with some effort and sits up in his bed.

He has unfinished business to attend to. He orders the guards to send in the members of his family and his inner circle of courtiers, the "friends of the emperor," who have been summoned to his camp. Though he appears frail and has suffered from illness throughout his life, Marcus is famously resilient. He has seemed on the verge of dying before, but this time the physicians have confirmed to him that he is unlikely to survive. Everyone senses that the end is near. He bids farewell to his beloved friends, his sons-in-law, and his four remaining daughters. He would have kissed each one of them, but the plague forces them to keep their distance.

His son-in-law Pompeianus, his right-hand man and senior general during the Marcomannic Wars, is there as always. His lifelong friend Aufidius Victorinus, another one of his generals, is also present, as are Bruttius Praesens, the father-in-law of Commodus, and another of his sons-in-law, Gnaeus Claudius Severus, a close friend and fellow philosopher. They gather solemn-faced around his bed. Marcus stresses to them that they must take good care of Commodus, his only surviving son, who has ruled by his side as his junior co-emperor for the past three years. He has appointed the best teachers available for him, but their influence is waning. Commodus became emperor when he was only sixteen; Marcus had to wait until he was forty. Young rulers, such as the Emperor Nero, tend to be easily corrupted, and Marcus can see that his son is already falling in with bad company. He asks his friends, especially Pompeianus, to do him the honor of ensuring that Commodus's moral education continues as if he were their own son.

Marcus appointed Commodus his official heir, granting him the title Caesar when he was just five years old. Commodus's younger brother, Marcus Annius Verus, was also named Caesar, but he died shortly thereafter. Marcus had hoped that the two boys would rule jointly one day. Any succession plans Marcus agreed with the Senate were always going to be precarious. However, at the height of the plague, as the First Marcomannic War broke out, it was necessary for Rome's stability to have a designated heir in case a usurper tried to seize the throne. During a previous bout of illness five years earlier, rumors spread that Marcus had *already* passed away. His most powerful general in the eastern provinces, Avidius Cassius, was acclaimed emperor by the Egyptian legion, triggering a short-lived civil war. Marcus immediately had Commodus rushed from Rome to the northern frontier to assume the *toga virilis*, marking his official passage to adulthood. After the rebellion was put down, Marcus continued to accelerate the process of appointing Commodus emperor. If Marcus had died without an heir, another civil war would probably have ensued.

Likewise, replacing Commodus with a substitute ruler at this stage would leave the whole empire vulnerable. The northern tribes might seize the opportunity to renew their attacks, and another invasion could mean the end of Rome. Marcus's best hope now would be that Commodus might follow the guidance of his trusted teachers and advisors. He is being swayed, however, by various hangers-on who constantly plead with him to return to Rome. As long as he remains with the army, under the watchful eye of his brother-in-law Pompeianus, there's still hope that Commodus may learn to rule with wisdom. Unlike his father, though, he shows no interest in philosophy.

In the middle of their conversation, Marcus suddenly slumps forward and loses consciousness. Some of his friends are alarmed and start to weep uncontrollably because they assume he is slipping away. The physicians manage to rouse him. When Marcus sees the faces of his grieving companions, rather than fearing his own death his attention turns to theirs. He watches them weeping for him just as he had wept for his wife and children and so many lost friends and teachers over the years. Now that he is the one dying, though, *their* tears seem unnecessary. It feels pointless to lament over something inevitable and beyond anyone's control. It's more important to him that they calmly and prudently arrange the transition to Commodus's reign. Though Marcus is barely conscious, things somehow seem clearer than ever before. He wants those gathered to remember their own mortality, to accept its implications, grasp its significance, and live wisely, so he whispers, "Why do you weep for me instead of thinking about the plague . . . and about death as the common lot of us all?"

The room falls silent as his gentle admonition sinks in. The sobbing quiets down. Nobody knows what to say. Marcus smiles and gestures weakly, giving them permission to leave. His parting words are, "If you now grant me leave to go then I will bid you farewell and pass on ahead of you."[3] As the news of his condition spreads through the camp, the soldiers grieve loudly—because they love him much more than they care for his son Commodus.

The following day, Marcus awakens early, feeling extremely frail and weary. His fever is worse. Realizing that these are his last hours, he summons Commodus. The series of wars against hostile Germanic and Sarmatian tribes that Marcus has been fighting for over a decade now is already in its final stages. He urges his son to bring them to a satisfactory conclusion by assuming personal command of the army, pursuing the remaining enemy tribes until they surrender, and overseeing the complex peace negotiations currently underway. Marcus warns Commodus that if he doesn't remain at the front, the Senate may view it as a betrayal after so much has been invested in the long wars and so many lives have been lost in battle.

However, unlike his father, Commodus is *scared witless* of dying. Gazing upon Marcus's withered body, rather than being inspired to follow his father's virtuous example, he feels repulsed and afraid. He complains that he risks contracting the plague by remaining among the legions in the north and that he yearns more than anything to return to the safety of Rome. Marcus assures him that soon enough, as sole emperor, he may do as he wishes, but he orders Commodus to wait just a few days longer before leaving. Then, sensing the hour of his death looming, Marcus commands the soldiers to take Commodus into their protection so that the youth cannot be accused of having murdered his father. Marcus can only hope now that his generals will talk Commodus out of his reckless desire to abandon the northern frontier.

Marcus wrote that nobody is so fortunate as not to have one or two individuals standing by his deathbed who will welcome his demise.[4] He says that in his own case, as emperor, he can think of hundreds who hold values at odds with his own and would be only too glad to see him gone. They do not share his love of wisdom and virtue, and they sneer at his vision of an empire that makes the freedom of its citizens its highest goal. Nevertheless, philosophy has taught him to be grateful for life and yet unafraid of dying—like a ripened olive falling from its branch, thanking both the tree for giving it life and the earth below for receiving its seed as it falls. For the Stoics, death is just such a natural transformation, returning our body to the same source from which we came. At Marcus's funeral, therefore, the people will not say that he has been lost but that he has been returned to the gods and to Nature. Perhaps his friends voiced this sentiment in their eulogies because it sounds like a reference to the Stoic teachings Marcus held dear. Never say that *anything* has been lost, they tell us. Only that it has returned to Nature.

Commodus, unfortunately, surrounds himself with sycophants who constantly plead with him to return home, where they can enjoy greater luxury. "Why do you continue to drink this frigid mud, Lord Caesar, when we could be back at Rome drinking pure waters running hot and cold?" Only Pompeianus, the oldest among his advisors, confronts him, warning him that to leave the war unfinished would be both disgraceful and dangerous. Like Marcus, Pompeianus believes the enemy will view it as a cowardly retreat and gain confidence for future uprisings; the Senate will view it as incompetence. Commodus is persuaded for a short while, but eventually the lure of Rome is too great. He gives Pompeianus the excuse that he must return there in case a usurper suddenly appears, plotting an uprising in his absence. After Marcus is gone, Commodus will hastily conclude the war by paying huge bribes to the leaders of hostile Germanic and Sarmatian tribes. Fleeing from the army camps will undermine, at one fell swoop, whatever credibility he had with the troops who were so steadfastly loyal to his father. Instead, he must turn to the populace of Rome for support, resorting to expensive crowd-pleasing gestures to win popularity and increasingly behaving like a *celebrity* rather than a wise and benevolent ruler. The Stoics observed that often those who are most desperate to flee death find themselves rushing into its arms, and that seems eminently true of Commodus. Marcus lived to fifty-eight despite his frailty and illness and the harsh conditions he endured in command of the northern legions. By contrast, Commodus is destined to spiral into paranoia and violence following repeated assassination attempts. His enemies in Rome will eventually succeed in murdering him when he is still only *thirty-one* years old. No number of bodyguards, as Marcus once said, is enough to shield a ruler who does not possess the goodwill of his subjects.

The successor chosen by an emperor is an important part of his legacy. However, the Stoics taught that we can't control the actions of others and that even supremely wise teachers, such as Socrates, have wayward children and students. When Stilpo, a philosopher of the Megarian school, one of the predecessors of Stoicism, was criticized over the disreputable character of his daughter, he reputedly said that her actions no more brought dishonor to him than his own brought honor to her. As things turned out, Marcus's real legacy would not be Commodus but the inspiration that his own character and philosophy provided for generations to come. Like all Stoics, Marcus firmly believed that virtue must be its own reward. He was also content to accept that events in life, let alone after death, are never entirely up to us.

Nevertheless, the Stoics taught that the wise man is naturally inclined to write books that help other people. Sometime during his first campaign on the northern frontier, Marcus, separated from his beloved Stoic friends and teachers back in Rome, started writing down his personal reflections on philosophy as a series of short notes and maxims. He probably began not long after the death of his main Stoic tutor, Junius Rusticus. Perhaps he wrote as a way to cope with this blow, becoming his own teacher as a substitute for conversations with Rusticus. These collected reflections are known today as *The Meditations*. How the text survived is a mystery: it may have fallen into Commodus's possession, unless Marcus bequeathed it to someone else. Perhaps it changed hands at the final meeting with his courtiers. Disappointed by the feckless character of his son, the dying emperor would at least know that one of his trusted friends was already safeguarding *The Meditations*—his true gift to subsequent generations.

As soon as Commodus has gone, Marcus beckons the young officer of the night watch to lean in close and whispers something hoarsely in his ear. Then he wearily covers his head with a sheet and lapses into sleep, passing away quietly during the seventh night of his illness. In the morning, his physicians pronounce the emperor dead, and the camp is thrown into a state of anguished confusion. As news quickly reaches them, the soldiers and the people fill the streets, weeping. According to Herodian, a Roman historian who witnessed firsthand the reign of Commodus, the whole empire cried out as if in a single chorus when word spread of Marcus's death. They grieved for the loss of him as their "Kind Father," "Noble Emperor," "Brave General," and "Wise, Moderate Ruler," and, in Herodian's opinion, "every man spoke the truth."

As the hubbub outside grows louder, the nervous guards ask their tribune, "What did he say?" The officer looks like he's about to speak but then pauses for a moment. He furrows his brow in puzzlement as he relays the dead emperor's message: *"Go to the rising sun,"* he said, *"for I am already setting."*[5]

## THE STORY OF STOICISM

Marcus Aurelius was the last famous Stoic of the ancient world. However, the story of Stoicism began almost five hundred years prior to his death, with a *shipwreck*. A wealthy young Phoenician merchant from the island of Cyprus named Zeno of Citium was transporting his cargo of purple dye across the Mediterranean.

Many thousands of fermented shellfish had to be painstakingly dissected by hand to extract just a few grams of this priceless commodity, known as *imperial* or *royal* purple because it was used to dye the robes of emperors and kings. The ship was caught in a violent storm. Zeno narrowly escaped with his life and washed ashore at the Greek port of Piraeus. He watched helplessly from the beach as his precious cargo sank beneath the waves and dissolved back into the ocean from which it came.

According to one story, Zeno lost *everything* in this shipwreck. Devastated, he found himself living as a beggar after making his way to nearby Athens: a penniless immigrant in a foreign city. Searching for guidance about the best way to live, he trudged for miles to the Oracle of Delphi, where the god Apollo, speaking through his priestess, announced that Zeno should *take on the color not of dead shellfish but of dead men*. He must have been fairly bemused by this cryptic advice. Feeling completely at a loss, Zeno made his way back to Athens and collapsed in a heap at a bookseller's stall. There he started reading what, by chance, turned out to be a series of anecdotes about Socrates, written by Xenophon, one of his most distinguished students. The words Zeno read struck him like a thunderbolt and completely transformed his life.

Greek aristocrats traditionally believed that virtue was associated with noble birth. Socrates, however, argued that classical virtues like justice, courage, and temperance were all just forms of moral wisdom, which could potentially be learned by anyone. He taught Xenophon that people should train themselves to acquire wisdom and virtue through self-discipline. After Socrates was executed, Xenophon faithfully wrote down many recollections of Socrates's conversations about philosophy. Perhaps it was at this moment that Zeno suddenly realized what the Oracle meant: he was to "take on the color of dead men" by thoroughly absorbing the *teachings* of *wise* men from previous generations, teachings such as the very philosophical doctrines he was now reading in Xenophon's *Memorabilia* of Socrates.

Zeno dropped the book, jumped to his feet, and excitedly asked the bookseller, "Where can I find a man like this today?" It so happened that a famous Cynic philosopher called Crates of Thebes was passing by at that very moment, and the bookseller pointed him out, saying, "Follow yonder man." Sure enough, Zeno became Crates's follower, training in the Cynic philosophy founded by Diogenes of Sinope. Stoicism therefore evolved out of Cynicism, and the two traditions remained very closely associated right down to the time of Marcus Aurelius.

When we speak of "cynicism" (lowercase c) today, we mean something like an attitude of negativity and distrust, but that's only very tenuously related to the meaning of capital-C "Cynicism." The ancient philosophy of Cynicism focused on cultivating virtue and strength of character through rigorous training that consisted of enduring various forms of "voluntary hardship." It was an austere and self-disciplined way of life. Zeno's followers would later call it a *shortcut* to virtue. Nevertheless, he wasn't completely satisfied with the Cynic philosophy and apparently found its doctrines lacking in intellectual rigor. He therefore went on to study in the Academic and Megarian schools of philosophy, founded by Plato and Euclid of Megara, respectively, two of Socrates's most famous students. All of these schools focused on different aspects of philosophy: the Cynics on virtue and self-discipline, the Megarians on logic, and the Academics on metaphysical theories about the underlying nature of reality.

Zeno appears to have been trying to synthesize the best aspects of different Athenian philosophical traditions. However, the Cynic and Academic schools were often seen as representing fundamentally different assumptions about what it means to *be* a philosopher. The Cynics sneered at the pretentious and bookish nature of Plato's Academy. The Academics, in turn, thought the doctrines of the Cynics were crude and too extreme—Plato reputedly called Diogenes "Socrates gone mad." Zeno must have seen his own position as a compromise. His followers believed that studying philosophical theory, or subjects like logic and cosmology, can be good insofar as it makes us more virtuous and improves our character. However, it can also be a *bad* thing if it becomes so pedantic or overly "academic" that it *diverts* us from the pursuit of virtue. Marcus learned the same attitude from his Stoic teachers. He repeatedly warned himself not to become distracted by reading too many books—thus wasting time on trifling issues in logic and metaphysics—but instead to remain focused on the practical goal of living wisely.

After studying philosophy in Athens for about two decades, Zeno founded his own school in a public building overlooking the *agora* known as the *Stoa Poikile*, or "Painted Porch," where he used to vigorously pace up and down as he discoursed on philosophy. The students who gathered there were originally known as Zenonians but later called themselves Stoics, after the *stoa*, or porch. It's possible the name "Stoic" also hints at the practical, down-to-earth nature of the philosophy. It arose on the streets of Athens, out in public, near the marketplace where Socrates once spent his time discussing wisdom and virtue. The name change from Zenonians to Stoics is significant because unlike other philosophical sects, the founders of Stoicism didn't claim to be perfectly wise. Zeno's attitude to his students perhaps resembled the one later described by Seneca, who did not claim to be an expert like a physician but saw his role more like that of a *patient* describing the progress of his treatment to fellow patients in the hospital beds beside him. This stood in marked contrast to the rival school of Epicureanism, for example, which *was* named after its founder. Epicurus *did* claim to be perfectly wise, and his students were required to memorize his sayings, celebrate his birthday, and revere his image.

Zeno told his students that he had come to value wisdom more than wealth or reputation. He used to say, "My most profitable journey began on the day I was *shipwrecked* and lost my entire fortune."[6] Even today it's not unusual for a client in therapy to arrive at the paradoxical revelation that losing their job may turn out to be the *best thing* that ever happened to them. Zeno learned to embrace the Cynic teaching that wealth and other external things are completely indifferent and that *virtue* is the true goal of life. In plain English, what the Cynics meant was that our character is the only thing that ultimately matters and that wisdom consists in learning to view everything else in life as utterly worthless by comparison. They believed that mastering this attitude required lifelong moral and psychological training in the voluntary endurance of hardship and renunciation of certain desires.

However, in contrast to the Cynics, other philosophers argued that "external goods"—such as health, wealth, and reputation—were also required for a good life, in *addition* to virtue. The problem is that these external things are partly in the hands of Fate, which seems to make a good life unattainable for many individuals. Socrates, for instance, was notoriously ugly by Athenian standards, lived in relative poverty, and died persecuted by powerful enemies. Would his life have been better, though, if he'd been handsome, wealthy, and praised by everyone? Didn't his greatness consist precisely in the wisdom and strength of character with which he handled these obstacles in life? As we'll see, Zeno's innovation was to argue that external advantages do have some value but of a completely different sort than virtue. They're not always *completely* indifferent. For Stoics, virtue is still the only true good—the Cynics were right about that—but it's also natural to prefer health to sickness, wealth to poverty, friends to enemies, and so on, within reasonable bounds. External advantages such as wealth may create more opportunities but in themselves they simply don't have the kind of value that can ever define a good life.

Zeno was profoundly inspired by his early training in Cynicism. Nevertheless, he sought to moderate and broaden its teachings by combining them with elements from the other schools of Athenian philosophy. His wide-ranging studies had convinced him that intellectual disciplines such as logic and metaphysics could potentially contribute to the development of our moral character. Zeno therefore established a curriculum for Stoicism divided into three broad topics: Ethics, Logic, and Physics (which included metaphysics and theology). The Stoic school he founded had a series of leaders, or "scholarchs," and a set of characteristic *core* doctrines, but students were also encouraged to think for themselves. After Zeno died, Cleanthes, one of his students, who had formerly been a boxer and watered gardens at night to earn a living, became head of the Stoic school; he was followed by Chrysippus, one of the most acclaimed intellectuals of the ancient world. Between them, these three developed the original doctrines of the Stoic school.

The teachings of Zeno and Cleanthes were simple, practical, and concise. True to his Cynic roots, Zeno focused on improving the character of his young students while avoiding long-winded academic debates. When someone complained that his philosophical arguments were very abrupt, Zeno agreed and replied that if he could he'd abbreviate the syllables as well. However, Chrysippus was a prolific writer and developed many arguments—we're told he wrote over seven hundred books. By his time, it had become necessary to defend Stoicism against philosophical criticisms leveled by other schools, especially the emerging Academic Skeptics, and that required formulating increasingly sophisticated arguments. On the other hand, Cleanthes, the teacher of Chrysippus, was not a great intellectual. According to legend, Chrysippus often said that it would be better if Cleanthes just cut to the chase and taught him the conclusions of the Stoic school so he could figure out better supporting *arguments* himself. Today many students of Stoicism adopt a similar attitude: they're attracted to the Stoic worldview but prefer to "update" it by drawing upon a wider range of arguments from modern science and philosophy. Stoicism was never intended to be doctrinaire. Chrysippus disagreed with Zeno and Cleanthes in many regards, which allowed Stoicism to keep evolving.

The original Stoic school survived for a couple of centuries before apparently fragmenting—into *three* different branches, according to one author. We're not sure why. Fortunately, by that time the Romans of the Republic had started to embrace Greek philosophy and felt a particular affinity for Stoicism. The celebrated Roman general who destroyed Carthage, Scipio Africanus the Younger, became a student of the last scholarch of the Stoic school at Athens, Panaetius of Rhodes. In the second century BC, Scipio gathered around himself a group of intellectuals at Rome known as the Scipionic Circle, which included his close friend Laelius the Wise, another influential Roman Stoic.

The famous Roman statesman and orator Cicero, who lived a couple of generations later, is one of our most important sources for understanding Stoicism. Although he was a follower of the Platonic Academy, Cicero nevertheless knew a great deal about Stoic philosophy and wrote extensively on the subject. On the other hand, his friend and political rival Cato of Utica was a "complete Stoic," as Cicero puts it, a living example of Stoicism, but didn't leave any writings about philosophy. After his death, making a stand against the tyrant Julius Caesar during the great Roman civil war, Cato became a hero and an inspiration to later generations of Stoics.

Following Caesar's assassination, his great-nephew Octavian became Augustus, the founder of the Roman Empire. Augustus had a famous Stoic tutor called Arius Didymus, which perhaps set a precedent for the Roman emperors who followed, most notably Marcus, to associate themselves with the philosophy. A few generations after Augustus, the Stoic philosopher Seneca was appointed rhetoric tutor to the young Emperor Nero, later becoming his speechwriter and political advisor—a position that clearly placed a strain on Seneca's Stoic moral values as Nero degenerated into a cruel despot. At the same time, a political faction called the Stoic Opposition, led by a senator called Thrasea, was attempting to take a principled stand against Nero and those subsequent emperors whom they considered tyrants. Marcus would later mention his admiration for Cato, Thrasea, and others associated with them, which is intriguing because these Stoics had been famous opponents, or at least critics, of imperial rule.

Emperor Nero, by contrast, was less tolerant of political dissent from philosophers, and he executed both Thrasea and Seneca. However, Nero's *secretary* owned a slave called Epictetus, who became perhaps the most famous philosophy teacher in Roman history after gaining his freedom. Epictetus himself wrote nothing down, but his discussions with students were recorded by one of them, Arrian, in several books of *Discourses* and a short *Handbook* summarizing the practical aspect of his teachings. The Stoics that Marcus knew personally were probably influenced by Epictetus, and some had likely attended his lectures. Indeed, we're told that Marcus was given copies of notes from these lectures by his main Stoic tutor, Junius Rusticus, so it's no surprise to find that Epictetus is the most quoted author in *The Meditations*. Marcus probably saw himself mainly as an adherent of Epictetus's version of Stoicism, although the two never met in person.

Nearly five centuries after Zeno the dye merchant founded the Stoic school, Marcus Aurelius was *still talking about dyeing things purple*. He warns himself to avoid dyeing his character with the royal purple and turning into a Caesar, instead aspiring to remain true to his philosophical principles. He (twice) reminds himself that his purple imperial robes are mere sheep's wool dyed in fermented shellfish mucus. He tells himself to dye his mind with the wisdom of philosophical precepts handed down from his Stoic teachers. Marcus Aurelius, indeed, viewed himself as a Stoic first and an emperor second.

## WHAT DID THE STOICS BELIEVE?

The Stoics were prolific writers, but probably less than 1 percent of their writings survive today. The most influential texts we have today come from the three famous Roman Stoics of the Imperial era: Seneca's various letters and essays, Epictetus's *Discourses* and *Handbook*, and Marcus Aurelius's *Meditations*. We also have some earlier Roman writings on Stoicism by Cicero and about a book's worth of fragments from the early Greek Stoics, as well as various other minor texts. That's woefully incomplete, but it does provide a *consistent* picture of the philosophy's core doctrines.

The schools of Hellenistic philosophy that followed the death of Socrates were often distinguished from one another in terms of their definition of the goal of life. For Stoics, that goal is defined as "living in agreement with Nature," which we're told was synonymous with living wisely and virtuously. Stoics argued that humans are first and foremost *thinking* creatures, capable of exercising reason. Although we share many instincts with other animals, our ability to think rationally is what makes us human. Reason governs our decisions, in a sense—the Stoics call it our "ruling faculty." It allows us to *evaluate* our thoughts, feelings, and urges and to decide if they're good or bad, healthy or unhealthy. We therefore have an innate duty to protect our ability to reason and to use it properly. When we reason *well* about life and live rationally, we exhibit the virtue of *wisdom*. Living in agreement with Nature, in part, means fulfilling our natural potential for wisdom; that's what it means for us to *flourish* as human beings.

The Stoics therefore took the name of *philosophy*, meaning "love of wisdom," quite literally. They loved wisdom, or loved virtue, above everything else. If "virtue" sounds a bit pompous, the Greek word for it, *arete*, is arguably better translated as "excellence of character." Something excels, in this sense, if it performs its function well. Humans excel when they think clearly and reason well about their lives, which amounts to living *wisely*. The Stoics adopted the Socratic division of *cardinal* virtues into wisdom, justice, courage, and moderation. The other three virtues can be understood as wisdom applied to our actions in different areas of life. Justice is largely wisdom applied to the social sphere, our relationships with other people. Displaying courage and moderation involves mastering our fears and desires, respectively, overcoming what the Stoics called the unhealthy "passions" that otherwise interfere with our ability to live in accord with wisdom and justice.

Wisdom, in all these forms, mainly requires understanding the difference between good, bad, and indifferent things. Virtue is good and vice is bad, but everything else is indifferent. Indeed, as we've seen, the Stoics followed the Cynics in maintaining the hard line that virtue is the *only* true good. However, Zeno went on to distinguish between indifferent things that are "preferred," "dispreferred," or completely indifferent. Put crudely, external things do have *some* value, but they're not worth getting *upset* over—it's a different *kind* of value. One way Stoics explained this was by saying that if we could put virtue on one side of a set of scales, it wouldn't matter how many gold coins or other indifferent things piled up on the opposing side—it should *never* tip the balance. Nevertheless, some external things are *preferable* to others, and wisdom consists precisely in our ability to make these sorts of value judgments. Life is preferable to death, wealth is preferable to poverty, health is preferable to sickness, friends are preferable to enemies, and so on.

As Socrates had put it earlier, such external advantages in life are good only if we use them wisely. However, if something can be used for *either* good or evil, it cannot truly be good in itself, so it should be classed as "indifferent" or neutral. The Stoics would say that things like health, wealth, and reputation are, at most, advantages or opportunities rather than being good in themselves. Social, material, and physical advantages actually give foolish individuals more opportunity to do harm to themselves and others.

Look at lottery winners. Those who squander their sudden wealth often end up more miserable than they could have imagined. When handled badly, external advantages like wealth do more harm than good. The Stoics would go further: the wise and good man may flourish even when faced with sickness, poverty, and enemies. The true goal of life for Stoics isn't to acquire as many external advantages as possible but to use whatever befalls us wisely, whether it be sickness or health, wealth or poverty, friends or enemies. The Stoic Sage, or wise man, needs nothing but uses everything well; the fool believes himself to "need" countless things, but he uses them all badly.

Most important of all, the pursuit of these preferred indifferent things must never be done at the *expense* of virtue. For instance, wisdom may tell us that wealth is generally preferable to debt, but valuing money more highly than justice is a vice. In order to explain the supreme value placed on wisdom and virtue, the Stoics compared reason, our "ruling faculty," to a king in relation to his court. Everyone in court is situated somewhere or other on the hierarchy of importance. However, the king is *uniquely* important because he's the one who assigns everyone else at court a role in the hierarchy. As mentioned earlier, the Stoics call reason, the king in this metaphor, our "ruling faculty" (*hegemonikon*). It's human nature to desire certain things in life, such as sex and food. Reason allows us to step back and question whether what we desire is actually going to be good for us or not. Wisdom itself is uniquely valuable because it allows us to judge the value of external things—it's the source of everything else's value. How therefore does it profit a man, the Stoics might say, if he gains the whole world but loses his wisdom and virtue?

In addition to believing that humans are essentially thinking creatures *capable of reason*, the Stoics also believed that human nature is inherently *social*. They started from the premise that under normal conditions we typically have a bond of "natural affection" toward our children. (If we didn't, as we now know, our offspring would be less likely to survive and pass on our genes.) This bond of natural affection also tends to extend to other loved ones, such as spouses, parents, siblings, and close friends. The Stoics believed that as we mature in wisdom we increasingly identify with our own capacity for reason, but we also begin to identify with others insofar as *they're* capable of reason. In other words, the wise man extends moral consideration to all rational creatures and views them, in a sense, as his brothers and sisters. That's why the Stoics described their ideal as *cosmopolitanism*, or being "citizens of the universe"—a phrase attributed both to Socrates and Diogenes the Cynic. Stoic ethics involves cultivating this natural affection toward other people in accord with virtues like justice, fairness, and kindness. Although this social dimension of Stoicism is often overlooked today, it's one of the main themes of *The Meditations*. Marcus touches on topics such as the virtues of justice and kindness, natural affection, the brotherhood of man, and ethical cosmopolitanism on virtually every page.

Another popular misconception today is that Stoics are *unemotional*. The ancient Stoics themselves consistently denied this, saying that their ideal was *not* to be like a man of iron or to have a heart of stone. In fact, they distinguished between *three* types of emotion: good, bad, and indifferent. They had names for many different types of *good* passion (*eupatheiai*), a term encompassing both desires and emotions, which they grouped under three broad headings:

1. A profound sense of *joy* or gladness and peace of mind,
   which comes from living with wisdom and virtue
2. A healthy feeling of *aversion* to vice, like a sense of conscience, honor, dignity, or integrity
3. The *desire to help* both ourselves and others, through
   friendship, kindness, and goodwill

They also believed that we have many irrational desires and emotions, like fear, anger, craving, and certain forms of pleasure that
are *bad* for us. Stoics did not believe that unhealthy emotions
should be suppressed; rather, they should be replaced by healthy
ones. However, these healthy emotions aren't entirely under our
control, and we're not always guaranteed to experience them, so
we shouldn't confuse them with virtue, the goal of life. For Stoics,
they're like an added bonus.

They also taught that our initial *automatic* feelings are to be
viewed as natural and *indifferent*. These include things like being
startled or irritated, blushing, turning pale, tensing up, shaking,
sweating, or stammering. They are natural *reflex* reactions, our
first reactions before we escalate them into full-blown passions.
We share these primitive precursors to emotion with some non-
human animals, and so the Stoics view them with indifference, as
neither good nor bad. Indeed, Seneca, as we'll see, noted the paradox that before we can exhibit the virtues of courage and moderation, we need to have at least some trace of fear and desire to
overcome.

Even the Stoic wise man, therefore, may tremble in the face
of danger. What matters is what he does next. He exhibits courage and self-control precisely by accepting these feelings, rising
above them, and asserting his capacity for reason. He's not en-
tranced by the siren song of pleasure or afraid of the sting of pain.

Some pains have the potential to make us stronger, and some pleasures to harm us. What matters is the use we make of these experiences, and for that we need wisdom. The wise man will *endure* pain and discomfort, such as undergoing surgery or engaging in strenuous physical exercise, if it's healthy for his body and, more important, if it's healthy for his character. He'll likewise forgo pleasures like eating junk food, indulging in drugs or alcohol, or oversleeping if they are unhealthy for his body or bad for his character. Everything comes back to the exercise of reason and the goal of living wisely.

By now you'll appreciate how much confusion is caused by people mixing up "Stoicism" (capital S) with "stoicism" (lowercase s). Lowercase stoicism is just a personality trait: it's mental *toughness* or the ability to endure pain and adversity without complaining. Uppercase Stoicism is a whole school of Greek philosophy. Being emotionally tough or resilient is just one *small* part of that philosophy, and lowercase stoicism neglects the entire social dimension of Stoic virtue, which has to do with justice, fairness, and kindness to others. Also, when people talk about being stoic or having a stiff upper lip, they often mean just suppressing their feelings, which is actually known to be quite *unhealthy*. So it's important to be very clear that's *not* what Marcus Aurelius and other Stoics recommended. Stoic philosophy teaches us instead to transform unhealthy emotions into healthy ones. We do so by using reason to challenge the value judgments and other beliefs on which they're based, much as we do in modern rational emotive behavior therapy (REBT) and cognitive-behavioral therapy (CBT).

In the following chapters you'll learn about the different ways in which Stoicism can be applied to life in order to overcome specific types of psychological problems, including pain, worry, anger, and loss. Stories about the life of Marcus Aurelius provide a human face for the philosophy and will furnish us with practical examples of Stoic strategies and techniques. We'll start by looking at Marcus's early life and education because that gets right to the heart of the matter by introducing *the Stoic use of language*.

# 2.

# THE MOST TRUTHFUL
# CHILD IN ROME

Marcus was born on April 26, 121 AD, and was "reared under the eye of Hadrian."[1] He took the name *Aurelius* later; throughout his childhood, he was known as Marcus Annius Verus, after his father and his grandfathers. The family lived in the small town of Ucubi in the Roman province of Hispania Baetica (in modern-day Spain) before moving to Rome. When he was about three years old, his father died—we don't know the circumstances. Marcus barely knew him but later wrote about his manliness and humility, drawing from what he learned of his father by reputation and what little he remembered.

Marcus was brought up by his mother and paternal grandfather, a highly distinguished senator who had served three times as consul. He was a close friend of the Emperor Hadrian and was the brother-in-law of Hadrian's wife, the Empress Sabina, Marcus's great-aunt. As a member of a wealthy patrician family with ties to the emperor, Marcus was naturally part of his grandfather's social circle, and though we're told he was loved by all, something about Marcus especially caught Hadrian's eye. The emperor heaped honors on him from an early age, enrolling him in the equestrian order when he was six years old, making him what's sometimes described as a Roman knight. When Marcus was eight, Hadrian appointed him to the College of the Salii, or leaping priests, whose main duty involved performing elaborate ritual dances in honor of Mars, the god of war, while dressed in ancient armor and bearing ceremonial swords and shields.

Hadrian nicknamed the boy Verissimus, meaning "truest" or "most truthful," a play on his family name of Verus, which means "true." It's as if he found Marcus, a mere child, to be the most plainspoken individual at court. Indeed, Marcus's family, though wealthy and influential, was notable for cherishing honesty and simplicity. Marcus's tendency toward plain speaking gave him a natural affinity for Stoic philosophy, which he would discover later. However, it set him at odds with the intellectual culture prevailing at Hadrian's court during the height of the Second Sophistic, a cultural movement celebrating formal rhetoric and oratory. By Hadrian's time, Greek art and literature had become highly fashionable. Greek intellectuals, particularly orators, were highly esteemed and became tutors to the Roman elite, allowing Greek culture to flourish in the heart of the Roman Empire.

Teachers of rhetoric, the formal study of the language used in giving speeches and part of any young aristocrat's curriculum in those days, were known as Sophists, reviving a Greek tradition that went back to the time of Socrates. They often included moral lessons, bits of philosophy, and other aspects of intellectual culture in their lessons. Hence our word "sophistication," which is loosely what they sought to impart. As Socrates had long ago observed, although Sophists often sounded like they were doing philosophy, their underlying goal was to win praise by displaying verbal eloquence rather than attaining virtue for its own sake. Put simply, while they spoke a lot about wisdom and virtue, they didn't necessarily live in accord with those values. They were usually more concerned with competing against one another to win public applause for their knowledge and eloquence. The *appearance* of wisdom therefore became more important to many Romans than wisdom itself. Even the emperor himself indulged in this. The *Historia Augusta*, one of our most important sources, says that although Hadrian was a somewhat talented writer of prose and verse in his own right, he often sought to ridicule and humiliate the teachers of these and other arts in an attempt to show he was more cultured and intelligent than them. He would get into pretentious arguments with certain teachers and philosophers, with each side issuing pamphlets and poems against the other—the ancient Roman equivalent of internet flaming or trolling.

For instance, the Sophist Favorinus of Arelate was renowned throughout the empire as one of its very finest intellectuals. He was well versed in the Skeptical philosophy of the Academy and won widespread acclaim for his rhetorical eloquence. He shamelessly buckled, though, in response to the Emperor Hadrian's dubious assertions about the correct usage of some word. "You're urging me down the wrong path," Favorinus told his friends, "if you don't allow me to regard the most learned of men as being the one who owns thirty legions."[2] Hadrian didn't like being wrong. Worse, he carried out merciless vendettas against intellectuals who disagreed with him. Indeed, when Favorinus eventually incurred Hadrian's disapproval, he was exiled to the Greek island of Chios. Nevertheless, for some reason Hadrian came to admire above all the integrity and plain speaking of a rather grave young noble, his Verissimus, who loved *real* wisdom more than the cultivated appearance of wisdom.

Hadrian was a talented, passionate, and mercurial man, the sort of person you'd describe as very *clever*, but not necessarily *wise*. Perhaps surprisingly, we're told he was a friend of Epictetus, the most important teacher of Stoicism in the Roman Empire. We might struggle to imagine the famous Stoic putting up with Hadrian's relentless one-upmanship. However, the emperor was clearly on very good terms with Epictetus's most famous student, Arrian, who wrote down and edited *The Discourses* and *Handbook*. As we'll see, Arrian rose to prominence during Hadrian's reign. Hadrian was no philosopher, though—he viewed philosophy in the same superficial manner as the Sophists did: a source for material to show off one's learning.

By contrast, Epictetus, in typical Stoic fashion, continually warned his students not to confuse academic learning with wisdom and to avoid petty arguments, hairsplitting, or wasting time on abstract, academic topics. He emphasized the *fundamental* difference between a Sophist and a Stoic: the former speaks to win praise from his audience, the latter to improve them by helping them to achieve wisdom and virtue.[3] Rhetoricians thrive on praise, which is vanity; philosophers love truth and embrace humility. Rhetoric is a form of entertainment, pleasant to hear; philosophy is a moral and psychological therapy, often painful to hear because it forces us to admit our own faults in order to remedy them— sometimes the truth hurts. Epictetus's own teacher, the Stoic Musonius Rufus, used to tell his students, "If you have leisure to praise me, I am speaking to no purpose." Hence, the philosopher's school, said Epictetus, is a doctor's clinic: you should not go there expecting pleasure but rather pain.

As the years passed, Marcus would grow increasingly aware

of his disillusionment with the values of the Sophists and his natural affinity with those of the Stoics. We can probably thank his mother for this to some extent. Domitia Lucilla was a remarkable woman who, like Marcus's father, came from a distinguished Roman patrician family. She was also immensely wealthy, having inherited a vast fortune, including an important brick-and-tile factory situated near Rome. However, Marcus would later say that he was particularly influenced by the simplicity and unpretentiousness of her way of life, "far removed from that of the rich."[4]

This love of simple living and distaste for the ostentatious impressed her son. Several decades later, Marcus revealed his distaste for the pretense and corruption of court life in *The Meditations*. He promised himself, though, that he would never again waste his time dwelling negatively on it. He added that it was only through recourse to philosophy that life at court even seemed bearable to him, and he bearable to those at court. He reminded himself that wherever it is possible to live, it is possible to live well, to live wisely, even at Rome, where he clearly felt it was a struggle to stay in tune with Stoic virtue. He found the insincerity of life at court a constant frustration, and he came to rely on Stoicism as a way of coping.[5]

Marcus also learned *generosity* from his mother. When his only sister married, Marcus gave her the inheritance his father had left him. Throughout his life, he received numerous other inheritances, and we're told he would typically give them to the deceased's next of kin. Decades later, during his reign as emperor at the outset of the First Marcomannic War, Marcus found that the state treasury was exhausted. He responded by holding a public auction, lasting two months, in which countless imperial treasures were sold off to raise funds for the war effort. His indifference toward wealth and the trappings of the imperial court turned out to be of great value, therefore, in responding to a serious financial crisis.

Marcus's mother was a lover of Greek culture, and she may have introduced her son to some of the intellectuals who later became his friends and teachers. Marcus mentions that his Stoic mentor, Junius Rusticus, taught him to write letters in a very simple and unaffected style, like one in particular that Rusticus sent Marcus's mother from Sinuessa, on the Italian coast.[6] Perhaps Rusticus and Marcus's mother had been friends for many years. Along with his mother's love of Greek culture, some of the old-fashioned Roman values instilled in Marcus during his upbringing doubtless paved the way for his later interest in Stoic philosophy. Indeed, that may be why he reminds himself of them in the opening passages of *The Meditations*.

Marcus began to build on these values by training in philosophy from an exceptionally young age. The *Historia Augusta* says that he was already wholly dedicated to Stoic philosophy while Hadrian was alive. However, he seems to have learned about philosophy first as a practical *way of life* when he was still a young boy living in his mother's house, long before he began studying philosophical *theory* under several eminent tutors. He first taught himself to endure physical discomfort and overcome unhealthy habits. He learned to tolerate other people's criticisms and to avoid being easily swayed by fine words or flattery.

Mastering our passions in this way is the first stage of training in Stoicism. Epictetus called it the "Discipline of Desire," although it encompasses both our desires and our fears or aversions. As we've seen, the Stoics were very much influenced by the Cynic philosophers who preceded them. Epictetus taught a form of Stoicism that held aspects of Cynicism in particularly high regard. It's said he was known for the slogan "endure and renounce" (or "bear and forbear"). Marcus seems to recall this saying in *The Meditations* when he tells himself that he must aim to *bear* with other people's flaws and *forbear* from any wrongdoing against them, while calmly accepting things outside of his direct control.[7]

In book 1 of *The Meditations*, Marcus, after contemplating the good qualities and lessons learned from his own family, next goes on to praise a mysterious unnamed tutor, probably a slave or freedman in his mother's household.[8] It's truly remarkable that Marcus seems to credit a humble slave with more influence upon his moral development than either the Emperor Hadrian or any of his rhetoric tutors, who included some of the most highly esteemed intellectuals in the empire. This unnamed man showed young Marcus how to endure hardship and discomfort with patience. He taught Marcus to be self-reliant and to have few needs in life. Marcus also learned from him how to turn a deaf ear toward slander and how to avoid sticking his nose into other people's concerns. This is very different from the example set by Hadrian or the famous Sophists competing to win the emperor's favor and the applause of crowds at Rome. The same tutor also persuaded Marcus early on not to side with the Green or Blue factions at the chariot races or with different gladiators in the amphitheater. As we've seen, the Cynics were renowned for training themselves to endure voluntary hardship (*ponos*) through their somewhat austere lifestyle and use of various exercises. They were also famous for cultivating indifference toward external things and disregarding both praise and condemnation from others. Doing so allowed them to speak the truth very plainly and simply. We'll never know whether Marcus's nameless tutor was influenced by Cynicism or whether he just happened to share similar values.

He certainly provided the child with a solid foundation for his future training in Stoicism, though.

So who first introduced Marcus to the formal *study* of philosophy? Astoundingly, he tells us that it was his *painting master*, Diognetus. They would have met when Marcus was aged around twelve, as he entered the next stage of his education. There are some striking passages in *The Meditations* in which Marcus appears to exhibit a painter's eye for visual details like the cracks on a loaf of bread, the lines on the face of an elderly person, or foam dripping from the mouth of a wild boar. These observations are used to illustrate Stoic metaphysical ideas: the beauty of something's apparent flaws and its worth become clearer when viewed as part of a larger picture. So it's tempting to wonder if they were inspired by philosophical conversations that Marcus had as a child with his painting tutor.

In any case, Diognetus taught Marcus not to waste his time with trivial matters and steered him away from popular amusements such as quail fighting—the Ancient Roman equivalent of today's video games, perhaps. He warned Marcus not to be duped by charlatans who hawked miracles and magic charms or by those (presumably early Christians) who professed to exorcise demons. Disdain for the supernatural and caution against wasting time and energy on diversions such as gambling are attitudes that Marcus may have learned from a Cynic or Stoic philosopher. Diognetus also taught him to tolerate plain speaking (*parrhesia*) and to sleep covered with a pelt in a camp bed on the ground, almost certainly references to the Cynic regime.[9] Indeed, the *Historia Augusta* confirms that around the time Diognetus would have become his tutor, Marcus adopted the dress of a philosopher and began training himself to endure hardship. However, his mother argued that sleeping on a mat like a legionary on campaign was inappropriate. With some effort she persuaded him to use a couch instead, albeit one still spread with animal pelts instead of normal bedding.

Marcus says that Diognetus taught him these and other aspects of "Greek training" (*agoge*). Although we don't know what all of these aspects were, we can infer what some may have been. Cynic philosophers often ate a very simple diet of cheap black bread and lentils, or lupin seeds, and drank mainly water. According to Musonius Rufus, the teacher of Epictetus, Stoics should likewise eat simple, healthy food that is easy to prepare, and they should do so with mindfulness and in moderation, not greedily. Like the Cynics, the Stoics would sometimes also train themselves to endure heat and cold. According to legend, Diogenes the Cynic did this by stripping naked and embracing frozen statues in winter or rolling in hot sand under the summer sun. Seneca described taking cold baths and swimming in the River Tiber at the beginning of the year—and cold showers are popular with those influenced by Stoicism today. Although Marcus doesn't mention these details, he may have adopted similar practices as a youth as part of his "Greek training" in enduring voluntary hardship. The French scholar Pierre Hadot believed that this phrase alluded to the notorious Spartan training, aspects of which may have influenced the austere lifestyle adopted by Cynic philosophers and some Stoics.

Indeed, philosophy in the ancient world was first and foremost a way of life. Today, "academic philosophy" as taught in universities has turned into a much more bookish and *theoretical* pursuit. Ancient philosophers, by contrast, were often recognizable because of their lifestyle and even the way they dressed. The Stoics, like the Cynics before them, traditionally wore a single garment called a *tribon* in Greek. This rudimentary cloak or shawl, made from undyed wool usually of a grayish color, was worn wrapped around the body, often with the shoulders exposed. Certain philosophers, like Socrates and the Cynics, also walked barefoot. Some Roman philosophers still dressed like this, although the style was perhaps occasionally viewed as antiquated and an affectation. Marcus, at least in his youth, wore the cloak of a philosopher, and as we can see from sculptures, he had a longish, well-kempt beard, which was probably typical for Stoics of that period.

Perhaps Diognetus dressed and lived as a philosopher himself and Marcus was inspired to imitate his example. Once again, it's striking that at the height of the Second Sophistic, when oratory and poetry were all the rage at the court of Hadrian, Marcus was drawn in an opposing direction. He was wrenched away from the sophistication and ostentation of *rhetoric* by the simplicity and honesty of Greek *philosophy*. In addition to introducing him to this way of life, Diognetus started encouraging the boy to write philosophical dialogues and attend the lectures of several philosophers. (He names three men but nothing more is known about them.) A few years later, aged around fifteen, Marcus briefly attended lectures at the house of a famous Stoic teacher called Apollonius of Chalcedon, who happened to be visiting Rome. Apollonius then departed for Greece, but, as we shall see, he would soon be recalled.

By this time, Marcus was already an aspiring Stoic. Apollonius and others must surely have introduced him to the teachings of Epictetus, arguably the most influential of all Roman philosophers. Epictetus, whose school had long since relocated from Rome to Greece, died when Marcus was still a boy, so they almost certainly never met. However, as Marcus's education proceeded, he would enjoy the company of older men who had most likely attended Epictetus's lectures and were studying *The Discourses* transcribed by Arrian. In *The Meditations*, Marcus names Epictetus as an exemplary philosopher alongside Socrates and Chrysippus,[10] and quotes him more than any other author. Indeed, Marcus clearly came to view himself as a follower of Epictetus. However, his family probably assumed that his education would focus on learning rhetoric from eminent Sophists, especially once he was designated a future emperor.

Hadrian's marriage was childless, so in his later years, when his health began to deteriorate, he adopted a successor. To everyone's surprise, he chose a relatively undistinguished man called Lucius Ceionius Commodus, who then became known as Lucius Aelius Caesar, starting a tradition that the *official heir* to the empire would assume the title Caesar. However, Lucius was in such poor health that he dropped dead little over a year later. Hadrian reputedly wanted Marcus, now sixteen, to become his successor, but he felt the boy was still too young. Instead, he chose an older man called Titus Aurelius Antoninus, who was already in his early fifties and had two daughters but no surviving sons. He was married to Marcus's aunt, Faustina. So, as part of a long-term succession arrangement, Hadrian adopted Antoninus on condition that he would in turn adopt Marcus, placing him in direct line to the throne. Hadrian thereby adopted Marcus as his grandson.

In early 138 AD, on the day of his adoption, young Marcus Annius Verus assumed Antoninus's family name, becoming forever known as Marcus Aurelius Antoninus. However, complicating matters, Lucius Aelius, the man Hadrian originally appointed as his successor and Caesar, had left behind a young son of his own, also called Lucius. Antoninus therefore adopted the child

Lucius, who thereby became Marcus Aurelius's new brother. Later, immediately following his own acclamation, Marcus would appoint his adopted brother co-emperor, at which point he became known as the Emperor Lucius Verus. It was the first time two emperors had ruled jointly in this way. Marcus presumably made the decision to share power with his brother at least in part to avoid the risk of unrest caused by having a rival dynasty with a claim on the throne. (We'll come back to the relationship between Marcus and his brother Lucius later.)

At first, Marcus was deeply dismayed that Hadrian had adopted him into the imperial household. He was reluctant to move from his mother's villa to the emperor's private home. When his friends and family members asked him why he was so perturbed, he rattled off a whole list of his concerns about life at court. Based on his later comments, we know he struggled with the insincerity and corruption of Roman politics. That night, though, after learning he was to become emperor, Marcus dreamt that he had arms and shoulders of ivory. Asked in the dream if he could still use them, he picked up a heavy load and discovered he had become much stronger. Exposed shoulders were the mark of a Cynic or Stoic philosopher's endurance against the cold, so he may have foreseen in this dream that his training in Stoic philosophy would grant him the strength and resilience required to fulfill his future role as emperor.

Marcus was now *second* in line to the throne and destined to succeed Antoninus. He was introduced to the circle of intellectuals at court, some of the finest rhetoricians and philosophers in the empire. He must also have observed the way the emperor bullied them. This was completely at odds with Marcus's values, as were Hadrian's growing suspicion, intolerance, and persecution of his supposed enemies. Later, during his own reign as emperor,

Marcus made a point of allowing his political opponents to go unpunished when they publicly ridiculed or criticized him. The most he ever did in response to outspoken critics was to address their remarks politely in speeches or pamphlets, whereas Hadrian would have had them banished or beheaded. Marcus famously pledged that not a single senator would be executed during his reign, and, as we will see, he maintained this promise even when several of them betrayed him during a civil war in the east. He believed that true strength consisted of one's ability to show kindness, not violence or aggression.

In his final years, Hadrian became something of a tyrant. He grew increasingly paranoid, paid agents to spy on his friends, and ordered a swath of executions. The Senate ended up hating him so bitterly that after his death they wanted to annul his acts and withhold the traditional honor of deification. However, the new emperor Antoninus reasoned with them that it would be better to act in a more conciliatory manner, for which he earned the cognomen *Pius*. Hadrian would doubtless have been infuriated by the fact that despite being mentioned several times elsewhere in the text, he is conspicuously absent from the first book of *The Meditations*, in which Marcus individually praises his family members and teachers. On the other hand, Marcus listed the virtues of Antoninus at great length more than once and made it clear that he represented his ideal role model as emperor.

Roman historians portray Antoninus, in many ways, as the opposite of his predecessor. Indeed, some of the traits Marcus praises in his adoptive father can be read as implicit criticisms of Hadrian. Antoninus was completely unpretentious. We're told that upon being acclaimed emperor, despite some resistance from the palace staff, he earned great respect from the people by minimizing the pomp of the imperial court. He often dressed as an ordinary citizen, without wearing the robes of state, to receive visitors, and he tried to continue living as he had previously done. Whereas his subjects came to humor Hadrian, wary of his changeable moods and quick temper, Antoninus was famous for his calm demeanor and for welcoming plain speaking at court and elsewhere. Unlike Hadrian, Antoninus would simply ignore any barbed remarks made at his expense.

The Stoics were happy to admit that some individuals *naturally* embodied virtues they sought to acquire through years of effort, by means of study and training in philosophy. Antoninus was such a man, according to Marcus. The traits he's described as possessing paint a vivid picture of the sort of character that Marcus wanted to develop through his training in Stoic philosophy. Once Antoninus had considered something and arrived at a decision, for example, he implemented it with unwavering determination.[11] In *The Meditations* Marcus contemplates how his predecessor never sought out empty praise or approval from others; instead, he was always willing to listen to other people's views and consider them carefully. He was meticulous in examining matters that required careful deliberation. He never rushed making a decision and was always willing to question his first impressions. He would patiently think over the issue until he was completely satisfied with his reasoning. He honored genuine philosophers, though he didn't necessarily agree with all of their doctrines. He didn't attack charlatans, but he wasn't taken in by them either. In other words, he was a very calm and rational man. His natural freedom from vanity helped him to follow reason more consistently and see things more clearly—unlike Hadrian, he didn't always have to be right.

Under Antoninus and later Marcus, the culture at Rome

would noticeably shift from favoring Sophists toward philosophers, particularly the Stoics. Marcus wanted to engage with Greek learning but in a totally different way than Hadrian. He genuinely sought to transform himself into a better person instead of merely scoring points against intellectual rivals. The seeds of that transformation were planted by his family, perhaps especially by his mother, but they were then nurtured by a series of exceptional tutors.

Nevertheless, young Roman noblemen were expected to undergo formal training in rhetoric. This began when they officially reached adulthood, symbolized by taking the *toga virilis* around the age of fifteen. Studying rhetoric in order to communicate more eloquently and persuasively would become Marcus's main obligation as a student, although it clashed with his growing interest in Stoic philosophy. Herodes Atticus and others trained him extensively in Greek, the language he would use to write *The Meditations*. However, once Emperor Antoninus adopted Marcus, his main tutor became Marcus Cornelius Fronto, the leading Latin rhetorician of the day.

Fronto was embraced as a close family friend, and he remained so until his death around 166 or 167 AD, possibly a victim of the plague during its initial outbreak in Rome. Fronto later wrote down his glowing impression of Marcus as a youth: he was innately predisposed to all the virtues before being trained in them, we're told, "being a good man before puberty, and a skilled speaker before donning the robes of manhood."[12] Fronto was important enough to Marcus to be one of the tutors cited in book 1 of *The Meditations*. However, Marcus mentions little about Fronto's influence on his character and reserves greater praise for Alexander of Cotiaeum, his Greek grammarian, a lower-grade teacher. Despite the importance of their relationship, therefore, Fronto didn't much inspire Marcus as a role model. He also tried to actively discourage his young student from becoming a Stoic.

We know Fronto worried that philosophers sometimes lacked the eloquence required by statesmen and emperors and risked making bad decisions under the influence of their peculiar doctrines. He wrote to Marcus saying that even if he achieved the wisdom of Zeno and Cleanthes, the founders of Stoicism, he would still be obliged, whether he liked it or not, to wear the purple imperial cloak "and not that of the philosophers, made of coarse wool."[13] Fronto meant that Marcus was required not only to dress like an emperor but also to speak like one, draping himself in purple and winning praise for his formal eloquence. In reality, though, Marcus preferred to dress down and talk plainly like a philosopher or, failing that, an ordinary citizen. Fronto's job was to imbue the boy with the cultural sophistication befitting his station in life and train him to become an effective political speechwriter and orator. This was a very difficult time for the young Caesar, as he felt torn between rhetoric and philosophy. Yet Fronto's influence gradually waned. Eloquence is one thing, wisdom another. We're told that Plato's saying was always on Marcus's lips: *those states prospered where the philosophers were kings or the kings philosophers*.

The contest between Sophists and Stoics over young Marcus had started shortly after Hadrian's death, when Antoninus summoned the philosopher Apollonius of Chalcedon back to Rome. The *Historia Augusta* claims that Antoninus instructed Apollonius to move into the imperial palace, the House of Tiberius, so that he could become Marcus's full-time personal tutor. However, Apollonius replied in laconic fashion: "The master ought not come to the pupil, but the pupil to the master."[14] Antoninus was initially unimpressed by this response and quipped that it was apparently easier for Apollonius to make the trip all the way from Greece to Rome than for him to get up and walk from his house to the palace. He probably assumed it was just arrogance for a tutor to insist that the emperor's son should come to his home for tuition like everyone else. Apollonius was the main philosopher whose lectures Marcus attended in his youth, which suggests that Antoninus eventually relented and allowed his son to mingle with other students outside the palace. As we'll see, many decades later, toward the end of his life, Marcus was still causing a stir by attending the public lectures of philosophers, as if he were a common citizen.

Marcus was impressed with Apollonius's skill and fluency as a teacher of Stoic doctrines. However, what he admired most was the man's character. The Sophists talked at length about wisdom and virtue, but it was all just words with them. Apollonius, on the other hand, was completely unpretentious about his intellectual prowess, and he never became the slightest bit frustrated when debating a philosophical text with students. He showed Marcus what it meant in practice for a Stoic to "live in agreement with Nature"—that is, how to consistently rely on *reason* as our guide in life. Indeed, Apollonius was no *mere* professor but exhibited the true constancy and equanimity of a Stoic even in the face of severe pain, long illness, and the loss of a child. Marcus also saw in him a clear example of what it meant for Stoics to engage in a course of action with great vigor and determination while simultaneously remaining relaxed and unperturbed about the outcome. (They referred to this as taking action with a "reserve clause," a strategy we'll examine in more detail later.) Marcus adds that Apollonius would accept favors graciously from friends, while neither demeaning himself by doing so nor showing any hint of ingratitude.[15] This man was an inspiration to the future emperor, in other words, and the sort of person that Stoicism promised to help him become.

Apollonius taught Marcus the doctrines of Stoic philosophy while showing him how to apply them in daily life. Marcus would have learned that the Stoics believed there was a relationship between the sincere love of wisdom and greater emotional resilience. Their philosophy contained within itself a moral and psychological therapy (*therapeia*) for minds troubled by anger, fear, sadness, and unhealthy desires. They called the goal of this therapy *apatheia*, meaning not apathy but rather freedom from harmful desires and emotions (passions). To say that Apollonius taught Marcus Stoic philosophy is therefore also to say that he trained Marcus to develop mental resilience through an ancient form of psychological therapy and self-improvement sometimes described as the Stoic "therapy of the passions." An important aspect of this training would have involved Apollonius showing Marcus how to maintain his equanimity by deliberately using language in the special *therapeutic* manner described by the Stoics.

However, before we turn to the Stoic use of language, we first have to understand a little more about the Stoic theory of emotions. The curious tale of an *unnamed* Stoic teacher provides our best introduction to this topic. We find it in *The Attic Nights*, a book of anecdotes written by Aulus Gellius, a grammarian who was a contemporary of Marcus Aurelius. Gellius was sailing across the Ionian Sea from Cassiopa, a town on Corfu, to Brundisium, in southern Italy, possibly en route to Rome. He describes one of his fellow passengers as an important and highly regarded Stoic teacher who had been lecturing in Athens. We can't identify the teacher with certainty; it's not impossible, though, that Gellius could have been referring to Apollonius of Chalcedon.

Out on open water their boat was caught in a ferocious storm, which lasted almost the whole night. The passengers feared for their lives as they struggled to man the pumps and keep themselves from drowning in a shipwreck. Gellius noticed that the great Stoic teacher had turned as white as a sheet and shared the same anxious expression as the rest of the passengers. However, the philosopher alone remained silent instead of crying out in terror and lamenting his predicament. Once the sea and sky calmed, as they were approaching their destination, Gellius gently inquired of the Stoic why he looked almost as fearful as the others did during the storm. He could see that Gellius was sincere and courteously answered that the founders of Stoicism taught how people facing such dangers naturally and inevitably experience a short-lived stage of fear. He then reached into his satchel and produced the fifth book of Epictetus's *Discourses* for Gellius to peruse. Today, only the first *four* books of the *Discourses* survive, although Marcus appears to have read the lost discourses of Epictetus and quotes from them in *The Meditations*. In any case, Gellius describes Epictetus's remarks, which he confidently asserts were true to the original teachings of Zeno and Chrysippus.

Epictetus reputedly told his students that the founders of Stoicism distinguished between two stages of our response to any event, including threatening situations. First come the initial impressions (*phantasiai*) that are imposed *involuntarily* on our minds from outside, when we're initially exposed to an event such as the storm at sea. These impressions can be triggered, says Epictetus, by a terrifying sound such as a peal of thunder, a building collapsing, or a sudden cry of danger. Even the mind of a perfect

Stoic Sage will initially be shaken by abrupt shocks of this kind, and he will shrink back from them instinctively in alarm. This reaction doesn't come from faulty value judgments about the dangers faced but from an emotional reflex arising in his body, which temporarily bypasses reason. Epictetus might have added that these emotional reactions are comparable to those experienced by non-human animals. Seneca, for instance, notes that when animals are alarmed by the appearance of danger, they take flight, but after they have escaped, their anxiety soon abates and they return to grazing in peace once again.[16] By contrast, the human capacity for thought allows us to perpetuate our worries beyond these natural bounds. Reason, our greatest blessing, is also our greatest curse.

In the *second* stage of our response, the Stoics say, we typically add *voluntary* judgments of "assent" (*sunkatatheseis*) to these automatic impressions. Here the Stoic wise man's response differs from that of the majority of people. He does not go along with the initial emotional reactions to a situation that have invaded his mind. Epictetus says the Stoic should neither assent to nor confirm these emerging impressions, such as anxiety in the face of danger. Rather, he rejects them as misleading, views them with studied indifference, and lets go of them. By contrast, the unwise are carried away by their initial impression of external events—including those that are terrible and to be feared—and continue to worry, ruminate, and even complain aloud about a perceived threat. Seneca gives a more detailed account of the Stoic model of emotion in *On Anger*,[17] which divides the process of experiencing a passion into three "movements," or stages:

FIRST STAGE: Initial impressions automatically impose themselves on your mind, including thoughts and emerging feelings called *propatheiai*, or "proto-passions," by the Stoics. For example, the impression *"The boat is sinking"* would quite naturally evoke some initial anxiety.

**SECOND STAGE:** The majority of people, like those on the boat, would agree with the original impression, go along with it, and add more value judgments, indulging in catastrophic thinking: *"I might die a terrible death!"* They would worry about it and continue to dwell on it long afterward. By contrast, Stoics, like the unnamed philosopher in the story, have learned to take a step back from their initial thoughts and feelings and withhold their assent from them. They might do this by saying to themselves, *"You are just an impression and not at all the things you claim to represent,"* or *"It is not things that upset us but our judgments about them."* The boat is sinking, but you might make it ashore; even if you don't, panicking won't help. Responding calmly and with courage is more important. That's what you'd praise other people for doing if faced with the same situation.

**THIRD STAGE:** On the other hand, if you have assented to the impression that something is intrinsically bad or catastrophic, then a full-blown "passion" develops, which can quickly spiral out of control. This actually happened to Seneca during a storm when he grew seasick and panicked so much that he foolishly clambered overboard and tried to wade ashore through the waves and rocks when he would have been much safer remaining on the boat.[18]

In other words, a certain amount of anxiety is natural. Indeed, the hearts of even the most experienced sailors might leap into their mouths when their ship looks like it's about to be overturned. Bravery would consist in carrying on regardless and dealing with the situation rationally. The Stoic likewise tells himself that although the situation may appear frightening, the truly important thing in life is how he chooses to respond. So he reminds himself to view the storm with Stoic indifference and to respond with wisdom and courage while accepting his initial nervous reaction as harmless and inevitable. What he *does not* do, though, is make things worse for himself by continuing to worry.

For this reason, once the pallor and anxious expression have left his face, the wise man's anxiety tends to abate naturally, and he regains his composure before long. He reevaluates his initial anxious impressions, confidently asserting that they are both false and unhelpful. On the other hand, the unwise and fearful perpetuate their own distress for much longer. Gellius read about this in the lost *Discourse* of Epictetus and learned that there is nothing *un-Stoic* about someone turning pale with anxiety for a while during a perilous situation like the one he'd just survived. It's natural and inevitable to experience feelings like these, as long as we don't escalate our distress by going along with the impressions accompanying them and telling ourselves that some awful catastrophe is about to happen.

Seneca likewise noted that certain misfortunes strike the wise man without incapacitating him, such as physical pain, illness, the loss of friends or children, or the catastrophes inflicted by defeat in war.[19] They graze him but do not wound him. Indeed, Seneca also points out that there is no virtue in enduring things we do not feel. This is important to note: for a Stoic to exhibit the virtue of temperance, he must have at least some trace of desire to renounce, and to exhibit courage *he must have at least these first sensations of fear to endure.* As the Stoics like to put it, the wise man is not made of stone or iron but of flesh and blood.

In *The Meditations*, Marcus himself writes that although he tells troubling impressions to go away, he is not angry with them because they have come according to their "ancient manner"; in other words, they arise in the way basic feelings also arise in animals.[20] That implies that, like the anonymous Stoic teacher on Gellius's storm-tossed boat, Marcus views them with indifference rather than judging them as inherently bad. Elsewhere he says that pleasant and unpleasant sensations in the body inevitably impinge on the mind because they're part of the same organism.[21] We shouldn't try to resist them, but rather we should accept their occurrence as natural, as long as we don't allow our mind to add the judgment that the things we're experiencing are good or bad. This is important, because people who confuse "Stoicism" with "stoicism" (i.e., having a stiff upper lip) often think that it's about suppressing feelings like anxiety, which they view as bad, harmful, or shameful. That's not only bad psychology, it's also totally in conflict with Stoic philosophy, which teaches us to accept our involuntary emotional reactions, our flashes of anxiety, as indifferent: *neither* good *nor* bad. What matters, in other words, isn't what we feel but how we respond to those feelings.

Although Marcus was reputedly introduced to philosophy at an unusually early age, it's believed that he didn't *wholeheartedly* commit his life *to* Stoicism until Junius Rusticus supplanted Fronto as his main tutor, when Marcus was in his early twenties. Looking back on this time, Marcus was grateful that when he first began to dabble in philosophy he didn't completely fall under the spell of a Sophist, like Fronto, or end up obsessively poring over books, working out logical puzzles, or speculating about physics and cosmology. Rather, he focused on Stoic ethics and its practical application in daily life. Whereas Fronto counseled Marcus to dress and speak more like an emperor, Rusticus did the opposite. He was among those who encouraged Marcus to set aside the vanity of status and dress down whenever possible rather than walking around in the formal attire of a Caesar (and later an emperor). This was exceptional behavior for a Roman of his status, incidentally, but the British Museum has a statuette in its collection that seems to confirm it really happened. It shows Marcus dressed not like an emperor but as a common citizen, apparently while visiting Egypt late in his life.

Rusticus also persuaded Marcus that he shouldn't be led astray by his initial enthusiasm for formal rhetoric; neither should he waste his time writing theoretical essays or trying to win praise by merely playing the role of the virtuous man. Indeed, Marcus says Rusticus convinced him to abstain from oratory, poetry, and fine language in general and to adopt the more down-to-earth and unaffected manner of speaking associated with Stoicism. In other words, Marcus went through a sort of *conversion* from rhetoric to philosophy, and this appears to have been a pivotal event in his life. Why was it such an upheaval, though? Whereas Sophistry is all about creating an appearance, philosophy is about grasping reality. Marcus's transformation into a fully-fledged Stoic therefore entailed a change in his fundamental values. It turns out that Stoic "plain speaking" isn't quite as easy as it sounds. It requires courage, self-discipline, and a sincere commitment to philosophical truth. As we'll see, this change in orientation and worldview went hand in hand not only with a more Stoic way of speaking but also with a whole new way of thinking about events.

# HOW TO SPEAK WISELY

We've seen that Marcus grew up at time when rhetoric was highly fashionable, particularly at the imperial court of Hadrian. He underwent a thorough training in speechwriting and oratory from a group of tutors, including Herodes Atticus and Fronto, the leading Greek and Latin rhetoricians of his day, respectively. However, from his early youth, Marcus had earned a reputation for speaking plainly and honestly. In stark contrast to Hadrian, who loved to make a show of his learning, Marcus tells himself that true philosophy is both simple and modest, and we should never be seduced into vanity or ostentation in this regard. Always take the shortest route, he says.[22] The short way is the way of Nature, which leads to the soundest words and actions. Simplicity frees us from affectation and the trouble it brings. For Stoics, this honesty and simplicity of language requires two main things: *conciseness* and *objectivity*. It would be an oversimplification to say that this just means to stop complaining, but in many cases the Stoics did advise along those lines. The point at which our language starts evoking strong emotions is precisely when we start saying things that involve strong value judgments, whether to others or ourselves. According to Stoic philosophy, when we assign intrinsic values like "good" or "bad" to external events, we're behaving irrationally and even exhibiting a form of self-deception. When we call something a "catastrophe," for instance, we go beyond the bare facts and start distorting events and deceiving ourselves. Moreover, the Stoics consider lying a form of impiety—when a man lies, he alienates himself from Nature.[23]

So how did the Stoics recommend we use language? Zeno, who wrote a *Handbook of Rhetoric*, didn't consider verbal eloquence an end in itself but rather a means for sharing wisdom by articulating the truth clearly and concisely in a manner adapted to the needs of the hearer. According to Diogenes Laertius, Stoic rhetoric identified five "virtues" of speech:

1. Correct grammar and good vocabulary
2. Clarity of expression, making the ideas easily understood
3. Conciseness, employing no more words than necessary
4. Appropriateness of style, suited to the subject matter and apparently also to the audience
5. Distinction, or artistic excellence, and the avoidance of vulgarity

Traditional rhetoric shared most of these values, with the notable exception of *conciseness*. However, the Stoic use of language was normally seen as being completely at odds with established forms of rhetoric.

The Sophists, as we've seen, sought to persuade others by appealing to their emotions, typically in order to win praise. The Stoics, by contrast, placed supreme value on grasping and communicating the truth by appealing to reason. This meant avoiding the use of emotive rhetoric or strong value judgments. We usually think of rhetoric as something used to manipulate *other* people. We tend to forget we're doing it to *ourselves* as well, not only when we speak but also when we use language to think. The Stoics were certainly interested in how our words affect others. However, their priority was to change the way we affect ourselves, our own thoughts and feelings, through our choice of language. We exaggerate, overgeneralize, omit information, and use strong language and colorful metaphors: "She's always being a bitch!"

"That bastard shot me down in flames!" "This job is complete bullshit!" People tend to think that exclamations like these are a natural *consequence* of strong emotions like anger. But what if they're also *causing* or perpetuating our emotions? If you think about it, rhetoric like this is designed to evoke strong feelings. By contrast, *undoing* the effects of emotional rhetoric by describing the same events more objectively forms the basis of the ancient Stoic therapy of the passions.

Indeed, one way of understanding the contrast between Stoic philosophy and Sophistic rhetoric is to view Stoicism as the practice of a kind of *anti*rhetoric or *counter*rhetoric. Whereas orators traditionally sought to exploit the emotions of their audience, the Stoics made a point of consciously describing events in plain and simple terms. Cutting through misleading language and value judgments and stripping away any embellishments or emotive language, they tried to articulate the facts more calmly and soberly. Marcus likewise told himself to speak plainly rather than dressing up his thoughts in fancy language. Indeed, nothing is so conducive to greatness of mind, he said, as the ability to examine events rationally and view them realistically by stripping them down to their essential characteristics in this way.[24] In the *Discourses* we're told that a philosopher, presumably *not* a Stoic, once grew so frustrated with his friends questioning his character that he screamed, "I can't bear it, you're killing me—*you'll turn me into him!*,"[25] pointing at Epictetus. That was a sudden display of histrionics: a blast of emotional rhetoric. Ironically, though, if he'd been more like Epictetus, he would have just stuck to the facts without getting worked up and said something like, "You criticized me; so be it." In truth, *nobody* was killing this man and he *could* bear it.

The way we talk and think about events involves making value judgments, which shape our feelings. Shakespeare's

Hamlet exclaims, "There is nothing either good or bad but thinking makes it so." The Stoics would agree that there's nothing good or bad in the external world. Only what is up to us can be truly "good" or "bad," which makes these terms synonymous with virtue and vice. Wisdom therefore consists in grasping external things objectively, as indifferent in this regard. Sometimes the Stoics describe this as staying with our initial impression of things before we impose value judgments. Epictetus gives many examples, such as when someone's ship is lost at sea, we should say only "the ship is lost" and not add value judgments or complaints like "Why me? This is awful!"[26] When someone bathes rather hastily, we should not react with disgust or even imply that he washed himself badly, but say only that he bathed quickly. When someone drinks a lot of wine, we should not say that he has done something terrible, only that he drank a lot of wine.[27] Marcus follows Epictetus's guidance when he says, for instance, that he should tell himself someone has insulted him in a matter-of-fact way, but not add the value judgment that it has done him any harm.[28] If you stick with the facts and don't unnecessarily extrapolate from them, you will put paid to many anxieties in life.

Zeno coined the Stoic technical term *phantasia kataleptike* to refer to this Stoic way of viewing events objectively, separating value judgments from facts. Pierre Hadot translates it as "objective representation," which is the term we'll use.[29] However, it literally means an impression that gets a grip on reality and thereby prevents us from being swept along by our passions. It anchors our thoughts in reality. Zeno even symbolized this concept by the physical gesture of clenching his fist—we still talk today of someone who looks at events in a matter-of-fact way as "having a firm grip on reality." Epictetus explained that a Stoic might say someone "has been sent to prison," but they should not allow themselves to go on about how *awful* it is and complain that Zeus has punished that person *unjustly*.[30] As an aspiring Stoic, you should begin by practicing deliberately describing events more objectively and in less emotional terms. Epictetus tells his students that if they can avoid being swept along with false and upsetting impressions, they will remain grounded in the objective representations they initially perceived.[31]

Sticking to the facts can, by itself, often reduce your anxiety. Cognitive therapists use the neologism "catastrophizing," or dwelling on the worst-case scenario, to help explain to clients how we project our values onto external events. They turn the noun "catastrophe" into a verb to help clients remember that viewing events in this way is actually an *activity* they're engaged in. Catastrophizing is also a form of rhetorical *hyperbole*, or exaggeration. An event like losing your job is not inherently catastrophic; we don't just passively perceive how bad it is. Rather, we actively *catastrophize* it, turning it into a catastrophe by imposing a value judgment upon it that blows things out of proportion.

In cognitive therapy, we learn to take greater ownership of or responsibility for the catastrophic value judgments that distress us. Modern cognitive therapists advise their clients to describe events in more down-to-earth language, like the Stoics before them. They call it "decatastrophizing" when they help clients downgrade their perception of a situation from provoking anxiety to something more mundane and less frightening. For instance, Aaron T. Beck, the founder of cognitive therapy, advised that clients suffering from anxiety should write "decatastrophizing scripts" in which they describe distressing events factually, without strong value judgments or emotive language: "I lost my job and now I'm looking for a new one" rather than "I lost my job and there's nothing I can do about it—it's just a total disaster!" Think about it: when you're distressed, don't you tend to exaggerate and use vivid, emotional language to describe things, both to yourself and other people? Decatastrophizing involves reevaluating the probability and severity of something bad happening and framing it in more realistic terms. Beck asks his clients, "Would it really be as terrible as you think?" Catastrophizing often seems to involve thinking, "What if?" What if the worst-case scenario happens? That would be unbearable. Decatastrophizing, on the other hand, has been described as going from "What if?" to "So what?": *So what if such-and-such happens? It's not the end of the world; I can deal with it.*

Another common method of decatastrophizing is for cognitive therapists to ask clients repeatedly, "What next?" Mental images of feared events often rapidly escalate to the worst, most anxiety-provoking part and then remain glued there as if the upsetting experience were somehow timeless. In reality, though, everything has a before, during, and after phase. Everything changes with time, and experiences come and go. Anxiety can often be reduced simply by moving the image past the worst point and imagining, in a realistic and noncatastrophic way, what's most likely to happen in the hours, days, weeks, or months that follow. Reminding himself of the transience of events is one of Marcus's favorite strategies, as we'll see in later chapters. One way of doing that is to ask yourself, "What, realistically, will most likely happen next? And then what? And *then* what?" And so on.

Beck's original cognitive therapy approach for anxiety was derived from something known as the "transactional" model of stress, developed by Richard Lazarus.[32] Imagine a seesaw, with your appraisal of the severity of a situation—how threatening or dangerous it is—on one side. On the other side is your appraisal of your own ability to cope, your self-confidence if you like. If you believe that the threat outweighs your ability to cope and the seesaw tips toward danger, then you'll probably feel extremely stressed or anxious. On the other hand, if you reckon that the severity of the threat is low and your ability to cope is high, then the seesaw will tip toward you, and you should feel calm and self-confident. The Stoics, like modern therapists, tried to modify both sides of this equation.

Normally, therefore, once you've arrived at a more realistic description of a feared situation, you will consider ways that you could potentially cope and get through it. Sometimes this involves creative problem-solving—brainstorming alternative solutions and weighing the consequences. The Stoics liked to ask themselves, "What virtues has Nature given me that might help me deal with the situation better?" You might also consider how other people cope so that you can try to model their attitudes and behavior. What would a role model like Socrates, Diogenes, or Zeno do? We can also ask "What would Marcus do?" if faced with the same situation. In modern therapy, clients model the behavior of others and develop "coping plans," which describe how they would deal with the feared situation if it actually happened. Considering what another person would do or what they would advise you to do can help you formulate better coping plans, and that will typically lead you to decatastrophize the situation and downgrade your appraisal of its severity. That means going from thinking of events as "totally unbearable" to picturing realistic ways you can bear them and deal with them. The more clearly formulated your coping plan is and the more confident you are about putting it into practice, *the less anxious you will tend to feel.*

When their *friends* were struggling emotionally, Stoics sometimes wrote them letters of consolation, helping them to view events in a less catastrophic, more constructive way. Six consolation letters written by Seneca exist today. For instance, he wrote to a woman called Marcia who had recently lost her son. Seneca's consolations to her include the argument that death is a release from all the pain of life, a barrier beyond which our suffering cannot extend, which returns us to the same restful state we were in before we were born. Moreover, Epictetus told his students that one of the Stoics he held in particularly high regard, Paconius Agrippinus, used to write similar letters to console *himself* whenever any hardship befell him.[33] When faced with fever, slander, or exile, he would compose Stoic "eulogies" praising these events as occasions to exercise strength of character. Agrippinus was truly a master decatastrophizer. He would reframe every hardship as an opportunity to cope by exercising wisdom and strength of character. Epictetus says that one day, as Agrippinus was preparing to dine with his friends, a messenger arrived announcing that the Emperor Nero had banished him from Rome as part of a political purge. "Very well," said Agrippinus, shrugging, "we shall take our lunch in Aricia," the first stop on the road he would have to travel into exile.[34]

You can start training yourself in this Stoic practice of objective representation right now by writing down a description of an upsetting or problematic event in plain language. Phrase things as accurately as possible and view them from a more philosophical perspective, with studied indifference. Once you've mastered this art, take it a step further by following the example of Paconius Agrippinus and look for positive opportunities. Write how you could exercise strength of character and cope wisely with the situation. Ask yourself how someone you admire might cope with the same situation or what that person might advise you to do. Treat the event like a sparring partner in the gym, giving you an opportunity to strengthen your emotional resilience and coping skills. You might want to read your script aloud and review it several times or compose several versions until you're satisfied it's helped you change how you feel about events.

Marcus tends to refer to this way of viewing events as entailing the *separation* of our value judgments from external events. Cognitive therapists have likewise, for many decades, taught their clients the famous quotation from Epictetus: "It's not things that upset us but our judgments about things," which became an integral part of the initial orientation ("socialization") of the client to the treatment approach. This sort of technique is referred to as "cognitive distancing" in CBT, because it requires sensing the separation or distance between our thoughts and external reality. Beck defined it as a "metacognitive" process, meaning a shift to a level of awareness involving "thinking about thinking."

> "Distancing" refers to the ability to view one's own thoughts (or beliefs) as constructions of "reality" rather than as reality itself.[35]

He recommended explaining this to clients using the analogy of colored glasses. We could look at the world *through* positive rose-tinted glasses or sad blue ones and just assume that what we see is how things are. However, we can also look *at* the glasses themselves and realize that they *color* our vision. Noticing how our thoughts and beliefs tinge our perception of the world is a prerequisite for changing them in cognitive therapy. Later generations of clinicians and researchers discovered that rigorous training in cognitive distancing, by itself, was sufficient in many cases to bring about therapeutic improvement. Greater emphasis on this cognitive skill is an integral part of what became known as the *mindfulness and acceptance* approach to CBT.

Sometimes merely remembering the saying of Epictetus, that "it's not things that upset us," can help us gain cognitive distance from our thoughts, allowing us to view them as hypotheses rather than facts about the world. However, there are also *many* other cognitive distancing techniques used in modern CBT, such as these:

- Writing down your thoughts concisely when they occur and viewing them on paper
- Writing them on a whiteboard and looking at them "over there"—literally from a distance
- Prefixing them with a phrase like "Right now, I notice that I am thinking . . ."
- Referring to them in the third person, for example, "Donald is thinking . . . ," as if you're studying the thoughts and beliefs of someone else
- Evaluating in a detached manner the pros and cons of holding a certain opinion
- Using a counter or a tally to monitor with detached curiosity the frequency of certain thoughts
- Shifting perspective and imagining a range of alternative ways of looking at the same situation so that your initial viewpoint becomes less fixed and rigid. For example, "How might I feel about crashing my car if I were like Marcus Aurelius?" "If this happened to my daughter, how would I advise her to cope?" "How will I think about this, looking back on events, ten or twenty years from now?"

There are several distancing methods found in the ancient Stoic literature. For instance, you can help yourself gain cognitive distance just by *speaking to* ("apostrophizing") your thoughts and feelings, saying something like, "You are just a feeling and not really the thing you claim to represent," as Epictetus in the *Handbook* advised his students to do.

The *Handbook* actually opens with a technique to remind ourselves that some things are "up to us," or directly under our control, and other things are not. Modern Stoics sometimes call this the "Dichotomy of Control" or the "Stoic Fork." Just recalling this distinction can help you recover a sense of indifference toward external things. Think of it this way. When you strongly judge something to be good or bad, you also commit yourself to saying that you want to obtain or avoid it. But if something is outside your control, then it's simply irrational to demand that you should obtain or avoid it. It's a *contradiction* to believe both that you must do something and also that it's not within your power to do so. The Stoics viewed this confusion as the root cause of most emotional suffering. They pointed out that only our own acts of volition, our own intentions and judgments if you like, are directly under our control. Sure, I can open the door, but that's always a *consequence* of my actions. Only my own voluntary actions themselves are truly under my control. When we judge external things to be good or bad, it's as though we forget what's under our control and try to overextend our sphere of responsibility. The Stoics view only their own actions as good or bad, virtuous or vicious, and therefore classify all external things as indifferent, because they're not entirely "up to us" in this sense.

As we've seen, of course, the Stoics still believe it's reasonable to prefer health to disease, wealth to poverty, and so on. They argue, however, that we deceive ourselves when we invest too much value in external things. They also trained themselves to gain cognitive distance by understanding that events don't seem the same to everyone: our own perspective is just one of many. For instance, the majority of people are terrified of dying, but, as Epictetus points out, Socrates wasn't afraid of death. Although he may have preferred to live, he was relatively indifferent to dying as long as he met his death with wisdom and virtue. This used to be known as the ideal of a "good death," from which our word "euthanasia" derives. However, for Socrates and the Stoics, a good death didn't so much mean a pleasant or peaceful death as one faced with wisdom and virtue. Knowing that not everyone sees a certain situation as catastrophic should make us more aware that the "awfulness" of it derives from our own thinking, our value judgments, and our way of responding rather than the thing itself. Awfulness (badness) is not a physical property. As Aristotle said, fire burns just the same in Greece as in Persia, but men's judgments about what's good or bad vary from one place to another. Marcus therefore compares our opinions to *beams of sunlight* shining on external objects, not unlike Beck's analogy of looking at the world through tinted glasses. By realizing that our value judgments are projections, Marcus says, we separate them from external events. He refers to this cognitive process as the "purification" (*katharsis*) of the mind.

In this chapter we saw how the values Marcus learned from his birth family, such as simplicity and plain speech, clashed with those of the Second Sophistic and the rhetoricians at Hadrian's court. This led him to embrace the Stoics' radical use of language as a *counter*rhetoric, through techniques such as redescribing events in more objective language, free from value judgments—

an ancient precursor to decatastrophizing in modern cognitive therapy.

Accepting this approach to describing our situation, whatever it may be, is a foundational step in learning the other Stoic practices. It leads to the next step: considering what resources or virtues you have that would allow you to cope better, or how a wise person might deal with the same situation. Whether we call it *cognitive distancing* or *katharsis*, we separate strong value judgments from external events by letting go of excessive attachment to things. You might find this a tricky concept at first, but coming back to Epictetus's famous saying—"It's not things that upset us but our judgments about things"—will serve you well as a guide.

We've seen that Marcus's disillusionment with court life and formal rhetoric gradually led him to embrace philosophy more deeply. His personal mentor Junius Rusticus would persuade Marcus to undergo a more thorough conversion to Stoic philosophy and embrace it wholeheartedly as a way of life.

# 3.

# CONTEMPLATING
# THE SAGE

A s a young man, Marcus Aurelius frequently became very *angry*, often struggling to avoid losing his temper. Later in life he would thank the gods that he had been able to restrain himself from doing something in those moments that he might otherwise have regretted. He'd seen the damage caused by Hadrian's temper. During one infamous tantrum, the emperor had poked out the eye of some poor slave with the point of an iron stylus, presumably to the horror of onlookers. Once he'd come back to his senses, Hadrian apologetically asked the man if there was anything he could do to make it up to him. "All I want is my eye back," came the reply.[1]

His successor, Antoninus, was famously gentle and even-tempered, quite the opposite of Hadrian. In the first book of *The Meditations*, Marcus contemplates his adoptive father's virtues several times, even referring to himself as Antoninus's *disciple*, but Marcus makes no mention of any virtues possessed by Hadrian. Marcus clearly viewed Antoninus as the model of an ideal ruler, everything he aspired to become himself. Indeed, over a decade after Antoninus's death, Marcus was still carefully meditating on his example.

The Stoics taught Marcus that anger is nothing but *temporary madness* and that its consequences are often irreparable, as in the case of the slave's eye. They also provided him with the psychological concepts and set of tools he needed to master his own feelings of aggression. Marcus clearly wanted to be more like the humble, peaceful Antoninus than the arrogant and volatile Hadrian. He needed help achieving this, though. Ironically, he credits the man who most frequently provoked his anger with teaching him how to control it. Marcus's Stoic mentor Junius Rusticus often infuriated him, but also showed him how to recover his normal frame of mind. As we'll see, the Stoics had many specific techniques for anger management. One of them is to wait until our feelings have naturally abated and then calmly consider what someone wise would do in a similar situation. Marcus also learned from Rusticus how to be reconciled with others as soon as they were willing to make amends. Perhaps that was how Rusticus conducted himself when he detected that Marcus was becoming angry, providing an example of gracious behavior that Marcus studied and emulated.

Whereas Apollonius was a professional philosophy lecturer, Rusticus, also an expert on Stoicism, probably acted more as a mentor or private tutor. A Roman statesman of consular rank, Rusticus was roughly twenty years Marcus's senior. He appears to have been the grandson of a famous Stoic called Arulenus Rusticus, a friend and follower of Thrasea, the leader of the Stoic Opposition—a political hero to Epictetus and his students. Rusticus himself was a highly esteemed man, both in private and public life. He was also intensely loyal to Marcus. Fronto, with typical hyperbole, says in his private letters that Rusticus "would gladly surrender and sacrifice his life" to preserve Marcus's little finger. Marcus clearly revered Rusticus, soon came to view himself as the Stoic's disciple, and remained devoted to him for decades, even after becoming emperor. For example, it was the custom in the imperial court for the emperor to greet his praetorian prefect with a kiss on the lips, but Marcus broke with this convention by always kissing Rusticus first when they met, as if he were greeting his own brother. This gesture made it clear to everyone that the philosopher occupied a special position at court. If Antoninus was Marcus's role model as an emperor, Rusticus undoubtedly provided the main example he sought to follow as a *Stoic*. As Marcus said elsewhere, philosophy was his mother, the court merely his stepmother.[2]

There's no doubt that Rusticus was the central figure in Marcus's development as a philosopher. However, Marcus makes it clear that one of the most important events in their relationship was when his tutor presented him with a set of notes on the lectures of Epictetus from his own personal library. Marcus probably meant the *Discourses* recorded by Arrian, which he quotes several times in *The Meditations*. As we've seen, Arrian was a student of Epictetus who transcribed eight volumes of his philosophical discussions, only four of which survive. We also have his shorter summary of Epictetus's sayings, the *Handbook*, or *Enchiridion*. Arrian was a prolific author in his own right and a highly accomplished Roman general and statesman. Hadrian made him a senator and later appointed him *suffect consul* for 131 AD, and he then served for six years as governor of Cappadocia, one of the most important military posts in the empire. During the reign of Antoninus, he retired to Athens, where he later served as *archon*, ruler and chief magistrate, before dying around the start of Marcus's reign. It's possible that Arrian is the missing link that connects Marcus and Rusticus to Epictetus.

Arrian was about a decade older than Rusticus, and they likely knew each other. Indeed, Themistius, a Roman philosopher of the fourth century, speaks of them together. Hadrian, Antoninus, and Marcus, he says, "pulled Arrian and Rusticus away from their books, refusing to let them be mere pen-and-ink philosophers."[3] The emperors didn't let Arrian and Rusticus write about courage while remaining safely at home, composing legal treatises while avoiding public life, or pondering the best form of administration while abstaining from participation in the government of Rome, we're told. Instead, they were escorted from the study of Stoic philosophy "to the general's tent and to the speaker's platform." Themistius adds that while serving as Roman generals, Arrian and Rusticus "passed through the Caspian Gates, drove the Alani out of Armenia, and established boundaries for the Iberians and the Albani." In reward for these military achievements, the two were appointed consuls, and they governed the great city of Rome and presided over the Senate. The examples of men like these who went before Marcus—statesmen and military commanders inspired by Stoicism—encouraged him to believe he could be both an emperor *and* a philosopher.

We know that Rusticus was appointed consul for the second time the year after Marcus was acclaimed emperor. He also served as urban prefect from 162 to 168 AD, effectively making him Marcus's right-hand man at Rome during the first phase of his reign. Rusticus died shortly after this period, perhaps another victim of the plague, and Marcus asked the Senate to erect several statues in his honor. As with his other tutors, Marcus kept a statuette of Rusticus in his personal shrine and offered sacrifices to his memory. So that leaves us with an odd question: *What exactly did Rusticus do to irritate the future emperor so badly?*

The answer may lie in the nature of their relationship. Marcus tells himself in *The Meditations* that when learning to read and write you cannot be a teacher without having first been a student, and that this is even truer for the art of living.[4] Students of Stoicism benefited from the wisdom of their teachers by treating them both as *models*, whose behavior they sought to emulate, and *mentors*, to whose advice they could listen. Rusticus certainly provided a living example of wisdom and virtue to Marcus. In *The Meditations* he mentions that Rusticus was one of three tutors, along with Apollonius of Chalcedon and Sextus of Chaeronea, who exemplified Stoicism for him as a way of life. He was also there to *counsel* him, though, offering guidance and moral correction. Indeed, Marcus said that it was Rusticus who showed him that he was in need of moral training and Stoic psychological therapy (*therapeia*). This may explain the tension in their relationship. Marcus clearly loved Rusticus dearly as a friend and looked up to him as a teacher, but he also found him exasperating at times, presumably because he frequently drew the young Caesar's attention to flaws in his character.

We can perhaps infer which aspects of Marcus's character Rusticus challenged based upon comments in *The Meditations*. For example, Rusticus taught him not to be pretentious, encouraging him to dress like a normal citizen when possible. He also taught Marcus to be a careful and patient student of philosophy, to read attentively rather than just skimming things, and not to be swayed too easily by speakers who have a silver tongue. Epictetus likewise told his students repeatedly that they should not speak about philosophy lightly, like the Sophists, but rather show its fruits in their very character and actions. In typically blunt fashion he told them that sheep don't vomit up grass to show the shepherds how much they've eaten but rather digest their food inwardly and produce good wool and milk outwardly.[5]

The most important change Rusticus brought about, however, was that he persuaded Marcus to sideline the formal study of Latin rhetoric, expected of a Roman noble, in favor of a greater commitment to Stoic philosophy as a way of life. Rusticus the philosopher and Fronto the rhetorician, Marcus's two most important tutors, appear to have vied for his attention for nearly a decade, but Rusticus finally won. Scholars date this "conversion" to around 146 AD, when Marcus was twenty-five. He confesses in a letter to Fronto that he has been unable to concentrate on his studies in Latin rhetoric. He is overcome with a mixture of joy and anguish after reading some books by a philosopher named Aristo. Most scholars believe this must have been Aristo of Chios, a student of Zeno's who had rebelled against his teachings and adopted a simpler and more austere version of Stoicism resembling Cynicism. Perhaps Rusticus or one of his other Stoic tutors shared these writings with Marcus. Aristo rejected the study of logic and metaphysics, arguing that the primary concern of philosophers should be the study of ethics, an attitude we can find echoed in *The Meditations*.

Marcus told Fronto that Aristo's writings tormented him, making him conscious of how far his own character fell short of virtue. "Your pupil blushes over and over again and grows angry with himself because, at the age of twenty-five, I have not yet absorbed any of these excellent teachings and purer principles into my soul."[6] The young Caesar was genuinely in turmoil. He felt depressed and angry and lost his appetite. He also mentions feeling envious of others, perhaps meaning that he yearned to dedicate himself to Stoicism and become like the philosophers he admired. It was around this time that Marcus began to distance himself from Sophists like Fronto and Herodes Atticus.

What was the *process* of being mentored by a Stoic philosopher actually like, though? Why did it have such a profound and lasting impact on Marcus? The Stoics wrote several books describing their psychotherapy of the passions, including one by Chrysippus, the third head of the school, titled *The Therapeutics*. Unfortunately, these are all lost to us today. However, a treatise titled *On the Diagnosis and Cure of the Soul's Passions* survives, written by Marcus's celebrated physician, Galen. A polymath with an eclectic taste in philosophy, Galen had initially studied under a Stoic called Philopater, and he drew upon early Stoic philosophy, quoting Zeno, in his own account of diagnosing and curing unhealthy passions. This may give us some clues about the nature of the Stoic "therapy" Marcus went through with Rusticus.

As a young man, Galen wondered why the Delphic Oracle's maxim to "know thyself" should be held in such high regard. Doesn't everyone *already* know himself? He gradually came to realize, though, that only the very wisest among us ever truly know ourselves. The rest of us, as Galen observed, tend to fall into the trap of supposing either that we are completely without fault or that our flaws are few, mild, and infrequent. Indeed, those who assume that they have the fewest flaws are often the ones most deeply flawed in the eyes of others. This is illustrated by one of Aesop's fables, which says that each of us is born with two sacks suspended from our neck: one filled with the faults of others that hangs within our view and one hidden behind our back filled with our own faults. We see the flaws of others quite clearly, in other words, but we have a blind spot for our own. The New Testament likewise asks why we look at the tiny splinter of wood in our brother's eye yet pay no attention to the great plank of wood obscuring our own view (Matthew 7:3–5). Galen says that Plato explained this well when he said that lovers are typically blind regarding the one they love. As we, in a sense, loves ourselves most of all, we are also most blind with regard to our own faults. The majority of us therefore struggle to attain the self-awareness required to improve our lives.

Galen's solution to this problem is for us to find a suitable mentor in whose wisdom and experience we can genuinely trust. Anyone can tell when a singer is truly dreadful, but it takes an expert to notice very subtle flaws in a performance. Likewise, it takes a person of moral wisdom to discern *slight* defects in another person's character. We all know that someone is angry when their face turns red and they start yelling, but a true expert on human nature would be able to tell when someone is just on the verge of getting angry, perhaps before they even realize it themselves. We should therefore make the effort to acquire an older and wiser friend: one renowned for honesty and plain speaking, who has mastered the same passions with which we need help, who can properly identify our vices and tell us frankly where we're going astray in life. What Galen is describing sounds somewhat like the relationship between a modern-day counselor or psychotherapist and their client. However, a better comparison would probably be with the mentoring or "sponsorship" provided by recovering drug or alcohol addicts to those who are in recovery and struggling with similar habits—the help of a more experienced fellow patient, as Seneca puts it. Of course, finding an appropriate mentor is still easier said than done.

Marcus wrote that anyone who truly wants to achieve wisdom through Stoicism will make it his priority in life to cultivate his own character and seek help from others who share similar values.[7] That seems like the role Junius Rusticus played for him. We should ask that person if they notice any unhealthy passions in us, says Galen, assuring them that we're not going to be offended if they speak frankly. Galen also explains that the novice is bound to feel that some of his mentor's observations are unfair, but he must learn to listen patiently and take criticism on the chin without becoming irritated. From what Marcus says, that was probably quite challenging for him at first, although Rusticus was good at smoothing things over.

Marcus had another Stoic tutor, called Cinna Catulus, about whom we know very little. Marcus observed that Catulus was a man who paid attention to his friends when they found fault in his character; even if they did so unjustly, he would always try to address matters and restore their friendship.[8] Through their own behavior, therefore, Rusticus and Catulus both showed Marcus that a wise man should welcome criticism from his friends.

The Stoics clearly inherited their love of plain speaking from their predecessors the Cynics, who were renowned for speaking very bluntly and criticizing even powerful rulers. In a sense, it was the duty, and privilege, of a true philosopher to speak truth to power. One of the most famous legends about Diogenes the Cynic tells how Alexander the Great sought out the philosopher. It's a juxtaposition of opposites: Diogenes lived like a beggar, and Alexander was the most powerful man in the known world. However, when Alexander asked Diogenes if there was anything he could do for him, the Cynic is supposed to have replied that he could step aside, as he was blocking the sun. Diogenes could speak to Alexander as if they were equals because he was indifferent to wealth and power. Alexander is said to have walked off and returned to his conquests, apparently without having gained much wisdom.

As was often the case, the Stoics adopted a more *moderate* approach, and they were concerned that their speech should not only be honest and simple but also appropriate to the needs of the hearer. There's no point in speaking plainly to people if it doesn't *benefit* them. Throughout *The Meditations*, Marcus makes many references to the value he places on speaking the truth, but he also consistently recognizes the importance of communicating it appropriately. For instance, Alexander of Cotiaeum, his childhood grammarian, made a lifelong impression on Marcus by the tactful way he would correct those making a verbal error.[9] If someone used a word incorrectly, Alexander would not overtly criticize the speaker. He never interrupted them or challenged them on the spot. Instead, the grammarian had a more artful and indirect way of steering them in the right direction. Marcus noticed that Alexander would subtly drop in the correct expression while replying or discussing some other topic. If the real goal for Stoics is wisdom, then sometimes just blurting out the truth isn't enough. We have to put more effort into communicating with others effectively.

Diplomacy was, of course, particularly important to Marcus. His duties as Caesar and later as emperor involved handling highly sensitive discussions, such as negotiations over peace treaties with foreign enemies. We can clearly see from his personal correspondence that he was a charming and tactful man with an impressive ability to resolve conflicts between his friends. Indeed, Fronto waxes lyrical about this, extolling his young student's ability to unite all his friends together in harmony, something the rhetorician compares to the mythic power of Orpheus to tame savage beasts through the music of his lyre. Throughout Marcus's reign, he doubtlessly averted many serious problems through his patient diplomacy and sensitive use of language. Indeed, he even reminds himself that he should always be tactful and honest with whoever he's speaking to, especially in the Senate.[10]

In addition to having this innate talent, Marcus learned a great deal from the Stoics about how a wise man should try to communicate with others. Apollonius of Chalcedon, for instance, was not a man to hold back his words, yet he balanced his self-confidence with open-mindedness. Marcus describes how another of his most beloved teachers, Sextus of Chaeronea, came across as both very serious and plainspoken, yet he was exceptionally patient with the unlearned, and even the opinionated. Correcting someone else's vices, Marcus says, is like pointing out that they have bad breath—it requires considerable tact. However, he noticed that Sextus won the respect of all sorts of people by skillfully adapting his conversation so that it seemed more charming than any flattery, even while he was speaking frankly or disagreeing with them. Clearly, Stoics like Marcus placed a lot more value on manners and civility than the Cynics did. The Stoics realized that to communicate *wisely*, we must phrase things *appropriately*. Indeed, according to Epictetus, the most striking characteristic of Socrates was that he never became irritated during an argument. He was always polite and refrained from speaking harshly even when others insulted him. He patiently endured much abuse and yet was able to put an end to most quarrels in a calm and rational manner.[11]

We can imagine that when Rusticus challenged Marcus over his behavior, his remarks, though sometimes provocative and close to the bone, were probably judicious enough that his young student benefited from them without feeling humiliated. How can we find mentors with such tact, though? Galen admits that you're not likely to meet many people like Diogenes the Cynic, who was brave enough even to speak plainly to Alexander the Great. What's required first is a more general openness to criticism: we should give everyone we meet permission to tell us what our faults are, according to Galen, and resolve not to be angry with any of them. Indeed, Marcus tells himself both to enter into every man's mind, to study their judgments and values, *and to let every man enter into his.*[12] If anyone gives him a valid reason to believe that he's going astray in terms of either thought or action, he says he will gladly change his ways. Marcus sought to make it his priority in life to get to the truth of matters, reminding himself that nobody has ever really been harmed in this way but that those who cling to error and ignorance harm themselves.[13] We're told this advice goes back to Zeno. Most men are eager to point out their neighbors' flaws, he said, whether we ask them to or not. So instead of resenting it, we should welcome criticism from others as one of life's inevitabilities and turn it to our advantage by making *all men* into our teachers. Galen therefore says that if we desire to learn wisdom, we must be ready to listen to anyone we encounter and show gratitude "not to those who flatter us but to those who rebuke us."[14]

This doesn't mean we should trust all opinions equally, of course. Marcus makes it clear that we must train ourselves to discriminate good advice from bad and learn not to preoccupy ourselves with the opinions of foolish people. It's prudent to listen carefully to most of the people we meet in life but not to give *equal* weight to all opinions. Rather, by welcoming criticism and accepting it dispassionately, we can gradually learn to sort through it rationally and discern good advice from bad. Sometimes, indeed, we learn most from the mistakes of others. However, as Galen observes, we should place more trust in the counsel of individuals who provide us with consistent evidence of their wisdom and virtue. Nevertheless, if we exercise caution we can learn from all people while we look for someone like Rusticus, a friend whose wisdom we can trust implicitly.

For a relationship of this kind to work, though, the student must be scrupulously honest with their mentor. In one passage,

Marcus imagines a wise teacher instructing someone to think of nothing he would be unwilling to say aloud, uncensored, as soon as it comes into his mind. Marcus doubts that the majority of us could really endure this for even a single day because we foolishly put more value on other people's opinions than on our own. And yet he aspired to this level of transparency. He says that we should imagine someone asking "What's going on right now in your mind?" without warning and that we should be able to answer truthfully without feeling the need to blush. Marcus says he wants his soul to be naked and simple, more visible even than the body that surrounds it. Elsewhere he goes even further and, like a Cynic, says we should never crave anything in life that requires walls or curtains. On one hand, these are expressions of Marcus's desire to work toward a lofty moral ideal: being so pure of heart that he has nothing to hide from anyone. However, he's also alluding to a very powerful *therapeutic* strategy. Being observed can help us develop greater self-awareness and correct our behavior, especially if we're in the presence of someone we admire, such as a trusted mentor. Even in the absence of your own Rusticus, however, just *imagining* that you're being observed by someone wise and benevolent can potentially have similar benefits, especially if you pretend that your innermost thoughts and feelings are somehow visible to them.[15]

If we wish to improve ourselves, Galen says that we must never relax our vigilance, not even for a single hour. How on earth do we do that? He explains that Zeno of Citium taught that "we should act carefully in all things—just *as if* we were going to answer for it to our teachers shortly thereafter."[16] That's a rather clever mind trick that turns Stoic mentoring into a kind of *mindfulness* practice. Imagining that we're being observed helps us to pay more attention to our own character and behavior.

A Stoic-in-training, like the young Marcus, would have been advised always to exercise self-awareness by monitoring his own thoughts, actions, and feelings, perhaps as if his mentor, Rusticus, were continually observing him. Epictetus told his students that, just as someone who walks barefoot is cautious not to step on a nail or twist his ankle, they should be careful throughout the day not to harm their own character by lapsing into errors of moral judgment.[17] In modern therapy, it's common for clients who are making progress to wonder between sessions what their therapist might say about the thoughts they have. For example, they might be worrying about something and suddenly imagine the voice of their therapist challenging them with questions like "Where's the evidence for those fears being true?" or "How's worrying like this actually working out for you?" The very notion of someone else observing your thoughts and feelings can be enough to make you pause and consider them. Of course, if you occasionally talk to a mentor or therapist about your experiences, it's much easier to imagine their presence when they're not around. Even if you don't have someone like this in your life, you can still envision that you're being observed by a wise and supportive friend. If you read about Marcus Aurelius enough, for instance, you may experiment by imagining that he's your companion as you perform some challenging task or face a difficult situation. How would you behave *differently* just knowing he was by your side? What do you think he might say about your behavior? If he could read your mind, how would he comment on your thoughts and feelings? You can pick your own mentor, of course, but you get the idea.

I think it's possible that this is, in part, what Marcus was doing by writing *The Meditations*. Rusticus probably died around 170 AD, while Marcus was away commanding the legions on the northern frontier during the First Marcomannic War. There is some evidence to suggest he may have started work on *The Meditations* around the same time. It's tempting then to wonder if he did so in response to the loss of his friend and tutor. As we've seen, Marcus described being surrounded by people who opposed his views and even wished him gone. It sounds as though he really felt the *absence* at this time of a friend like Rusticus who shared his philosophical beliefs and most cherished values.

If Marcus did start creating these notes for himself shortly after the loss of his Stoic mentor, his purpose may have been to assume responsibility for mentoring *himself*. Even today, writing exercises such as keeping a therapy journal are a popular form of self-help. However, in addition to aphorisms crafted by Marcus and sayings he quoted from famous poets and philosophers, *The Meditations* contains little snippets of dialogue. These could be quotations from lecture notes, such as the copy of Epictetus's *Discourses* that Rusticus gave him. Or they could be fictional dialogues invented by Marcus, using his imagination to conjure up an *inner* mentor. Perhaps they were even fragments of *remembered* conversations Marcus may have had with his tutors many years earlier. For example, one of them can be paraphrased as follows:

TEACHER: Piece by piece, one action after another, you must build up your life and be content if each individual act, as far as Fate permits, achieves its goal.

STUDENT: But what if there is some external obstacle that prevents me from achieving my goal?

TEACHER: There can be no obstacle to a man's efforts to approach things wisely, justly, and with self-awareness.

STUDENT: But what if some outward aspect of my behavior is hindered?

TEACHER: Well, then a cheerful acceptance of that hindrance is required, along with a tactful shift to doing what circumstances allow. This will enable you to substitute another course of action, one in keeping with the overall scheme of life that we're talking about.[18]

Galen suggested that imitating a role model is more appropriate in our youth. Later in life, as we take more responsibility for our own character, it becomes important to follow specific philosophical principles and practice living by them. Over the years, with more experience, we should develop more self-awareness and become able to spot our own errors without needing the help of a mentor. Moreover, we gradually learn to weaken passions such as anger through disciplined practice and checking their expression at an early stage. Doing this frequently will eventually make us less prone to experiencing such feelings in the first place. Marcus had trained in philosophy for over three decades by the time Rusticus passed away. So as he began writing *The Meditations*, he was probably well prepared to enter the next phase in his psychological development as a Stoic.

## HOW TO FOLLOW YOUR VALUES

The term "mentor" comes from Homer's *Odyssey*. Athena, the goddess of wisdom and virtue, disguises herself as a friend of Odysseus named Mentor so that she can counsel his son Telemachus, who is in grave danger. She remains by their side during the ultimate battle against Odysseus's enemies, encouraging the hero toward victory. Marcus said that even aspiring Stoics should not be ashamed to seek the help of others, just as an injured soldier besieging a fortress does not blush to accept a leg up from his comrades in mounting the battlements.[19] Not everyone has a Rusticus to get them over the ramparts, however. If you can find someone in whom you can trust, like Galen describes, that's great. In truth, though, most people will probably have to rely on other modeling strategies, as Marcus perhaps did *after* the death of Rusticus. These fall into two main categories: *writing* and *imagining*.

Even if you don't have a real-life mentor following you around, you can still benefit from the concept by using your imagination. Marcus, like other ancient philosophers, conjured the images of various advisors and role models in his mind. He also believed it was important to consider the character and actions of famous historical philosophers. At one point he says that the writings of "the Ephesians," possibly meaning the followers of Heraclitus, contained the advice to think constantly of individuals from previous generations who demonstrated exemplary virtue. As we've seen, the story of Zeno begins with him being given the cryptic advice to "take on the color of dead men" by studying the wisdom of previous generations. Marcus tells himself to focus his attention on the minds of wise men, particularly their underlying principles, and carefully consider what these men avoid and what they pursue in life. In *The Meditations*, he names the philosophers he most admires: Pythagoras, Heraclitus, Socrates, Diogenes the Cynic, Chrysippus, and Epictetus. Of course, you might even choose Marcus himself as a role model if you're studying his life and philosophy.[20]

Your first step is to *write down* the virtues exhibited by someone you respect. Listing the qualities you most admire in another person, just as Marcus does in the first book of *The Meditations*, is a simple and powerful exercise. He explains in a later chapter that he contemplates the virtues of those who lived with him in order to raise his spirits: the energy of one, the modesty of another, the generosity of a third, and so on.[21] Nothing cheers our soul, he says, like the people close to us exhibiting virtue in their lives, and for that very reason we should treasure these examples and keep the memory of them fresh. Writing things down will often make the image more vivid and memorable. Stoics considered this a healthy source of joy. Writing down your ideas about what makes another person admirable, mulling them over, and revising them gives you an opportunity to process them. With practice, you will be able to *visualize* the character traits you're describing more easily.

Over a decade after Antoninus's death, for example, Marcus was still reminding himself to remain a faithful disciple to him in all areas of life.[22] Although not a philosopher himself, Antoninus seems to have *naturally* possessed many of the virtues praised by the Stoics. In *The Meditations*, Marcus said that it was Antoninus who showed him that an emperor could win the respect of his subjects without bodyguards, expensive robes, precious ornaments, statues, and all other such trappings of his station in life. His adoptive father taught Marcus that it was possible for him, despite his status as Caesar, to live in a manner close to that of a private citizen, without losing status or neglecting his responsibilities. Following the example of Antoninus, he therefore reminds himself not to be "stained purple" and turned into a Caesar.[23] Rather Marcus sought to dye his mind deeply with the same virtues he observed in others, striving, as he put it, to remain the person philosophy sought to make him.

Marcus contemplates Antoninus's vigorous commitment to reason, his simple piety, his unshakable inner peace and calm demeanor. Marcus even says that his father was like Socrates in his ability to abstain from things that the majority are too weak to do without and to enjoy things in moderation that most people cannot enjoy without going to excess. He tells himself that if he can emulate all of these virtues, then he will be able to meet his own final hour with the same equanimity and clear conscience that Antoninus showed on his deathbed.

In addition to the virtues of real people, the Stoics were also known for contemplating the hypothetical character of an *ideal* Sage, or wise person. There are several passages where Marcus appears to be doing this. These descriptions inevitably seem a bit more abstract and grandiose. For example, he says that the perfect wise man is like a true priest of the gods, at one with the divine element of reason within himself. He is neither corrupted by pleasure nor injured by pain, and he remains untouched by insults. The true Sage is like a fighter in the noblest of fights, dyed deep with justice. With his whole being, he accepts everything that befalls him, as assigned to him by Fate. He seldom concerns himself with what others say or do unless it's for the common good. He naturally cares for all rational beings, as though they were his brothers and sisters. He is not swayed by the opinions of just anyone, but he gives special heed to the wise who live in agreement with Nature.[24] Marcus is trying here to describe human perfection to himself and to envisage an ideal Sage who completely embodies the Stoic goals of life.

In addition to asking ourselves what qualities the ideal wise person might have, we can ask what qualities we might hope to possess in the distant future. For instance, what sort of person would you hope to be after having trained in Stoicism for ten or twenty years? At one point, Marcus seems to be describing the long-term goals of the Stoic therapy process he went through with Rusticus. He says that in the mind of one who has been chastened and thoroughly purified there is no festering sore beneath the surface, and nothing that would not bear examination or would hide from the light. There is no longer anything servile or phony about someone who has achieved this, he adds, and they are neither dependent on others nor alienated from them.[25] Those are both therapy goals for Stoics and the goals of life.

Writing down the virtues possessed by a hypothetical wise man or woman, or those we aspire to ourselves, is usually a very beneficial exercise. It may also be useful for you to formulate descriptions of two or three specific individuals and compare these to a more general description of an ideal. These could be real acquaintances from your life, historical figures, or even fictional characters. The important thing is to process the information by reflecting on it and revising it where necessary. Allow some time to pass and then come back to review and improve your descriptions. Consider how specific virtues, such as wisdom, justice, courage, and moderation, might be exhibited by role models you've chosen. In general, thinking things over and looking at these ideas from different perspectives—however you choose to do it—can be helpful in terms of self-improvement. Having spent some time on writing exercises, you will more easily be able to picture things in your mind's eye. The best way to do this is to imagine a role model whose strengths you've identified coping with a challenging situation. The Stoics asked themselves, "What would Socrates or Zeno *do*?" Marcus likely asked himself how Rusticus and his other teachers would cope with the difficult situations he faced in life. He undoubtedly asked himself what Antoninus would do. Psychologists call this "modeling" someone's behavior. We've already touched upon it briefly in our discussion of decatastrophizing in cognitive therapy. You might want to ask yourself, for example, "What would Marcus *do*?"

In addition to visualizing people to model their *behavior*, we can also model their *attitudes*. Stoics might ask themselves, "What would Socrates or Zeno *say* about this?" You can imagine your personal role model—or even a whole *panel* of Stoic Sages—giving you advice. What would they tell you to do? What advice would they give? What would they have to say about how you're currently handling a problem? Pose these types of questions to yourself as you picture them in your imagination and try to formulate what the response would be. Turn it into a longer discussion if that helps. Again, if you're modeling Marcus Aurelius, ask "What would Marcus *say*?"

Modeling is typically followed by the "mental rehearsal" of behavior change: picturing yourself acting more like your role models or imagining yourself following their advice. This often takes several attempts. Think of it as trial-and-error learning. Imagine yourself coping with the challenges you expect to face and exhibiting the virtues you want to learn. You'll probably find it more helpful to picture yourself improving in small increments rather than immediately mastering the whole situation. That's known as the benefit of "coping imagery" over "mastery imagery." Don't try to run before you can walk by setting unrealistic goals. Just rehearse a few simple changes in your behavior to get started. Small changes can often have big consequences anyway.

When teaching people to employ Stoic practices, I've found it helpful to have a simple framework for daily Stoic practices. It involves a "learning cycle" with a beginning, middle, and end, which then repeats each day. In the morning you prepare for the day ahead; throughout the day you try to live consistently in accord with your values; and in the evening you review your progress and prepare to repeat the cycle again the next day. I'll refer to the Stoic exercises used at the beginning and end of each day as the *morning* and *evening* meditations. Having a daily routine like this makes it much easier to be consistent in your practice.

This framework also fits in neatly with our discussion of modeling and mentoring. During your *morning meditation*, consider what tasks you have to complete and what challenges you must overcome. Ask yourself, "What would my role model do?" and try to imagine them dealing with the same situations you're about to face. Mentally rehearse the virtues you want to exhibit. Throughout the day, try continually to be self-aware, as if a wise mentor or teacher is observing you. We call this "Stoic mindfulness" today, but the Stoics meant something similar by *prosoche*, or paying attention to yourself. Keep an eye on how you use your mind and body, particularly the value judgments you make in different situations, and watch out for subtle feelings of anger, fear, sadness, or unhealthy desires, as well as bad habits.

During your *evening meditation*, review how things actually went, perhaps going over the key events of the day two or three times in your mind's eye. What would your imaginary *mentors* say? What advice might they give you about doing things differently next time? This is your opportunity to learn from experience and prepare for the morning, when you'll plan your behavior and rehearse things again in an ongoing cycle of self-improvement. You might ask yourself, for example, "What would Marcus Aurelius say about how I fared today?"

The ancients did something similar. Galen said that his own daily routine involved contemplating a famous poem about philosophy called "The Golden Verses of Pythagoras." Seneca and Epictetus mention it as well, and it may have influenced other Stoics. Galen recommends reading its verses twice, first silently and then aloud. He suggests that we call to mind each day the areas for improvement that our mentor has helped us identify. We should do this as frequently as possible but at the very least, he says, "at dawn, before we begin our daily tasks, and toward evening, before we are about to rest."

Regarding the *morning meditation*, Galen says that as soon as you rise from bed and begin considering each of the tasks ahead, you should ask yourself two questions:

1. What would the consequences be if you acted as a slave to your passions?
2. How would your day differ if you acted more rationally, exhibiting wisdom and self-discipline?

Marcus discusses how to prepare for the day ahead at least four times in *The Meditations*. He mentions that the Pythagoreans used to contemplate the stars each morning, thinking of their consistency, purity, and nakedness as symbolic of man living with wisdom, virtue, and simplicity. He likewise tells himself on awakening that he is rising to fulfill his potential for wisdom and not just to be a puppet of bodily sensations, swayed by pleasant feelings or turned aside by discomfort. He tells himself to love his nature and his capacity for reason, and to do his best to live accordingly. As we'll see later, he also gives himself very specific advice about how to deal with difficult people without becoming frustrated or resentful.[26]

This famous passage from "The Golden Verses," which Epictetus quoted to his students, describes the *evening meditation*:

*Allow not sleep to close your wearied eyes,*
*Until you have reckoned up each daytime deed:*

*"Where did I go wrong? What did I do? And what duty's left
        undone?"*
*From first to last review your acts and then*
*Reprove yourself for wretched acts, but rejoice in those done
        well.*[27]

You can ask yourself these three very simple questions:

1. **What did you do badly?** Did you allow yourself to be
   ruled by irrational fears or unhealthy desires? Did you
   act badly or allow yourself to indulge in irrational
   thoughts?
2. **What did you do well?** Did you make progress by acting wisely? Praise yourself and reinforce what you want
   to repeat.
3. **What could you do differently?** Did you omit any opportunities to exercise virtue or strength of character?
   How could you have handled things better?

As we've seen, young Stoics being observed or questioned by
a trusted mentor became deeply mindful of their thoughts and
actions. To some extent, knowing that you are going to cross-
examine yourself at the end of the day can have a similar effect.
It forces you to pay more attention to your conduct throughout
the day. Marcus reminded himself of a pithy saying from Heraclitus: "We ought not to act and speak as if we were asleep."[28] We
need to make an effort to awaken our self-awareness, in other
words. Following this daily routine, in a sense, helps us to do that
by acting like a mentor to *ourselves.*

This regimen will make you more aware of your thoughts,

feelings, and actions. You can also foster self-awareness by questioning yourself regularly throughout the day in the way the Stoics describe. For example, Marcus frequently examines his own character and actions, perhaps posing the sort of questions a Stoic mentor might have asked. He asks himself, in different situations, "What use am I now making of my soul?"[29] He probed his own mind, scrutinizing the fundamental values he was taking for granted. "Whose soul do I now have?" he would ask. "Am I behaving like a child, a tyrant, a sheep, a wolf, or am I fulfilling my true potential as a rational being? For what purpose am I currently using my mind? Am I being foolish? Am I alienated from other people? Am I letting myself be dragged off course by fear and desire? What passions are there right now in my mind?" You might also ask yourself, "How's this actually working out?" Sometimes it's necessary to interrupt the things you're doing out of habit so that you can ask yourself whether they're actually healthy or unhealthy for you in the long run.

The Stoics employed the Socratic method of questioning, the *elenchus*, which exposes contradictions in the beliefs of the person being questioned—a bit like the cross-examination of a witness in a court of law. They believed above all that the wise man is consistent in both his thoughts and actions. Foolish people, by contrast, vacillate, driven by contradictory passions, which flutter from one thing to another like butterflies. That's why we often hear the Stoics praising the wise man for remaining "the same" no matter what he faces—even his facial expression and demeanor remain consistent come rain or shine. Marcus quite probably underwent this sort of questioning from Rusticus and his other Stoic tutors as part of the Stoic therapy. One of the main things it tends to highlight is any contradiction between the values we use to guide our own lives, or the things we desire, and the values we use to judge other people, or what we find praiseworthy and blameworthy. Therapists today would call this a "double standard."

This sort of Socratic questioning forms part of an approach called "values clarification," which has been around since the 1970s but has recently gone through a resurgence of popularity among therapists and researchers.[30] By deeply reflecting on our values each day and attempting to describe them concisely, we can develop a clearer sense of direction in life. You might do this by posing questions to yourself such as:

- What's ultimately the most important thing in life to you?
- What do you really want your life to stand for or represent?
- What do you want to be remembered for after you're dead?
- What sort of person do you most want to be in life?
- What sort of character do you want to have?
- What would you want written on your tombstone?

These questions are similar to the well-known therapy technique of imagining the eulogies at your own funeral and asking yourself what, ideally, you would want people to remember you for. Think of Ebenezer Scrooge in Dickens's *A Christmas Carol*, who has a sort of moral epiphany after the Ghost of Christmas Future confronts him with a troubling vision of people reacting to his death and tombstone.

Another useful values clarification technique for students of Stoicism involves making two short lists in side-by-side columns headed "Desired" and "Admired":

1. **Desired.** The things you most desire for yourself in life
2. **Admired.** The qualities you find most praiseworthy and admirable in other people

These two lists are, at first, virtually never identical. Why are they different, and how would your life change if you desired for yourself the qualities you find admirable in other people? As the Stoics might put it, what would happen if you were to make *virtue* your number one priority in life? The most important aspect of this values clarification exercise for Stoics would be to grasp the true nature of man's highest good, to elucidate our most fundamental goal, and to live accordingly. Everything in Stoicism ultimately refers back to the goal of grasping the true nature of the good and living accordingly.

Once you clarify your core values, you can compare them to the Stoic cardinal virtues of wisdom, justice, courage, and moderation. People find it surprisingly helpful to set aside even a few minutes per day to reflect deeply upon their values. Indeed, values clarification has become an integral part of modern evidence-based treatments for clinical depression. Clarifying our values and trying to live more consistently in accord with them can help us gain a greater sense of direction and meaning in life, leading to greater satisfaction and fulfillment. Try brainstorming small ways in which you can do things that satisfy your core values each day. Don't be too ambitious; just begin with small changes. Then during your evening meditation, you might literally give yourself "marks out of ten for virtue," or rather for living up to your core values. This will encourage you to think more deeply about ways you can progress toward embodying your values. Remember: the fundamental goal of life for Stoics, the highest good, is to act *consistently* in accord with reason and virtue.

In this chapter we've looked at the role Junius Rusticus played in Marcus's life as a Stoic tutor and mentor: he persuaded Marcus, as a young Caesar, that he would benefit from moral training and Stoic therapy of the passions. We've reconstructed an account of Stoic therapy (*therapeia*) based on the description given by Marcus's personal physician, Galen, which draws on Chrysippus's lost *Therapeutics*, and combined this account with relevant passages from *The Meditations*.

We've also described how to benefit from similar practices today, whether or not you have a real mentor you can turn to. The mentor's role can be seen in terms of modeling both *behaviors* and *attitudes*. You can use different writing and visualization exercises to simulate the Stoic process of mentoring. We've also seen how "The Golden Verses of Pythagoras" provided Galen, Seneca, and Epictetus with a framework for Stoic therapy by dividing the day into three stages: morning meditation, mindfulness during the day, and evening meditation.

We introduced the concept of values clarification from modern therapy. Reflecting upon and clarifying your core values can help combat depression and other emotional problems, especially once you make a consistent effort to live more in accord with your truest values each day. You can compare these values to the Stoic virtues and explore them from different perspectives by following the daily routine. Keep coming back to the question "What's the most important thing in life?" Or, as the Stoics would say, "What is the true nature of the good?" Even setting aside a few minutes each day to clarify your values and do things that are consistent with them can be very beneficial. Remember: small changes of this kind can often have surprisingly large *effects*.

The ideas in this chapter will help you apply the many other Stoic concepts and techniques that you're about to learn by providing you with a framework for your daily practice. This simple "learning cycle" alone, when used properly, will be enough for many people to see improvements in their character and emotional resilience, especially combined with their own reading and study of the Stoic texts. Self-scrutiny of this kind appears to have been an important aspect of training in ancient Stoicism. As Socrates said, "The unexamined life is not worth living."

# 4.

# THE CHOICE
# OF HERCULES

Marcus put his head in his hands and groaned. It wasn't the devastation caused by the Antonine Plague or the growing threat of barbarian invasion from the North that made him despair for the future of Rome. Rather, it was a party thrown by his brother, Lucius Verus. Lucius and Marcus had always been quite different characters even though they ruled together, but as the years passed, their lives grew further apart. Whereas Marcus increasingly turned to philosophy as his guide, Lucius became notorious for being a hedonist and something of a hell-raiser.

The family ties of Roman nobles could be convoluted. Lucius was not only Marcus's adoptive brother but also his son-in-law, having married Marcus's daughter Lucilla. It was therefore said that Marcus looked on him more like a son than a brother. Upon being acclaimed emperor, Marcus's first act had been to have Lucius appointed co-emperor to rule jointly with him, the first arrangement of its kind in Roman history. Lucius was given Marcus's family name, Verus; formerly he had been known as

Lucius Aelius Aurelius Commodus. Lucius was a handsome and charismatic young man who probably looked more comfortable than Marcus in the purple robes of an emperor.

> [Lucius] Verus was well-proportioned in person and genial of expression. His beard was allowed to grow long, almost in the style of the barbarians; he was tall, and stately in appearance, for his forehead projected somewhat over his eyebrows. He took such pride in his yellow hair, it is said, that he used to sift gold-dust on his head in order that his hair, thus brightened, might seem even yellower.[1]

However, although Marcus and Lucius both held the title of emperor, Lucius was clearly subordinate to Marcus and obeyed him in a manner comparable to that of a provincial governor or an army lieutenant.

One reason Marcus had appointed a co-emperor was that Lucius arguably had a claim on the throne: as we've seen, Lucius's natural father died before he could succeed Hadrian. So it was wise of Marcus to persuade the Senate that he should share power with his brother in order to avoid the rise of opposing factions. The Senate feared nothing more than civil war tearing the empire apart, and this measure helped ensure political stability. The histories also imply that Marcus's poor health influenced the decision. As Lucius was younger by nine years and in much better physical condition, he was primed to outlive Marcus and become his successor. Joint rule meant, of course, that if one emperor died suddenly the other would remain in power, reducing the risk of conflict over the succession.

Moreover, the historian Cassius Dio described Lucius as a younger and more vigorous man "better suited for military enterprises." As far as we're aware, Lucius never saw any military service as a young man, but at first he was perhaps more popular with the legions than Marcus. His father had at least served briefly as governor and military commander of Pannonia. As soon as Marcus and Lucius were acclaimed as co-emperors, Marcus sent Lucius to address the legions on his behalf and effectively began treating him as his representative with the military. Marcus and his advisors obviously had the impression that Lucius could be a general in the making. He turned out to be completely useless in this role because he lacked the sense of duty and self-discipline necessary for military life, preferring instead to spend his time drinking and entertaining his friends.

Indeed, Lucius was known for his love of extravagant parties, in marked contrast to his brother. The party that caused Marcus so much concern cost roughly the equivalent of an entire legion's annual pay. The main expense seems to have been the extravagant gifts the Emperor Lucius showered on his guests. They first received exquisite carving knives and platters and live animals of the same type as they were eating during each course, a menagerie of birds and four-legged creatures. Then they were given fine goblets made from semiprecious stones and Alexandrine crystal. Next, silver, gold, and jeweled cups, garlands entwined with gold ribbons and out-of-season flowers, and golden vases containing rare ointments were handed out. The guests were entertained by private gladiatorial bouts and they drank and played dice until dawn. Finally, carriages with mules dressed in silver trappings carried them home; the carriages were theirs to keep, along with the handsome young slave boys who had been serving them. You can't buy good friends, though, and the extravagance attracted a retinue of greedy and dissolute hangers-on who encouraged the worst aspects of Lucius's character.

The *Historia Augusta* paints Lucius in a very negative light overall, as a vain and self-indulgent buffoon. The picture painted of Lucius contrasts dramatically with that of Marcus as a bona fide Stoic. Even if the stories exaggerate Lucius's vices, there's probably at least a grain of truth in them. For instance, despite ruling as Marcus's co-emperor for nearly a decade, Lucius is virtually relegated to a footnote in *The Meditations*. Marcus says only that he's grateful for having had a brother "who by his character was able to stimulate me to cultivate my own nature, and yet at the same time heartened me by his respect and affection," perhaps damning Lucius with faint praise.[2] Marcus speaks with artful vagueness here but perhaps meant that he became more determined to strengthen his own character after observing his brother's vices spiraling out of control. However, Marcus was relieved that Lucius remained loyal to him, showing "respect and affection" rather than dividing the empire by siding with those who opposed his rule. We can tell that this was a very real danger from the civil war instigated against Marcus six years after Lucius's death by his most celebrated general, Avidius Cassius.

In their youth, Marcus and Lucius both shared a love of hunting, wrestling, and other active pursuits, and both trained in Stoic philosophy. However, whereas Marcus increasingly dedicated himself to the study of rhetoric and philosophy and diligently worked his way up through ascending roles in public office, Lucius seems to have done very little except enjoy a life of leisure. While the younger brother was at the chariot races, gladiatorial games, or banquets with his friends, Marcus was poring over books, gaining crucial knowledge of Roman law and the bureaucracy of government. You could say Lucius chose pleasure before work; Marcus, work before pleasure.

My interpretation is that Lucius organized his whole life

around the pursuit of empty pleasures as a form of emotional avoidance. Psychologists now know that people often engage in habits they consider pleasurable—from social media to crack cocaine—as a way of distracting themselves from or suppressing *unpleasant* feelings. In Lucius's case, alcohol and other diversions perhaps offered him a way to escape worry about his responsibilities as emperor. As we'll see, there's nothing wrong with pleasure unless we begin craving it so much that we neglect our responsibilities in life or it replaces healthy and fulfilling activities with ones that are not.

Chasing empty, transient pleasures can never lead to true happiness in the long run. However, pleasure can be tricky—it can lure us in by posing as something it's not. What we're all really seeking in life is the sense of *authentic* happiness or fulfillment the Stoics called *eudaimonia*. Lucius, though, was looking for it in entirely the wrong places: cheering on the carnage of the arena, heaping lavish gifts on dubious friends, and drinking himself into oblivion. Of course, the banqueting habits of a decadent Roman emperor might seem an extreme example of someone allowing their hedonistic urges free rein. However, the basic psychology of desire isn't much different today. People still confuse pleasure with happiness and often find it difficult to imagine another perspective on life. By contrast, the Stoics taught Marcus that we all seek a deeper and more lasting sense of fulfillment. They taught him that this could only be obtained by realizing our inner potential and living in accord with our core values, not being led astray by superficial feelings. Marcus's and Lucius's lives diverged in this regard until they were heading in quite opposite directions.

There's something *strangely familiar* about this tale: the opposing paths our two young Caesars found themselves on as co-emperors could have been lifted from a moral fable. Indeed, while attending the lectures of Apollonius and other Stoics, Marcus must surely have thought of his brother as he listened attentively to their many exhortations to embrace philosophy as a way of life. One of the most famous of these was known as "The Choice of Hercules." This ancient allegory about choosing our path in life plays a special role in the history of Stoicism. The story goes that by chance, shortly after his shipwreck, Zeno had picked up and read the second book of Xenophon's *Memorabilia*. It portrays Socrates arguing that the virtue of self-control makes men noble and good, whereas pursuing a life of pleasure does not. Socrates begins by quoting a well-known verse from Hesiod:

> Wickedness can be had in abundance easily: smooth is the road and very nigh she dwells. But in front of virtue the gods immortal have put sweat: long and steep is the path to her and rough at first; but when you reach the top, then at length the road is easy, hard though it was.

Socrates then goes on to recount "The Choice of Hercules," which he had learned from Prodicus of Ceos, one of the most highly regarded Greek Sophists.

One day, as a young man, Hercules was walking along an unfamiliar path when he came upon a fork in the road, at which he sat down and began to contemplate his future. Unsure which path to take, he found himself suddenly confronted by two mysterious goddesses. The first appeared as a beautiful and alluring woman dressed in fine clothing. She was called Kakia, although she (falsely) claimed that her friends called her Eudaimonia, meaning happiness and fulfillment. She barged in front of her companion and pleaded very insistently with Hercules to follow her path. It led, she promised, to by far the easiest and most pleasant way of life, a shortcut to true happiness. She told him that he could live like a king, avoiding hardship and enjoying luxury beyond most men's wildest dreams, all delivered to him through the labor of others.

After listening to her for a while, Hercules was approached by the second goddess, Arete, a less boastful and more modest woman, who nonetheless shone with natural beauty. To his surprise, she wore a grave expression. She warned him that her path led in a very different direction: it would be long and difficult, and would require a great deal of hard work. Speaking plainly, she told Hercules that he would suffer. He would be doomed to walk the earth in rags, reviled and persecuted by his enemies. "Nothing that is really good and admirable," cautioned Arete, "is granted by the gods to men without some effort and application." Hercules would be called upon to exercise wisdom and justice and to face mounting adversity with bravery and self-discipline. Overcoming great obstacles through courageous and honorable deeds, the goddess said, was the only true path to fulfillment in life.

Hercules famously chose the heroic path of Arete, or "Virtue," and was not seduced by Kakia, or "Vice." Armed with a wooden club and dressed in the pelt of the Nemean lion, symbolic of a more primitive and natural way of life, he wandered from one place to another, as if the whole world were his home. The gods forced him to undertake the legendary Twelve Labors, including slaying the Hydra and ultimately entering Hades, the Underworld itself, to capture Cerberus with his bare hands. He died in extreme agony, betrayed by his jealous wife, who tricked him into wearing a robe soaked in blood contaminated with the Hydra's poison. However, Zeus was so impressed by his mortal son's greatness of soul that he granted him an *apotheosis*, elevating him to the status of a god in his own right.

Not surprisingly, Hercules was the mythic hero most admired by Cynic and Stoic philosophers. His labors embodied their belief that it's more rewarding to face hardship voluntarily and cultivate strength of character than to take the easy option by embracing comfortable living and idleness. Hence, the satirist Lucian, a contemporary of Marcus, portrayed the legendary sale of Diogenes the Cynic at a slave auction as follows:

BUYER: Is there anyone whom you strive to emulate?

DIOGENES: Yes, Hercules.

BUYER: Then why aren't you wearing a lion-skin? Though I'll admit that your club looks like his.

DIOGENES: Why, this old cloak is my lion-skin, and like him I'm fighting a campaign against pleasure, not at anyone else's bidding, but of my own free will, since I've made it my purpose to clean up human life.[3]

Like the Cynics before them, the Stoics saw the myth of Hercules as an allegory about the virtues of courage and self-discipline. "What do you think Hercules would have amounted to," Epictetus asks his students, "if there had not been monsters such as the Nemean lion, the Hydra, the stag of Artemis, the Erymanthian boar, and all those unjust and bestial men for him to contend with? Why, if he had sat at home, wrapped up asleep in bedsheets, living in luxury and ease, he would have been no Hercules at all!"[4] Epictetus tells his students that just as Hercules cleansed the earth of monsters—without complaining—they should set about conquering themselves by purging the base desires and emotions from their hearts.

For Stoics, in other words, the tale of Hercules symbolizes the epic challenge of deciding who we really want to be in life, the promise of philosophy, and the temptation of giving in to pleasure and vice. The moral is that it often requires a Herculean effort to keep to the right path. But wasn't Hercules's life *unpleasant*? As we'll see, from the Stoic perspective Hercules remained *cheerful*, despite the terrible things he endured. He enjoyed a profound sense of inner satisfaction knowing that he was fulfilling his destiny and expressing his true nature. His life had something far more satisfying than pleasure: it had *purpose*.

All of this must have been familiar to Marcus and Lucius from the education they received in Stoicism. Lucius gradually lost interest, though, and turned his back on philosophy. Indeed, while Marcus was busy studying and tirelessly engaged in public office, Lucius was gaining notoriety for his debauchery and his growing infatuation with popular Roman spectator sports. He got himself in hot water by siding with the Greens at the races and thereby offending fans of rival teams, particularly the Blues. He took a golden statue of the Greens' most prized horse, Volucer, everywhere he went. He also had an enormous crystal wine goblet made that he named in its honor, which "surpassed the capacity of any human draught," another testament to his notoriety for binge drinking.

By contrast, Marcus, like Hercules in the fable, chose to avoid these sorts of distractions, or at least keep them to a minimum. The unnamed slave from whom he learned so much as a child had wisely counseled him not to take the side of the Greens or the Blues in the chariot races or back different factions in the gladiatorial lists. These were the main forms of public entertainment in imperial Rome, and it seems the "masses" were just as addicted to them as many of us are to spectator sports and reality television today.

Marcus came to loathe all such public events, but he was obliged to attend them at the insistence of his friends and advisors. He seems to have found unnecessary bloodshed vicious and barbaric. Indeed, as emperor, Marcus began to impose many restrictions on the cruelty of the games. He insisted that the gladiators before him use blunted weapons so that they would be fighting like athletes, without any risk to their lives. The thrill of the chariot races was likewise about bloodlust, as horses and charioteers were frequently maimed or killed in this dangerous sport. Marcus tried to see beyond the excitement of the crowd. He adopted a more philosophical attitude to the events unfolding before his eyes, asking himself, Is this *really* what people consider fun?

For Stoics, feelings of pleasure in themselves are neither good nor bad. Rather, whether our state of mind is good or bad, healthy or unhealthy, depends on the things we take enjoyment *in*. Marcus compares Roman society to the idle pageantry of a procession, where people seem distracted by trivialities, but he reminds himself that he must take his place in it with good grace. Nevertheless, a man's worth can be measured by the things upon which he sets his heart.[5] Enjoying the suffering of others is bad. Taking pleasure in watching men risk death or serious injury would therefore be considered a vice by the Stoics. In contrast, enjoying seeing people flourish is good. You might think that's obvious; however, we can be blinded by pleasure to its consequences for both others and ourselves. Marcus had been taught by his Stoic tutors to examine the sources and consequences of pleasure very closely. He was therefore able, to some extent, to see beyond the prejudices of his own culture. We should like-

wise learn to enjoy things that are good for us and others, not
things that are bad for us. Indeed, there's a type of inner gratifi-
cation that comes from living consistently in accord with our
deepest values, which can make ordinary pleasures feel superficial by comparison. Marcus has that in mind when he repeatedly
tells himself that the goal of his life is not pleasure but *action*.

At first the people ridiculed Marcus as a snob and a bore
because at the games they could see that he was reading legal doc-
uments and discussing them with his advisors. He'd been told
that he had to show his face at these events to keep the crowds
happy, but he wanted to use the time to address the serious business of running the state. Even his tutor and close friend, Fronto,
denounced him for being too serious:

> On occasion, in your absence, I have criticized you in quite se-
> vere terms in front of a small circle of my most intimate friends.
> There was a time when I would do so, for instance, when you
> entered public gatherings with a more gloomy expression than
> was fitting, or pored over a book at the theatre or during a ban-
> quet (I am speaking of a time when I myself did not yet keep
> away from theatres and banquets). On such occasions, then, I
> would call you an insensitive man who failed to act as circum-
> stances demanded, or sometimes even, in an impulse of anger,
> a disagreeable person.[6]

Fronto came around to Marcus's way of thinking in the end.
He gradually realized that there was more to life than socializing among the Roman patrician class, whom they both came
to view as lacking any genuine warmth or friendliness. Marcus
also faced criticism from the old guard for promoting men such
as his future son-in-law Pompeianus based on merit rather than

nobility of birth. He picked his friends carefully, based on the character traits he most admired rather than what seemed congenial to those of his social class. His friends' company wasn't always fun—sometimes they spoke plainly and criticized him— but he embraced them because they shared his values and helped to improve him as a person. He clearly preferred the company of his family and most trusted friends over socializing with the Roman elite. He admits in *The Meditations* that he craves the simpler but idyllic family life at his peaceful villas in the Italian countryside. Although this was undoubtedly a healthier and more modest way to spend his leisure time compared with Lucius's riotous banqueting, it was nevertheless a yearning Marcus would soon have to set aside, when the Marcomannic Wars required him to leave Rome for the northern frontier.

Though Marcus shrewdly put away his papers at the amphitheater, he still insisted on working. While he discussed political decisions with his advisors, onlookers assumed he was chatting with them about the games like everyone else. He even found ways to glean life lessons from the games. In wild beast fights he observed gladiators, half eaten and covered with wounds, begging to be patched up so they could throw themselves back into the fight. This reminded Marcus of the way we continue to give in to unhealthy desires despite knowing the harm they do us. Perhaps it also reminded him of his brother, who had abandoned philosophy and embraced a life of debauchery that was clearly destroying him.

Marcus kept Lucius somewhat in check as long as they were together. However, shortly after the two brothers were acclaimed as co-emperors, the Parthian king Vologases IV invaded the Roman client-state of Armenia. The governor of nearby Cappadocia (in modern-day Turkey) rushed to engage the enemy, but his legion was surrounded and annihilated. He was forced to take his own life. This was a humiliating defeat for the Romans, and the conflict rapidly escalated into a major military crisis.

Marcus's presence was still required at Rome, so he sent Lucius to Syria to take command of the troops massed in the East. However, a journey that should have taken a few weeks ended up taking nine months. The histories allege that Lucius wasted his time hunting and partying along the way. Marcus accompanied him as far as Capua, in southern Italy, before he had to turn back to Rome. As soon as his older brother was gone, Lucius "gorged himself in everyone's villa" until he became so ill that Marcus had to rush to attend to him at nearby Canusium. Pleasures, as we've seen, can blind us to their consequences if we're not careful. Lucius's overindulgence would increasingly lead him to neglect both his own welfare and that of the empire.

The *Historia Augusta* deals harshly with the Emperor Lucius, complaining that when he finally reached Syria, and throughout the course of the Parthian War, away from Marcus's supervision, the weaker and more degenerate features of his character prevailed.

> For while a legate [a Roman general] was being slain, while legions were being slaughtered, while Syria meditated revolt, and the East was being devastated, [Lucius] Verus was hunting in Apulia, travelling about through Athens and Corinth accompanied by orchestras and singers, and dallying through all the cities of Asia that bordered on the sea, and those cities of Pamphylia and Cilicia that were particularly notorious for their pleasure-resorts.

When Lucius eventually reached Antioch, the capital of Syria, far from Marcus's gaze, he gave himself over entirely to riotous living. He also shaved off his beard to humor his mistress, Panthea. This confirmed that he was turning his back on philosophy once and for all in order to pursue a more self-indulgent lifestyle. The philosopher's beard had become a surprisingly politicized symbol after years of persecution under previous regimes; for some, at least, shaving it off implied abandoning one's most cherished beliefs and values. A few generations earlier, presumably speaking of Emperor Domitian's persecution of philosophers, Epictetus had defiantly exclaimed that if the authorities wanted to cut off his beard, they'd have to cut off his head first.

Marcus had already sent the Roman general Avidius Cassius, a notoriously strict disciplinarian, to take command of the troops in Syria, dragging the dissolute eastern legionaries out of the brothels and drinking houses and knocking the flowers from their hair. No sooner had Lucius arrived to take command, though, than his personal entourage took the place of soldiers in the fleshpots and resorts of the East. The gossip was that Lucius indulged in numerous adulterous love affairs with women and young men in Syria, even though he was married to Marcus's young daughter, Lucilla. It was there that he picked up the habit of playing dice until dawn. He wandered through taverns and brothels late at night disguised as a commoner, it's said, getting drunk, ending up in fights, and coming home black and blue. When he was out drinking he liked to smash the cups in the cookshops by throwing coins at them, which presumably started a few brawls. He'd get so inebriated after feasting through the night that he'd typically fall asleep at the banqueting table and have to be carried to his bedroom by the servants.

Indeed, Lucius was notorious for being a heavy drinker. Based on the available information, it seems possible he suffered from alcoholism, accompanied by symptoms of anxiety and depression. During the Parthian War, for example, he wrote to Fronto complaining in desperation of "the anxieties that have rendered me very miserable day and night, and almost made me think that everything was ruined." He's probably referring to problems negotiating with the hostile Parthians, but he was clearly overwhelmed by emotional distress. Binge drinking, casual sex, gambling, and partying became his way of coping, albeit badly, with the pressures of his role. The Stoics believed that entertainment, sex, food, and even alcohol have their place in life—they're neither good nor bad in themselves. However, when pursued *excessively*, they can become unhealthy. So the wise man sets reasonable limits on his desires, and he exercises the virtue of moderation: "Nothing in excess." When doing what feels pleasurable becomes *more important* than doing what's actually good for us or our loved ones, though, that's a recipe for disaster. There's a world of difference between healthy pleasures and unhealthy ones. Lucius had definitely crossed that line.

After the Romans secured victory over the Parthians following six years of war, Lucius finally returned from Syria to celebrate his triumph with Marcus. However, once back at Rome, he paid even less regard to his older brother, and his behavior continued to degenerate. People scoffed that he must have been taking actors prisoner rather than Parthian soldiers because he proudly brought back so many from the East. Nevertheless, Lucius shamelessly invited Fronto, a great rhetorician, to write a history of the war giving Lucius credit for all Rome's achievements. The truth was that Lucius had left Avidius Cassius and his other generals in command and stayed as far away from the action as possible, touring the region like a celebrity with his entourage of hangers-on. As we'll see, this negligence was no small matter. Avidius Cassius was able to step into his shoes and gradually became almost as powerful as an emperor himself throughout the eastern provinces.

Lucius hadn't been home long, though, before the First Marcomannic War broke out along the northern frontier. This time both emperors rode out from Rome together in their military attire. Marcus evidently didn't think it was a good idea for his brother to go alone, and he didn't feel comfortable leaving him back at Rome unsupervised. Lucius wanted to remain at Aquileia, in northern Italy, where he could hunt and banquet, but Marcus insisted they needed to cross the Alps to Pannonia, which had been overrun by the Marcomanni and their allies. After the Romans repulsed the initial barbarian incursion, the co-emperors returned to Aquileia at Lucius's insistence because he yearned to be near Rome. However, in early 169 AD, Lucius was struck with a sudden fainting spell, and he died three days later after being bled by his physicians. We can't be sure what killed him. There were even rumors Marcus had him poisoned. However, his loss of consciousness, inability to speak, and sudden death are signs of the plague, which was prevalent in nearby cities and legionary camps around this time. Ironically, despite Lucius's reputation as the younger and hardier of the two co-emperors, he only made it to age thirty-nine, while Marcus, with his notorious frailty, reached nearly sixty.

We might think Marcus was relieved to be rid of his wayward brother, but he probably felt his loss greatly. It came at a time of mounting crises, as disease spread throughout the empire and Marcus was forced to leave Rome for the first time to take up his command on the northern frontier. He must have felt increasingly isolated, in great personal danger, and under a tremendous amount of political pressure. As we'll see, though, it was within this crucible that *The Meditations* took shape.

# HOW TO CONQUER DESIRE

We mentioned Prodicus's "Choice of Hercules" earlier, but Marcus cites another famous allegory about desire in his notes. It's one of Aesop's fables, called "The Town Mouse and the Country Mouse." A town mouse once visited his cousin in the countryside, where he was welcomed with a simple meal of rustic food: a crust of bread and some dry oats. However, the town mouse laughed at his cousin's unsophisticated tastes and peasant fare. Boasting of the luxury and abundance to be found in the town, he insists that the country mouse come back to the city with him for a taste of the good life. The country mouse agrees, and they return to the house where the town mouse lives hidden to feast like kings upon the finest scraps from the owner's table. However, two dogs hear them scratching around and come hurtling into the room barking, which sends the mice scurrying for cover in fear for their lives.

Once they've reached the safety of a mouse hole and caught their breath, the shaken country mouse thanks his cousin for his hospitality but says he'll be returning to his humble rural dwelling right away. Although the country fare is modest, he prefers the peace and quiet of his own home and a simple life to the dangers of the city. The town mouse's perilous habits aren't really the good life at all. They come at too high a cost. The country mouse says he would rather dine like a peasant than risk being eaten alive by ravenous dogs. Reflecting on the moral of this story, Marcus calls to mind "the alarm and trepidation" with which the town mouse perpetually lives because of his greed.[7] I can't help but think that Marcus Aurelius saw himself as the country mouse and his brother Lucius as the town mouse.

Just because Marcus saw the "pleasures" that ensnared Lucius as empty and superficial doesn't mean there was no joy in his own life. We shouldn't be fooled by the gravity of *The Meditations*, which consists of semiformal exercises, into thinking that the author had a gloomy personality. His private letters prove that Marcus was a good-humored and surprisingly affectionate man who spent his youth enjoying a wide variety of sports and hobbies. He liked painting, boxing, wrestling, running, fowling, and boar hunting, and the *Historia Augusta* adds that he was very skilled at playing various ball games. Of course, as the years passed and his responsibilities increased, he dedicated his life to handling the affairs of state and to his training in Stoic philosophy, which helped guide his actions. However, we're told he was loved by those close to him and seemed pleasant and approachable to others. He was described as austere but not excessively so, humble but not passive, and serious but never gloomy. He clearly took great pleasure in the company of his friends and family.

Marcus was probably a much happier man than his hedonistic brother Lucius was. True, he didn't experience the highs of all the wild parties Lucius threw, but neither did he suffer the lows, the painful consequences of overindulgence. What he gained instead was the more profound and lasting happiness that the Stoics claimed was the result of living in accord with wisdom and virtue, or at least some glimmer of that ideal state. Indeed, he made it clear that his goal was to achieve the utmost joy in his heart and maintain a "cheerful serenity" throughout the whole of his life. Having glimpsed this inner peace, Marcus was convinced that it was possible to live consistently in that state of mind, even if he was criticized by those around him or was gored by wild beasts.[8] Socrates himself had remained cheerful while in prison awaiting his execution, and even as he raised the hemlock cup to his lips. At least that was the story. However, Marcus also saw this healthy attitude of cheerfulness in the face of adversity with his own eyes, as exhibited by his beloved Stoic tutors. They had taught the young Marcus that inner calm and happiness are the natural consequences of a life lived well, in accord with genuine wisdom and self-discipline. More importantly, though, he had witnessed evidence of this being their actual way of life, embodied in the actions of these great men even in the face of terrible adversity.

Modern English isn't well equipped to capture some of the distinctions made in ancient Greek philosophy, especially when it comes to describing emotions and sensations. We use the word "pleasure" very broadly to encompass almost any positive feeling. However, the Stoics distinguished between the sort of pleasure (*hedone*) we get from "external" things like food or sex or flattery and the deeper sense of inner joy (*chara*) that Marcus is talking about. Stoic joy is profound. It comes from achieving your fundamental goal in life and experiencing genuine fulfillment, which make ordinary pleasures seem trivial by comparison. Ordinary pleasures often ruffle our minds, especially when indulged in too much. Stoic joy never does this—it's synonymous with inner peace and knows no excess.[9] The Stoics refer to it as the pure form of "joy" that someone experiences who is living a truly great life and has attained genuine personal fulfillment (*eudaimonia*). Of course, none of us are there yet, but all of us may, potentially, glimpse the goal as long as we're heading in the right direction.

There are two more key points about Stoic joy worth emphasizing:

1. The Stoics tended to view joy not as the goal of life, which is wisdom, but as a by-product of it, so they believed that

trying to pursue it directly might lead us down the wrong path if it's sought at the *expense* of wisdom.

2. Joy in the Stoic sense is fundamentally *active* rather than passive; it comes from perceiving the virtuous quality of our own deeds, the things we do, whereas bodily pleasures arise from experiences that *happen* to us, even if they're a consequence of actions like eating, drinking, or having sex.

Marcus therefore says that it's not in feelings but in actions that your supreme good resides.[10]

The wise man's sense of delight comes from one thing alone: *acting consistently in accord with virtue.*[11] Nevertheless, Marcus does elsewhere mention two *additional* sources of joy. Together these correspond with the three core relationships that Stoic ethics encompassed: our *self*, *other people*, and the *world as a whole*.

1. **Contemplating virtue in yourself.** As we've just seen, Marcus says that the most important source of both "serenity" and "joy" for a Stoic comes from letting go of attachment to external things and focusing on living wisely, particularly by exercising virtue (justice) in our relations with others.

2. **Contemplating virtue in others.** Marcus also tells himself that when he wants to gladden his heart, he should meditate on the good qualities of those close to him, such as energy, modesty, or generosity. That's essentially what he's doing in book 1 of *The Meditations* when he lists the virtues of his family members and teachers at length, and it helps to explain the important role of these friendships in his life.

3. **Welcoming your fate.** Marcus also tells himself that rather than *desiring* things that are absent, as many do, he should reflect on the pleasant aspects of things he already has before him and contemplate how he would miss them if they were not there.[12]

The Greek word for joy (*chara*) is closely related to that for gratitude (*charis*). Indeed, the Stoics encourage you to appreciate the external things Fortune has given you. Marcus cautions, however, that you must exercise moderation in this regard. You should not fall into the habit of *overvaluing* external things and becoming overly attached to them. You can check this, he says, by asking yourself whether you would be upset if the things you value were ever taken away. The Stoics wanted to develop a healthy sense of gratitude in life, unspoiled by attachment. So they practiced calmly imagining change and loss, like a river gently flowing past, carrying things away. The wise man loves life and is grateful for the opportunities it gives him, but he accepts that everything changes and nothing lasts forever. Marcus therefore wrote that it is a characteristic of the Stoic Sage "to love and welcome all that happens to him and is spun for him as his fate."[13] People today often feel that this is similar to a famous Latin phrase coined by the nineteenth-century German philosopher Friedrich Nietzsche: *amor fati*, or love of one's fate.

The Stoics emphasize gratitude, but they also accept that there's nothing wrong with taking pleasure in healthy experiences, as long as it's not carried to excess. As mentioned earlier, they certainly didn't think that pleasurable experiences were a *bad* thing. Rather, pleasure, and its sources, is morally "indifferent," *neither* good nor bad.

In other words, the Stoics weren't killjoys. Marcus was convinced he could obtain as much healthy enjoyment from the simple things that befell him in life as pleasure-seekers like his brother did from ravenously indulging their unhealthy desires.[14] Socrates had likewise claimed, paradoxically, that those who practice self-control actually obtain *more* pleasure from things like food and drink than those who indulge in them to excess. Hunger is the best relish, he said, whereas if we overeat we spoil our appetites. Hedonists might accuse Stoics of missing out on life's pleasures, but Stoics would respond with this paradox: the life of someone like Marcus, who exercises moderation, is surely more pleasant and involves less self-inflicted suffering than the life of someone like Lucius, who lacks self-control and indulges himself far too much.

However, an even deeper paradox lies in the notion that, ultimately, the virtue of self-discipline itself might become a greater source of "pleasure" than food or other external objects of our desire. More accurately, exercising moderation may become a source of personal satisfaction and inner fulfillment that outweighs the ordinary pleasures it seeks to overcome. It's important to remember, though, that we're talking about self-discipline that's exercised wisely, not any sort of self-denial that might actually be foolish or unhealthy. For Stoics the *intrinsic* value of wisdom, as an end in itself, always surpasses everything else, including the pleasure and other external benefits that may accrue as the result of living wisely. Those are more like an added bonus than the real goal of life.

# STEPS FOR CHANGING DESIRES

So how do you get rid of unhealthy desires and learn to experience greater fulfillment in life, like the Stoics describe? Most of us find ourselves seeking hedonistic pleasures and indulging in bad habits that can seem difficult to break. Of course, in cases of genuine addiction to drugs or alcohol, you should seek *professional* advice. However, psychologists working in the 1970s developed reliable ways of changing ordinary habits and cravings. These methods are still being applied by therapists today to issues like snacking on unhealthy foods or fingernail biting. Some of our most persistent habits may be ways of avoiding unpleasant feelings, which leave deeper problems unresolved. However, spending too much time chasing empty pleasures can also prevent us from pursuing activities that we may find genuinely rewarding, such as living more fully in alignment with our core values. Arguably, that's the most serious problem of all.

For example, people today often complain that they feel "addicted" to social media. They spend many hours online checking messages out of a kind of habit or compulsion, feeling agitated, bored, or uneasy if they try to abstain for any length of time. They obsess about social networks, computer games, television programs, etc., in the same way Lucius did about chariot races and gladiatorial bouts. On reflection, though, few would conclude that this is the most fulfilling way to spend their lives. Nobody has ever had the words "I wish I'd watched more television" or "I wish I'd spent more time on Facebook" engraved on their tombstone. If these empty and passive pleasures provide no lasting sense of fulfillment or satisfaction, the Stoics would caution us against spending too much time on them.

In particular, people suffering from clinical depression may find that unsatisfying pleasures have come to replace the more fulfilling activities that once gave their lives meaning. They can easily end up becoming forms of distraction or sources of emotional numbing.

So you should carefully evaluate your habits and desires in terms of the bigger picture: how much do these pursuits actually contribute to your long-term happiness or sense of fulfillment in life?

I'm going to recommend a simple framework for evaluating and changing your behavior based on a combination of cognitive-behavioral therapy and ancient Stoic practices. It consists of the following steps:

1. Evaluate the consequences of your habits or desires in order to select which ones to change.
2. Spot early warning signs so that you can nip problematic desires in the bud.
3. Gain cognitive distance by separating your impressions from external reality.
4. Do something else instead of engaging in the habit.

In addition, consider how you might introduce other sources of healthy positive feelings by:

1. Planning new *activities* that are consistent with your core values.
2. Contemplating the qualities you admire in *other people*.
3. Practicing *gratitude* for the things you already have in life.

## 1. EVALUATING THE CONSEQUENCES OF DESIRES

How do you identify *which* habits to change? Modern therapists often help their clients weigh the pros and cons of different courses of action in order to choose among them. Sometimes this is called a "cost-benefit analysis" or "functional analysis." Of course, people with habits they want to break, such as overeating or smoking, normally say, "I *already* know this is bad for me!" Nevertheless, if you're not sure something is a bad habit or an unhealthy desire, you should weigh the consequences of following the desire against those of exercising moderation or doing something else.

For instance, if you regularly watch television for an hour after work, what are the long-term pros and cons of that habit? What could you do instead that would be more consistent with your true values in life, and how would that work out in the long run? Some philosophers, as we've seen, claim that the mere act of exercising moderation could become more gratifying itself than indulging in bad habits. Alternatively, you may want to do a "substitute behavior" that's high on your list of personal values but that might take a little effort to get done, such as phoning a loved one or reading a book. Remember, the purpose of this exercise is not just to reduce bad habits but to introduce more activities that are *intrinsically* valued and rewarding, like the Stoic virtues. For instance, if it's important to you to be a good parent, schedule activities that allow you to behave in a manner consistent with this value. Embracing these types of opportunities will help you become more like the sort of person you want to be in life, even if it's only for a few minutes each day at first. What would happen if you spent more time exercising the virtues you admire, doing things that you find inherently valuable and fulfilling, and less time indulging in the sort of habits that may feel pleasurable but aren't actually good for you?

In fact, really thinking through consequences of behaviors and picturing them vividly in your mind may be enough in some cases to eliminate the behavior. Epictetus therefore told his students to envision the consequences of an action and determine how it would work out for them over time. We can observe Marcus employing this method, asking himself what each action means for him and wondering whether he'll have cause to regret it in the future.[15] As we've noted, the Stoics liked to break decisions down into simple dichotomies. In "The Choice of Hercules," likewise, there are basically two paths forward:

1. The path of vice, or following excessive desires and irrational emotions (unhealthy passions)
2. The path of virtue, or exercising self-discipline and following reason and your true values in life

The Stoics often reminded themselves of the paradox that unhealthy emotions such as fear and anger actually do us more harm than the things we're upset about. Likewise, learning self-control may ultimately do us more good than obtaining all the external things we desire. The virtues of courage and moderation improve our character and our lives in general when they are exercised wisely, whereas most of the things we crave just give us fleeting pleasure.

Therapists find it helpful to ask their clients of their habits, "How's that working out in the long run?" Often that simple question is enough to motivate behavior change. However, what we'll call Stoic "functional analysis" can be done much more thoroughly on paper. You might write down the short-term pros and cons of a course of action followed by longer-term consequences. Simply realizing that your desires produce negative results can *sometimes* change the way you feel and behave. Other times, though, you may need to picture repeatedly the negative effects of bad habits in a very detailed, clear, and vivid manner in order to change them. You may find it also helps to picture the *positive* consequences of refraining from the desire, mastering it, or doing the opposite of it. It can be helpful to visualize two paths ahead of you, just like the fork in the road that confronted Hercules: for example, quitting smoking versus continuing, exercising versus doing nothing. Spend time picturing how these two paths would grow apart over time, where they might lead you several months or even years from now.

Your primary goal at this stage is to identify which desires or habits you want to overcome and to be clear about the consequences of doing so. Your secondary goal is to boost your *motivation* by developing a strong sense of contrast between the two paths ahead of you and the benefits of change. Motivation is a well-established key to success when it comes to breaking habits, so it makes sense to begin by doing what you can to boost it. To break a habit you must have a desire for change. However, it's possible to *increase* your desire for change, so that's something you should work on.

## 2. SPOT EARLY WARNING SIGNS

Now that you've considered what sort of habits or desires might conflict with your values and be worth changing, your next step is to "catch them in the wild" by noticing when they're actually happening. The key is to spot them early so that you can nip them in the bud. This requires patient self-monitoring, especially looking out for the early warning signs of the feelings or behavior you want to change. When done properly, this sort of self-monitoring is effectively a form of training in *Stoic mindfulness*.

Keep a written daily record of the situations in which you notice the desire emerging. This can be as simple as tallying each time you sense even the slightest inclination to engage in the habit, the first inkling of the desire. It could also be a more detailed record sheet, including rows with columns for the date/time, the external situation ("Where were you?"), the early warning signs you notice, and/or a rating from zero to ten of the strength of the urge and possibly also the level of actual pleasure you experienced if you gave in to it. If you find it helpful, you might also want to record any thoughts you had that facilitated or excused the desire, such as "Just this once won't hurt!" or "I can always stop tomorrow," or "I just don't have the willpower."

| Date/Time/Place | Early Warnings | Urge (0–10) | Pleasure (0–10) | Thoughts |
|---|---|---|---|---|
|  |  |  |  |  |

Your first goal should be to study yourself and identify the trigger or "high-risk" situations where the problem tends to arise. Maybe you eat junk food for comfort on particularly high-stress days at work or after you've had a fight with a loved one. Look for subtle early warning signs of the behavior that you'd previously overlooked. Become more aware of your thoughts, actions, and feelings so you can catch the desire emerging at an earlier and earlier stage. Look out for signs that typically precede the desire.

To continue the junk food example, you may notice that you look at candy in the store and picture yourself eating it. If you're a smoker, perhaps you become tense or fidget when you're craving a cigarette. Simple things that people do when engaging in habitual behaviors are hard for them to detect, even though they may be quite visible to an observer—for instance, the expression on their face, the look in their eyes, the way they use their hands, and so on. These early warnings may include the sort of facilitating thoughts mentioned above, such as "I could do with a treat" or "Just this once won't hurt."

Many common habits that people want to quit turn out to be of the hand-to-face types, such as fingernail biting, smoking, drinking, or snacking on junk food. People often fidget with their hands before engaging in these habits, such as stroking their chin just before biting their fingernail. Noticing these *precursors* for the first time can often weaken the habit. A Stoic mentor or a friend you've enlisted would be an invaluable asset to you in situations like this. Instruct the person to bring the habit to your attention with a simple gesture like tapping their nose and walking away. People often find it very irritating to be lectured about something they weren't even aware they were doing. If you're working alone, you will need to act as though another person is carefully observing you and imagine what they might see.

Learning to catch things at an early stage makes it easier to derail the chain of behaviors that leads to the full desire or passion emerging. Raising awareness of the subtle elements of a behavior also makes it feel less automatic. For instance, most adults can tie their own shoelaces automatically, without thinking about it. However, if you try to teach a child how to do it, you may find yourself suddenly all thumbs. What was habitual and automatic when we didn't think about it often becomes very clumsy and awkward when we are forced to analyze the steps or do it in a slightly different manner. That's unhelpful if you're performing before an audience or playing a sport, where thinking too much about your behavior can cause self-consciousness and disrupt routine actions. Ask someone who's about to perform a skilled action, like putting in golf, whether they begin doing it by breathing in or out—that will often be enough to confuse them and put them off. The same principle, that self-awareness disrupts the automatic quality of the behavior, can be very *helpful* when you actually want to break a bad habit.

## 3. GAIN COGNITIVE DISTANCE

Once you've spotted the early warning signs of a craving or habit, you can also help yourself change by noticing the *separation* between your current perspective and external reality. We've already introduced the concept of cognitive distancing from modern psychotherapy. It provides a way of understanding one of the most important psychological practices in Stoicism: that of "separating" our values from external events. When a desire or habit emerges, you can take note of thoughts that encourage it—"I wonder what's happening online"—and also thoughts or excuses that facilitate it—"It won't hurt if I just check my social media messages for a second." Observing these in a detached way, almost as if they were someone else's thoughts, will help you gain cognitive distance and will weaken the urge to act on them. The Stoics do this, as we've seen, in a number of ways. Following them, you might "apostrophize" the thought, speaking to it as if to another person, and say, "You are just a thought and not at all the thing you claim to represent"—the thing itself having no intrinsic value. You might also adapt Epictetus and say "It's not things that make us crave them but our judgments about things." We are the ones who choose to assign value to things that look appealing.

It's as though strong desires and feelings of pleasure are telling us "This is good!" Strong desire makes us forget that there are other ways of viewing the things we crave. However, pausing and gaining cognitive distance, by defusing your thoughts from reality, tends to weaken the strength of your feelings and the hold they have over your behavior.

There are many different ways of gaining cognitive distance. One is to imagine how a role model might perceive the same situation differently. Suppose you're craving a hamburger. You might use the verbal technique of asking yourself, "What would Socrates do about this desire?" Socrates, as it happens, was careful about his diet and preferred to eat modestly. He thought that self-control was more important than pleasure, as we've seen, and if we avoid overeating, we will obtain more enjoyment from our food anyway. You could also ask, "How would Marcus cope if he had the same sort of cravings?" Of course, you might prefer to pick a role model of your own, perhaps someone you know personally, a friend, colleague, or family member, or even a celebrity or fictional character. First, consider what the role model you choose would say to themselves about the desire. How would they react to the initial awareness of the urge? Then consider what they would actually do. Of course, you don't have to imitate them, but viewing the experience from different perspectives can weaken the strength of the feeling. You may be inspired to problem-solve and think creatively of alternative ways to respond. On the other hand, when people feel overwhelmed by desires or emotions, they can often only imagine *one* way of looking at events.

Marcus also talks about the importance of breaking things

down into their components and reflecting on each part in isolation. The idea is that when we analyze something in terms of its elements and focus on each in turn, asking ourselves whether it alone is enough to overwhelm us, the whole experience will tend to seem more bearable. Similar "divide-and-conquer" techniques are employed in modern cognitive therapy to overcome problematic desires and emotions. We may as well borrow the term used by the early twentieth-century psychotherapist Charles Baudouin, who was influenced by Stoicism, to describe this psychological technique: "depreciation by analysis."[16] That means breaking any problem down into small chunks that seem less emotionally powerful or overwhelming.

For instance, when engaged in certain actions, such as bad habits of the kind we've been discussing, Marcus advised pausing and asking of each step: "Does death appear terrible because I would be deprived of this?" That gave him a way of isolating each part of a habit in turn and casting its value in question.[17] For example, someone smoking a cigarette might ask with each puff whether losing that sensation would really be the end of the world. Someone compulsively checking social media might stop and ask if not reading each individual notification would really be so unbearable. If you practice self-awareness in this way, you'll often (but not always) realize that the pleasure you obtain from such habits is actually *much less* than you previously assumed.

Marcus led the dance of the Salii, the ancient leaping warrior-priests, and trained in boxing and wrestling as a youth. He draws on these experiences, making the astute psychological observation that you can spoil the delights of song and dance just by pausing to analyze them into their parts—for example, breaking a melody down into individual notes, in your mind, and asking yourself of each small part: "Would this be enough to overcome me?"[18] Likewise, in the *pankration*, an ancient sport combining boxing, wrestling, kicking, and choking, analyzing each of your opponent's moves individually can help you learn to overcome them without feeling overwhelmed. Marcus therefore advised himself to analyze events into their component parts in order to break the spell of passion.

You've already learned about the concept of Stoic indifference, or *apatheia*. It has a very specific meaning—freedom from harmful desires or passions—that the Stoics distinguished from *ordinary* indifference. It's not about being coldhearted or uncaring. Whereas Stoics believed that the only true good is wisdom and virtue, we tend to slip into the habit of thinking about external things as if they were more important than fulfilling our own nature. We've seen how the Stoics particularly emphasized suspending value judgments about external things. They did this by using language to describe events as objectively as possible. As we've seen, they called this firm grip on reality *phantasia kataleptike*, or the "objective representation" of events.

You can see how this concept could apply to managing unhealthy desires. People often talk about the things they crave in language that's bound to excite their own desire, even when they realize they're fostering unhealthy habits: "I'm dying for some chocolate. Why is it *so* good? It tastes like heaven! This is better than sex." (It's mainly vegetable fat, some cacao, and a load of refined sugar.) That's another example of rhetoric working against you. On the other hand, when you describe food, or anything else you crave, in down-to-earth language, you can feel detached from it. Hadrian, who is thought to have died from a heart attack, greatly admired an extravagant dish jokingly called the *tetrapharmacum*, or "fourfold remedy," reputedly invented by Lucius Verus's father. It consisted of pheasant, wild boar, ham, and a sow's udder, all wrapped in pastry. By contrast, Marcus would sometimes look at roasted meats and other delicacies and murmur to himself, "This is a dead bird, a dead fish, a dead pig."[19] An exquisite wine is just fermented grape juice, and so on.[20] Viewed from a different perspective, in other words, the things people crave are often nothing to get excited about.

Sometimes these objective representations resemble the notes an ancient physician or natural philosopher may have made documenting their observations of physical phenomena. In modern cognitive therapy, we also suggest that clients think of themselves as scientists, approaching behavior change as an experiment with an attitude of curiosity, detachment, and objectivity. Marcus even applied this way of looking at the world to his sex life. We noted earlier that he had struggled to overcome feelings of anger as a young man. He also briefly mentions having sexual desires that he considered it better not to act upon. In book 1 of *The Meditations* Marcus says that, looking back, he's grateful he chose to preserve his sexual innocence for a few years into his adulthood.[21] He's also thankful that when he was later troubled by strong sexual cravings, he overcame them and "never touched Benedicta or Theodotus"—possibly a female and male slave in the household of his father, the Emperor Antoninus. We can see that Marcus applied depreciation by analysis to sexual desires. At one point, for instance, he described sex to himself, perhaps as an ancient physician might, as merely the rubbing together of body parts followed by a convulsion and the ejaculation of some mucus.[22] Not very romantic, but that's the point—he was aiming to neutralize *inappropriate* sexual urges of the kind he struggled to overcome. (He had thirteen children, though, so he wasn't completely opposed to sex.) The point isn't to obliterate all desire but rather to moderate unhealthy or excessive desires, which place too much importance on certain types of pleasure.

## 4. DO SOMETHING ELSE

You've identified which desires you want to overcome, learned how to spot their early warning signs, and practiced how to pause and gain distance from them. In a sense, the best thing to do next is *nothing*. In other words, do not respond any further to the feelings of desire. You can certainly come back to those feelings later if you need to. Take a time-out instead of acting on the desire. You might want to leave the situation where you're experiencing temptation. Many types of urges only last a minute or so at a time, although they may recur throughout the day. You only have to deal with the present moment, though, one instance of an urge or craving at a time. So having caught those feelings early and reminded yourself that it's mainly your thinking that's causing your feelings, just refrain from acting on the desire or go and engage in a different activity instead, something healthy that you find intrinsically rewarding. You are always free to *do something else*.

For example, suppose you're in the habit of drinking a glass of wine every evening after work, but that's gradually turned into a bottle of wine, perhaps sometimes two bottles. That's not going to be healthy for you in the long run. Perhaps you've also decided your evenings would be better spent reading or going to evening classes instead, because that's the sort of person you'd rather be. You know that being at home in the early evening is your trigger situation for engaging in this habit. You've noticed that it starts when you feel bored and agitated, and you tell yourself that you need a drink to relax. Now you're getting better at catching the urge to drink as soon as it begins to appear. You notice your thoughts, and you're aware of how they influence your feelings. You tell yourself, "It's not the wine that makes me feel desire but the way I'm thinking about it." So having paused and taken a step back from those feelings, the next step is to not pour yourself a glass of wine and to refrain from doing so long enough for the desire to abate. Additional temptations won't last long, and you can deal with the feeling again in exactly the same way, one step at a time, if it comes back.

Instead of pouring a glass of wine, do something else: perhaps leave the house for a change of scenery. Do something that gives you a sense of genuine accomplishment rather than just a fleeting and empty sensation of pleasure. If you're determined to break this sort of habit, you can remove temptation by getting rid of any bottles and wine glasses in your house and making a commitment not to buy replacements. You can engage in healthy "substitute behaviors" instead, like drinking fruit smoothies or herbal teas. Of course, what you do will depend on the type of habit that you want to overcome, but you get the general idea.

Ideally, as we've seen, your goal is to replace unfulfilling habits and desires with activities that you find more intrinsically rewarding. When we discussed values clarification earlier, we touched on this aspect of Stoicism, which has to do with acting in more "virtuous" ways. Sometimes, though, *not* doing something, the very act of overcoming a bad habit, might be considered a virtue, something to be valued for its own sake. One of the techniques Marcus employs most frequently in *The Meditations* is to ask himself what virtue or resource Nature has given him to cope with a particular situation. This is closely related to the question of what character traits we admire most in other people. Marcus says we typically praise the virtue of self-control or moderation in others, which stops us from being carried away by our pleasures.[23] We don't normally admire anyone for how much junk food they've eaten, but we praise their strength in overcoming bad habits such as eating too much junk food.

The Stoics thought that if we want to improve ourselves, we should be guided more by the qualities we admire in other people and our true values and principles than by avoiding pain and seeking pleasure. That sort of hedonistic life isn't satisfying, and, as "The Choice of Hercules" implies, we can't flourish as human beings and achieve things we can be proud of until we endure certain feelings of pain or discomfort or forgo certain pleasures.

This perspective arguably comes more to the fore when people have children and they begin to think about what it means to be a good parent. If you want to be a role model for your children, you should ask yourself what sort of person you are and what qualities you want to exhibit. Developing your own character by exercising moderation wisely in your daily life may then become more of a priority than the simple pursuit of pleasure. Of course, the Stoics would go further and argue that we should exercise wisdom, self-discipline, and moderation, not because it sets a good example for our children but because doing so is an end in itself—virtue is its own reward. We aim for wisdom and strength of character not because we're hoping to gain something else but simply because that's who we want to be in life.

You've also learned how Stoics studied the attitudes and behaviors of role models. For Marcus that included individuals from his own life like Antoninus Pius and Junius Rusticus, and also wise historical figures like Heraclitus, Socrates, and Diogenes the Cynic. The people we often admire have a fairly take-it-or-leave-it attitude toward bodily pleasures such as food and drink, like the attitude Marcus attributed to Socrates and observed in Antoninus. They don't *crave* these pleasures or feel *addicted* to them. They place more value on their own character and integrity. On the other hand, they are able to enjoy pleasures in a healthy way, within reasonable bounds, remembering that they are temporary and not wholly under our control.

Again, it's enlightening to consider the double standard between the things you desire for yourself and the things you find admirable in others. Many people find the suggestion that they should abandon certain pleasures almost shocking at first. However, the same people often praise and admire others who exercise endurance or self-control and forgo certain pleasures for the sake of wisdom and virtue. Epictetus used Socratic questioning to highlight this sort of contradiction, hidden from view in people's underlying values. Really seeing that two beliefs are incompatible can weaken one or both of them and help you clarify your core values. The two-column technique that involves listing the things you typically *desire* in your own life and comparing them to qualities you *admire* in other people can highlight inconsistencies between the two perspectives. What would happen if you started to desire more of the traits you admire in other people? For example, suppose you replaced your desire to eat chocolate assuming you had one, with the desire to be a fairly self-disciplined person and make healthy choices more consistently? For Stoics the supreme goal is always virtue rather than pleasure. However, healthy pleasures and even a deeper sense of joy may follow as the consequence of living in accord with virtue.

# ADD HEALTHIER SOURCES OF JOY

We saw earlier that Marcus mentions three sources of rational joy. The first and most important is the joy that Stoics experience by glimpsing their own progress toward wisdom and virtue, and thereby fulfilling their potential in life. In addition to *replacing* unhealthy habits with more intrinsically valuable activities, you can schedule beneficial activities every day. For example, you might set aside ten minutes each day to write stories for your children. While that might not replace a bad habit, it does introduce a good one, if that's something that gives you a sense of fulfillment. It's like setting aside time each day to exercise the Stoic virtues and become more like the people you admire.

What about the joy Marcus says we can obtain by contemplating the virtue of *others*? That's related to what we've been saying about modeling the attitudes and behavior of others. You might want to set aside time to write down a description of the qualities you most admire in other people, as Marcus does in book 1 of *The Meditations*, or visualize them in your mind's eye. Contemplating the virtues of people who are close to you may have the added benefit of helping to improve your relationship with them. Also, how does thinking about the qualities you admire in others affect you, and how might you learn and benefit from this experience?

Finally, remember what Marcus said about feeling *gratitude* instead of desire. In a sense, to desire something is to imagine having what you don't have, the presence of something that's absent. Gratitude, on the other hand, comes from imagining the absence of things that are currently present: What would it be like if you didn't have this? If we don't occasionally picture loss, reminding ourselves what life might be like without the things and people we love, we would take them for granted. Keep a journal of people and things that you're grateful for, perhaps also focusing on what you can learn from them. As Marcus says, though, it's important to do this in such a way that you don't end up becoming overly attached to external things. Stoics try to avoid that by reminding themselves that external things, and other people, are not entirely under our control, and one day they will be gone. The wise man is grateful for the gifts life has given him, but he also reminds himself that they are merely on loan—everything changes and nothing lasts forever. Epictetus told his Stoic students to imagine they're guests at a banquet being handed a sharing plate, not greedily holding on to it and scoffing the lot but politely taking an appropriate share and then handing the rest along. That's how Stoics think about life in general: they aim to be grateful for external things without becoming overly attached to them.

We've now seen how the Stoics aspired to find happiness in healthy ways, through gratitude for the things they have, admiration for the strengths of others, or pride in their own ability to act with dignity, honor, and integrity. Also, remember that for Stoics ordinary pleasure and pain aren't good or bad but merely *indifferent*. Their main concern is to avoid becoming *hedonistic* by placing too much value on physical pleasures, indulging in them, and craving them excessively. A preference, or "light" desire, for pleasurable things and avoiding pain and discomfort is natural for Stoics, within reasonable bounds.

We can apply some of the guidance they left us about how to master our desires today using the framework I described. Evaluate certain habits or desires rationally in terms of their consequences. Write down the long-term pros and cons of indulging in the habit versus overcoming it. Close your eyes and visualize a fork in the road representing two paths, picturing as vividly as you can first the future with *unhealthy* passions, then the future with wise actions in accord with reason. You can adapt the daily routine mentioned earlier to look like this:

1. **Morning Meditation.** Think of the rising sun, the stars, and your small space within the whole cosmos. Mentally rehearse the key events of the day, imagining how Socrates, Zeno, Marcus Aurelius, or your own role model would cope with habits or desires. Picture how you plan to cope with any challenges and what inner resources or virtues you can employ.

2. **During the Day.** Practice Stoic mindfulness by looking for early warning signs of the habits or desires you want to overcome. Try to catch them early and nip them in the bud. Pause and practice accepting any feelings of unease with Stoic indifference. Gain cognitive distance from your thoughts and refrain from acting on your feelings. Engage in healthy substitute behaviors instead, which contribute to a genuine sense of fulfillment. You could also keep a written log or tally of certain habits, as described in this chapter.

3. **Evening Meditation.** At the end of the day, review how well you fared in terms of acting in accordance with your values—that is, virtues. In relation to desires, consider what you did well, what you did badly, and what you could do differently tomorrow. If it helps, imagine answering these questions before a wise Stoic mentor or even a panel of Sages, and consider what advice

they might give you. Use what you learn to help prepare for the next day's morning meditation.

As we'll see in the following chapters, you can adapt this
basic Stoic routine, and some of the same techniques, to help you
cope with other challenges in life, such as pain, anxiety, and anger.
You'll therefore be learning to use similar techniques, but in a
slightly different way.

# 5.

# GRASPING THE NETTLE

Marcus Aurelius was known for his physical *frailty*, due to chronic health problems, but he was also known for his exceptional *resilience*. For instance, the historian Cassius Dio wrote:

> To be sure, he could not display many feats of physical prowess; yet he had developed his body from a very weak one to one capable of the greatest endurance.[1]

How do we explain this seeming paradox? How did a man so weak and sickly become known for toughness and endurance? Perhaps the answer lies in his *attitude* toward pain and illness, and the Stoic techniques he used to cope with them.

Marcus was nearly fifty, an old man by Roman standards, at the outbreak of the First Marcomannic War. Nevertheless, he donned the military cape and boots, rode forth from Rome, and stationed himself on the front line. He spent much of his time at the legionary fortress of Carnuntum, on the other side of the Alps, by the banks of the Danube in modern-day Austria. Cassius Dio tells us that at first Marcus was too frail to endure the frigid northern climate and address the legions assembled before him. It was a dangerous and physically grueling environment, even for an emperor. To make things worse, with large numbers of men living in close proximity, the military camps were especially vulnerable to outbreaks of the plague. Nevertheless, Marcus typically shrugged off the hardships of life on the northern frontier by quoting the poet Euripides: "Such things accursed war brings in its train." They were to be expected, in other words.

Despite his health problems and the inhospitable environment, Marcus would spend over a decade commanding the legions along the Danube. In *The Meditations*, he thanks the gods that his body held out for such a long time under such physical duress.[2] He survived the two Marcomannic Wars and the Antonine Plague, nearly making it to the age of sixty at a time when the odds of doing so were poor. Indeed, although he suffered from recurring health problems, he managed to live longer than most of his contemporaries. Still, the sudden transition to military life must have been a tremendous physical challenge for him. It's therefore no surprise that his writings frequently reveal evidence of his psychological struggle to cope with *physical* problems.

He'd been preparing himself to face this inner battle for most of his life, though. Over the years, Marcus had gradually learned to endure pain and illness by utilizing the psychological strategies of ancient Stoicism. During the war, in writing *The Meditations*, he reflected on these techniques as part of his ongoing practice. These notes reflect a state of mind attained from more than three decades of rigorous Stoic training. In other words, his attitude toward pain and illness during the northern campaign didn't come naturally to him; he had to *learn* it.

*The Meditations* isn't our only insight into Marcus's thinking, though. In the early nineteenth century, the Italian scholar Angelo Mai uncovered a treasure trove of ancient letters between the Latin rhetorician Marcus Cornelius Fronto and several other notable individuals, including his student Marcus Aurelius. We can't date the individual letters precisely, but they appear to span the whole period of Marcus and Fronto's friendship, until the latter's death around 167 AD at the height of the Antonine Plague.

Their correspondence is remarkable for several reasons. For the first time, scholars could peek into Marcus's private life and witness his true personality. Far from the popular caricature of a Stoic as someone coldly austere, Marcus shows remarkable warmth and affection toward Fronto and his family. His style of writing is casual and good-humored. He tells Fronto, for instance, of the time he was riding in the countryside, dressed as a regular citizen, when a shepherd rudely accused his companions of being a band of common rogues. Marcus rode laughing into the flock, playfully scattering the sheep to break up the argument. However, the shepherd wasn't amused and threw his cudgel at them, yelling as the young men fled the scene. It's difficult to imagine that twenty years later the author of these affable and easygoing letters would find himself gravely noting down Stoic meditations upon seeing the severed body parts littering the frigid battlefields of Pannonia.

There's something else, though, about these letters that stands in marked contrast to *The Meditations*: the amount of small talk, and sometimes even griping, that goes on about various health conditions. Fronto was roughly twenty years Marcus's senior and was particularly fond of complaining to him about his assorted aches and pains. In one instance, Fronto lists the regions of his body most afflicted during the night by widespread pain—"my shoulder, elbow, knee, and ankle"—which he says prevented him from writing to Marcus in his own hand.[3]

In another letter he writes,

> After your departure I was seized by a pain in the knee, mild enough, it is true, for me to be able to walk with due caution and use a carriage. Tonight the pain has set in more violently, but not so badly that I cannot easily bear it when lying down, if it does not get any worse.[4]

Sometimes Marcus gets drawn into gossiping with Fronto about his own health problems.

> As to my present state of health, you will be able to judge that easily enough from my shaky handwriting. It is true that as regards my strength, that is beginning to come back, and nothing remains, besides, of the pain in my chest; but the ulcer is working on my windpipe.[5]

This particular letter was written before Marcus was acclaimed emperor. It shows that by the age of forty, perhaps much earlier, he was *already* suffering from the kind of symptoms that would afflict him throughout his reign. In these letters, though, there's no evidence of the Stoic techniques for coping that we find a decade or more later in *The Meditations*.

As a youth, Marcus was fit and enjoyed physical activity, as we've seen. While at Rome, he was trained to fight in armor, probably by gladiators, using blunted weapons for practice. He also enjoyed hunting and particularly loved to spear wild boar from horseback. He went fowling as well, hunting birds with nets and spears.

So our overall picture of Marcus in his youth is one of a strong, athletic young man. As he aged into his forties and fifties, though, he became physically frail, and that seems to be how subsequent generations remembered him. Writing in the fourth century, for instance, the Emperor Julian imagines Marcus's skin looked *diaphanous* and *translucent*. Marcus even referred to himself in a speech as a weak old man, unable to take food without pain or sleep without disturbance. *The Meditations* also mentions him obtaining remedies for coughing up blood and spells of giddiness.[6] He particularly suffered from chronic chest and stomach pains. He could manage only small amounts of food, taken late at night. Scholars have offered different diagnoses, the most common being chronic stomach ulcers, although he probably suffered from multiple health problems.

After the initial plague outbreak at Rome, Marcus's court physician, Galen, prescribed him the ancient compound known as *theriac*, a mysterious concoction made from dozens of exotic ingredients, everything from bitter myrrh to fermented viper's flesh and a small quantity of opium. Marcus believed that regular doses of theriac helped him endure the pain in his stomach and chest as well as his other symptoms. He stopped using it for a time because it was making him too drowsy, but he resumed taking a modified version with a reduced quantity of opium. He therefore seems to have taken theriac judiciously and in a mild form.

In any case, the medicine clearly didn't eliminate the pain

and discomfort Marcus felt. Like many people who suffer from chronic pain, he had to develop other ways of coping. Over the years, therefore, Marcus came to depend on the *psychological* techniques of Stoicism as a way of living with health problems, especially as things became tougher for him after joining the army on the Danube. During the misery of the Antonine Plague and the carnage of the Marcomannic Wars, he must have witnessed countless people dealing with their own suffering, some better than others. Over the course of his life, he learned a great deal by studying how a handful of exemplary individuals endured severe pain and illness. He interpreted that wisdom through the lens of Stoicism and then distilled it into *The Meditations*.

In marked contrast to the Marcus of Fronto's letters, he states very bluntly in *The Meditations* that the wise man neither strikes a tragic attitude nor whines about what befalls him. He's certainly not referring to his rhetoric teachers, Fronto and Herodes Atticus. However, when he wrote these words, he probably had their rivals in mind: his philosophy teachers, the men who trained him in Stoicism and provided him with a living example of mental resilience. For example, the way Apollonius of Chalcedon endured severe pain and several long illnesses made a lifelong impression on Marcus. Apollonius had maintained his equanimity through it all, never allowing any setback to knock him off course, always remaining committed to his life's goal of acquiring wisdom and sharing it with others.[7]

However, Claudius Maximus, another one of Marcus's Stoic tutors, seems to have left an even more powerful impression on him. Marcus mentions Maximus's illness and death three times in *The Meditations*. Like Apollonius, Maximus was completely resolute in his commitment to the pursuit of wisdom despite severe illness. He wasn't a Stoic professor, like Apollonius, but a high-ranking Roman statesman and accomplished military commander. He was also a tough and profoundly self-reliant individual, renowned for his commitment to Stoicism—the sort of man who stood upright of his own accord, as Marcus liked to put it, rather than having to be set upright by anyone else. He remained unwavering in his resolve and cheerful in the face of any predicament.[8] It seems likely that Maximus became ill and died not long after the Senate appointed him proconsul of Africa in 158 AD, and his loss seems to have affected Marcus quite deeply.

Indeed, Marcus appears to compare Maximus to the Emperor Antoninus. Both men showed impeccable strength of character, self-discipline, and endurance in the face of pain and illness. Antoninus took good care of his health, so that throughout most of his long life he seldom required the aid of physicians. However, he did suffer from severe headaches, and as he grew older, he became so doubled over that wooden splints were required to keep his torso upright. Marcus noticed that while recovering from a severe headache, his adoptive father would simply get right back to his duties as emperor with renewed determination. He didn't waste time worrying about his ailments or allow the pain to stop him for long. As Marcus was writing *The Meditations*, he found himself looking back on the peaceful manner in which Antoninus had passed away over a decade earlier, at the venerable age of seventy-four.[9] Like Maximus, Antoninus was always contented, always cheerful. It's said that even as he lay dying, with his last breath he whispered the word *equanimity* to his guard, which was emblematic both of his character and of his reign. We can clearly see that Marcus's attitude toward pain and illness was shaped by studying the characters of these men. Perhaps he also wanted to become *less* like Fronto and the other Sophists, whose love of high-flown rhetoric risked amplifying their complaints by turning common misfortunes into personal tragedies.

Although Marcus was a Stoic, he also drew inspiration from another, more surprising source when it came to coping with pain and illness: the *rival* philosophical school of Epicurus. The Epicureans believed that the goal of life was pleasure (*hedone*). They described pleasure, though, in a notoriously paradoxical manner, as consisting mainly of a state of freedom from pain and suffering (*ataraxia*). Minimizing the emotional distress caused by pain and illness was therefore extremely important to them.

Marcus quotes from a letter purportedly written by Epicurus nearly five hundred years earlier. We know from another source that Epicurus was afflicted by severe kidney stones and dysentery, which eventually caused his death:

> When I was ill, my conversation was not devoted to the sufferings of my body, nor did I chatter about such matters to those who visited me but I continued to discuss the main elements of natural philosophy as before, and this point especially, how it is that the mind, while being aware of the agitations in our poor flesh, is unperturbed and preserves its specific good. Nor did I allow the doctors to assume grand airs, as though they were engaged in something important, but my life proceeded as well and happily as ever.[10]

Marcus must have been struck by the contrast between this letter and the sort of correspondence he had been having decades earlier with Fronto. Just as most of us do, Marcus had engaged in precisely the sort of chatter and complaints about the "sufferings of the body" that Epicurus had warned against. Although he was in poor health, Epicurus didn't complain or dwell on his symptoms. In fact, he used his illness as an opportunity to converse in a dispassionate manner about how the mind can remain contented while the body suffers terrible pain and discomfort. He simply carried on doing what he loved: discussing philosophy with his friends.

Marcus quotes this letter and then exhorts himself always to act as Epicurus did: remain focused on the pursuit of wisdom even in the face of illness, pain, or any other hardship. This advice, he says, is common not only to Epicureanism and Stoicism but to all other schools of philosophy. Our main concern should always remain the use we are making right now, from moment to moment, of our own mind.[11]

Marcus returns to the teachings of Epicurus concerning pain and illness several times in *The Meditations*. He's particularly interested in one of Epicurus's famous maxims, or *Principal Doctrines*, which contains advice for coping with pain. We should remind ourselves, Epicurus said, that pain is always bearable because it is either acute or chronic but never both. The Church Father Tertullian neatly summed up the same idea by saying that Epicurus coined the maxim "a little pain is contemptible, and a great one is not lasting." You can therefore learn to cope by telling yourself that the pain won't last long if it's severe or that you're capable of enduring much worse if the pain is chronic. People often object to this by saying that their pain is *both* chronic and severe. However, earlier in *The Meditations*, Marcus paraphrased the same quote from Epicurus as follows: "On pain: if it is unbearable, it carries us off, if it persists, it can be endured."[12] The point is that chronic pain beyond our ability to endure would have killed us, so the fact we're still standing proves that we're capable of enduring much worse. Although this can be hard for some people to accept, participants in my online courses who have suffered for many years with chronic pain have reported that this Epicurean maxim has been a great help to them, just as it was for many people throughout previous centuries. We have to *practice* to keep looking at things this way, though, just as we must practice to overcome unhealthy habits and cravings.

Why exactly did the ancients find this particular strategy so helpful as a way of coping with pain? When people are really struggling, they focus on their *inability to cope* and the feeling that the problem is spiraling out of control: "I just can't bear this any longer!" This is a form of *catastrophizing*: focusing too much on the worst-case scenario and feeling overwhelmed. However, Epicurus meant that by focusing instead on the *limits* of your pain, whether in terms of duration or severity, you can develop a mind-set that's more oriented toward coping and less overwhelmed by worry or negative emotions about your condition.

Marcus also found it helpful to think of his pain as confined to a particular part of the body rather than allowing himself to become consumed by imagining it as more pervasive. Pain wants to dominate your mind and become the whole story. However, people who handle pain well usually view it objectively, as something more limited in nature, which makes it easier for them to see themselves coping with it in various ways. Indeed, elsewhere in *The Meditations*, Marcus adds a Stoic twist to Epicurus's saying. "Pain is neither unendurable nor everlasting, if you keep its limits in mind *and do not add to it through your own imagination.*"[13] The Stoics were typically happy to assimilate aspects of Epicureanism and other philosophical teachings, but they tweaked them to be more compatible with their own core doctrines. Marcus meant that pain is tolerable if we remember that our attitude toward it is what really determines how upset we become. It's not our pains or illnesses that upset us but our judgments about them, as the Stoics would put it. This is one of the main therapeutic tools in the armamentarium of Stoic pain management.

Marcus also noted that most other forms of physical discomfort can be dealt with in essentially the same manner. He compares coping with pain to coping with difficulty eating and drowsiness, two problems we know he suffered from personally. He also mentions oppressive heat, bringing to mind the Cynic notion of learning to endure intense heat and cold. When faced with any of these discomforts, Marcus would simply warn himself, "You are giving way to pain."[14] Then he'd apply the same coping skills, whether he was struggling in a blizzard along the Danube or suffering fatigue from riding for days from his base at Aquileia in northern Italy to the legionary fortress of Carnuntum. Pain, discomfort, fatigue—they're all just unpleasant sensations.

He was right. The skills people use to cope with pain—even very severe pain—are similar to ones that can be used to deal with other uncomfortable sensations. For instance, during ordinary forms of physical exercise, such as jogging or yoga, there are opportunities to practice essentially the same coping strategies. We can learn to tolerate the harmless sensations of fatigue and discomfort experienced while doing these sorts of activities. Taking cold showers also allows us to practice the same techniques. If we learn these strategies well enough, then we may be able to call upon them to cope with severe pain or serious physical injury in a crisis, even if we're caught off guard. Everyday tolerance of minor physical discomforts can help us build lasting psychological resilience, in other words. You could call this a form of *stress inoculation*: you learn to build up resistance to a bigger problem by voluntarily exposing yourself repeatedly to something similar, albeit in smaller doses or a milder form.

Over time, Marcus observed many people around him afflicted by different illnesses and facing death in various ways. He also learned specific coping strategies and techniques from his Stoic teachers. Indeed, Marcus described several different Stoic strategies for dealing with pain and illness in *The Meditations*. The most important thing he observed in those individuals who coped well was their ability to "withdraw" or "separate" their mind from bodily sensations. We've already introduced this Stoic technique, which I've called *cognitive distancing*. It requires learning to withhold value judgments from unpleasant feelings, viewing them as morally *indifferent*, neither good nor bad in themselves, and ultimately *harmless*. This takes practice, of course, and an understanding of the underlying concepts.

It was mainly through the Stoic teachings of Epictetus that Marcus found a way to conceptualize this powerful technique. One of the most famous stories about Stoic endurance happens to be about Epictetus. He was originally a slave and came to be owned by Epaphroditus, a secretary to Emperor Nero. According to the Church Father Origen, Epaphroditus took hold of Epictetus in anger one day and cruelly twisted his leg. Epictetus didn't react but remained completely composed. He merely warned his master that the bone was about to snap. Epaphroditus continued twisting it, and that's exactly what happened. Rather than complain, Epictetus responded matter-of-factly: "There, did I not tell you that it would break?"

Epictetus alludes to his being lame in the *Discourses* but never mentions the cause. Instead, he uses his disability as an example to teach his students about coping with illness. Disease is an impediment to our body, he tells them, but not to our freedom of will unless we make it so. Lameness, he says, is an impediment to the leg but not to the mind.[15] Epictetus was no more perturbed by his crippled leg than he was by his inability to grow wings and fly—he simply accepted it as one of the many things in life that were beyond his control. He viewed his lameness as an opportunity to exercise wisdom and strength of character. Later in life he gained his freedom and began teaching philosophy. Perhaps his master felt remorse. In any case, this story powerfully illustrates the famous indifference of Stoics to physical pain. If this story is true, Marcus would certainly have heard about it.

## HOW TO TOLERATE PAIN

It may seem natural to assume that pain is intrinsically bad, but the Stoics employ a barrage of arguments to persuade their followers that pain and pleasure are neither good nor bad. For instance, one way of illustrating the indifference of pain would be to point out that, like other externals, pain can be used either wisely or foolishly, for good or for bad. An athlete might learn to endure the pain and discomfort of extreme physical exertion. In that case, deliberately exposing themselves through hard exercise to painful, or at least uncomfortable, sensations might be something beneficial insofar as it helps them to build endurance. Of course, someone who avoids discomfort is probably going to avoid strenuous exercise. Pain and discomfort can become advantages in life if they provide opportunities for us to develop our strengths. It's also true that many ordinary people, at certain times, exhibit indifference to pain—such as when they're injured while saving their own life. Some people, of course, such as masochists, even *enjoy* the sensation of pain. Pain is just a sensation, in other words; what matters is how we choose to respond to it.

Epictetus tells his students how to cope with pain and illness several times in the *Discourses*. Like Epicurus before him, he believed that complaining and chattering too much about our problems just makes them worse, and, more importantly, it harms our character. Marcus agreed that collective whining is bad for the soul: "No joining others in their wailing, no violent emotion."[16] Modern cognitive therapists likewise find that distress escalates when people tell themselves "I can't cope!" Their distress lessens when they begin looking at things more rationally and objectively and acknowledge various ways they can *potentially* cope now or have coped in a similar situation in the past. In part, this is an observation about the *rhetoric* of pain. We should be wary of telling ourselves "This is unbearable!" and so on, because that's usually just hyperbole that adds to our sense of despair.

Epictetus tells his students that it's one thing to have a pain in the head or in the ear, but they should not go a step further and say, "I have a pain in the head—*alas!*" They shouldn't imply that the pain is some kind of catastrophe. He explained that he wasn't denying them the right to groan, just that they shouldn't do so *inwardly* by actually buying into the notion that they've been harmed. Just because a slave is slow in bringing them a bandage they shouldn't cry aloud and torment themselves, complaining "Everyone hates me!" ("For who would *not* hate such a man?" he adds sardonically.) He summed up his practical advice by telling his students to respond to troubling events or unpleasant sensations by literally saying *This is nothing to me*. This perhaps overstates things. Stoics can still "prefer" to avoid pain and illness when possible. Once it's already happening, though, they try to accept the fact with indifference.

In addition to the maxim of Epicurus, Marcus mentions many Stoic strategies for bearing pain and illness by viewing them with studied indifference. Most of these strategies were influenced by the *Discourses* of Epictetus.

1. Separate your mind from the sensation, which I call "cognitive distancing," by reminding yourself that it is not things, or sensations, that upset us but our judgments about them.

2. Remember that the fear of pain does more harm than pain itself, or use other forms of functional analysis to weigh up the consequences for you of fearing versus accepting pain.

3. View bodily sensations objectively (objective representation, or *phantasia kataleptike*) instead of describing them in emotive terms. ("There's a feeling of pressure around my forehead" versus "It feels like I'm dying—an elephant might as well be stamping over and over on my head!")

4. Analyze the sensations into their elements and limit them as precisely as possible to their specific site on the body, thereby using the same depreciation by analysis that we used in the previous chapter to neutralize unhealthy desires and cravings. ("There's a sharp throbbing sensation in my ear that comes and goes," not "I'm in total agony.")

5. View the sensation as limited in time, changeable, and transient, or "contemplate impermanence." ("This sensation only peaks for a few seconds at a time and then

fades away; it will probably be gone in a couple of days.")
If you have an acute problem like toothache, you'll have
forgotten what it felt like years from now. If you have a
long-term problem such as chronic sciatica, you'll know
it sometimes gets worse and so at other times it must
be less severe. It makes a difference if you can focus on
the notion that this shall pass.

6. Let go of your struggle against the sensation and accept it as natural and indifferent, what is called "Stoic
acceptance." That doesn't mean you shouldn't take
practical steps to deal with it, such as using medication
to reduce pain, but you must learn to live with the pain
without resentment or an emotional struggle.

7. Remind yourself that Nature has given you both the
capacity to exercise courage and the endurance to rise
above pain and that we admire these virtues in other
people, which we discussed in relation to contemplating and modeling virtue.

We'll look at each of these strategies in turn.

## COGNITIVE DISTANCING

The most important pain-management strategy mentioned by
Epictetus and Marcus is the one we've called "cognitive distancing." It's summed up in a phrase that will already be familiar to
you: "It's not events that upset us but our judgments about events."[17]
If we apply that to the concept of pain, it means that the pain
isn't what upsets us but rather our judgments about it. When we
suspend the activity of assigning value judgments to the pain, our
suffering is alleviated. It's always within our power to do this in

any situation—it's up to us how much importance we choose to invest in bodily sensations.

Marcus describes the suspension of value judgments as the "withdrawal," "separation," or "purification" (*katharsis*) of the mind from, in this case, bodily sensations of pain and illness. He also likes to explain the suspension of judgment by saying that pain and pleasure should be *left where they stand*, in the parts of the body to which they belong. Even if the body, the closest companion of the mind, is "cut or burned, or festers or decays," we can preserve our ruling faculty in a peaceful state as long as we don't judge bodily sensations as being intrinsically good or bad.[18]

Marcus also calls this being "indifferent to indifferent things."[19] There's a particularly important passage where he spells out the subtleties of Stoic psychology in this regard.[20] We should keep our ruling faculty undisturbed by external things, including bodily sensations of pain and pleasure. He says this means not allowing it to unite with them but rather drawing a line around the mind, marking its boundaries, with bodily sensations on the other side, as if viewed from a distance—*over there*. On the other hand, when we allow ourselves to make strong value judgments about external sensations such as pain, we merge our minds with them and lose ourselves in the experience of suffering.

It's important to note that Marcus isn't asking us to deny that pain (or pleasure, for that matter) is part of life, even for the Stoic wise man. He notes that sensations of pain and pleasure will inevitably find their way into our consciousness because of the natural sympathy that exists between the mind and the body. He stresses that you should not try to *suppress* the sensations, because they are natural, and you should not assign judgments to them as good or bad, helpful or harmful. This delicate balance is central to modern mindfulness and acceptance-based cognitive therapy, which teaches clients neither to suppress unpleasant feelings nor to worry about them. Instead, you should learn to accept them while remaining detached from them.

For Marcus, what matters is that we stop looking at pain and illness through the lens of *harm*. Those judgments originate *within* us. They are projected outward onto bodily sensations and other external events. It's important to remember that whether we view something as helpful or harmful depends entirely upon our goals. Most people take for granted assumptions they have about their goals in life, so much so that they are rarely aware of them. If my goal is to look handsome, then if I break my nose, I'm bound to view it as harmful rather than helpful. But if my most cherished goal is survival and I break my nose while narrowly escaping certain death, I'd probably view it with relative indifference. The Stoics want us to go through a radical upheaval in our underlying values so that our supreme goal is to live with wisdom and its accompanying virtues. They want us to treat physical pain and injuries with indifference. In fact, these misfortunes can even provide an opportunity for us to exercise greater wisdom and strength of character. Marcus tells himself:

> Do away with the judgment, and the notion "I have been harmed" is done away with; do away with that notion, and the harm itself is gone.[21]

So do the Stoics not care at all about physical health? Yes, they do. They classify it as a preferred indifferent. It's natural and reasonable for us to prefer health to sickness. Physical health provides us with more opportunity to exercise our will and influence external events in life. In itself, health is not really good or bad. It's more like an opportunity. A foolish person may squander the advantages good health provides by indulging in his vices. A wise and good person, by contrast, may use both health and illness as opportunities to exercise virtue. Was Epictetus "harmed" when his leg was broken if we suppose that this was one of the events that set him on the path to becoming a great philosopher? He would say that what matters, ultimately, is the harm we do to our own character. By comparison, a mangled leg is trivial.

If we can learn to withhold our judgment that pain is terrible or harmful, then we can strip away its horrific mask, and it no longer appears so monstrous to us.[22] We're just left with the banal observation that our flesh is being stimulated "roughly," as Epictetus liked to put it. It's just a sensation. Through our judgment that it is intrinsically bad, unbearable, or catastrophic, though, we escalate the *mere* sensation of bodily pain into the inner turmoil of emotional suffering. For instance, Marcus elsewhere addresses (apostrophizes) his impressions and bodily sensations, saying,

> Go away, I entreat you by the gods, as you did come, for I do not want you. But you have come according to the ancient fashion. I am not angry with you: only go away.[23]

"I am not angry with you," he says to the painful feeling, because he does not perceive it as bad or harmful. It enters the mind in the age-old manner, through sensation, a natural physiological process that humans share with animals. Ironically, you don't need to try to suppress or resist unpleasant feelings as long as you abandon the belief that they are bad. If you accept them with indifference, then they do you no harm. When your conscious mind, your ruling faculty, invests too much importance in bodily sensations, it becomes "fused and blended" with them, and it is pulled around by the body like a puppet on strings.[24] However, you always have the potential within you to rise above physical sensations and view them with studied indifference.

## FUNCTIONAL ANALYSIS

Once you've gained cognitive distance, you're in a better position to consider the *consequences* of your value judgments ("functional analysis"). Given that suffering arises from our negative value judgments, the Stoics say that the *fear* of pain does us far more harm than pain itself because it injures our very character. Pain, by contrast, is harmless if you learn to accept it with an attitude of indifference. Epictetus stated this very succinctly: "For death or pain is not fearsome, but rather the *fear* of pain or death."[25] To live life fully, you have to get out of your comfort zone, as we say today. Fear of pain makes cowards out of us all and limits our sphere of life.

It's important to have a firm grasp of a behavior's negative consequences if we want to change it. For example, blood phobia might prevent someone from having medical tests they require— for some women it's even an obstacle to giving birth. Indeed, most people are frightened of pain and illness to varying degrees. Realizing that fear of pain may be doing you more harm than the pain itself can motivate you to start regularly practicing the psychological skills required to overcome intolerance of pain and discomfort.

## OBJECTIVE REPRESENTATION

Marcus also learned to describe external events and bodily sensations to himself as *natural processes*, adopting the language of *objective representation*. As noted earlier, we can compare this to the neutral and detached way a physician might document the symptoms of illness in a patient. Epictetus and Marcus both do this when they describe painful and unpleasant sensations merely as "rough" movements, or agitations, occurring in the flesh.

> Thoughts such as these reach through to the things themselves and strike to the heart of them, allowing us to see them as they truly are.[26]

It's as if we were describing the problems of *another* person: with greater objectivity and detachment. I might say to myself, for example, "The dentist is working on Donald's teeth," thereby thinking of it dispassionately from a third-person perspective.

## DEPRECIATION BY ANALYSIS

Marcus also tells himself to avoid overwhelming his mind by worrying about the future or ruminating about the past. When we focus our attention on the reality of the here and now it becomes easier to conquer. By viewing things objectively, isolating the present moment and dividing it into smaller parts, we can tackle them one at a time, using the method we've called depreciation by analysis. He says, for example, that we should ask of each present difficulty, "What is there in this that is unbearable or beyond endurance?"[27] Indeed, Marcus notes that the power of events to afflict us is greatly diminished if we set aside thoughts of the past and future and focus only on the present moment, the here and now, in isolation.

This divide-and-conquer strategy is still used in modern cognitive-behavioral therapy to combat unpleasant feelings; clients might be encouraged to focus on the present moment and deal with overwhelming experiences one step at a time. The Stoics move between this perspective and one that modern scholars call the "view from above," which involves picturing your current situation from high above, as part of the whole of life on Earth, or even the whole of time and space. One strategy divides events up into smaller parts, and the other imagines the whole of existence and an event's minuscule place within it. Both strategies can help us view external events, such as pain and illness, with greater indifference.[28]

## CONTEMPLATING FINITUDE AND IMPERMANENCE

Having described any painful sensations or symptoms of illness to ourselves in objective language and analyzed them into their component parts, we can usually also view them as being confined to a particular location in the body. Marcus consistently reminds himself to view pain and pleasure as belonging to the parts of the body where they're located—in other words, to think of the smallness of the sensation in contrast with the expansiveness of his observing consciousness. He thereby taught himself to think of pain remaining "over there" at a distance.

Let the affected part of the body complain if it must, he says. The mind doesn't need to agree and go along with it by judging the sensation to be very bad and harmful.[29] Think of the pain in your body as if it's the barking of an angry dog; don't start barking along with the dog by groaning about your own pain. It's always within your power to consider the sensation as belonging to the body and limited to a specific location. You can choose to leave it there rather than becoming fused with it through worry and rumination.

> The mind, too, can preserve its calm by withdrawing itself, and the ruling faculty comes to no harm; as for the parts that are harmed by pain, let them declare it, if they are able to.[30]

Therapists today help their clients objectify pain in this way by attributing an arbitrary shape or color to it, such as a black circle. This technique, called "physicalizing" the feeling, can help you picture it in your mind's eye, from a detached perspective, at a particular location in the body. You might even think of yourself as looking at physical pain or another symptom of illness through a glass window, separating the body from the mind, or imagining the pain as temporarily outside of the body on the other side of the room.

In addition to viewing unpleasant sensations as limited spatially to the affected part of the body, Marcus frequently reminds himself to consider their duration and to view them as limited in *both* time and space. He employs this strategy with externals in general but particularly with painful sensations and symptoms of illness. It resembles advice given by Epicurus, to focus on the fact that acute pain is temporary. You might be familiar with the Persian saying "This too shall pass," quoted by Abraham Lincoln, which makes a similar point. We can also remind ourselves how many unpleasant sensations have already come and gone in the past as a way of highlighting their transience.

This approach is one of Marcus's favorite strategies for encouraging an attitude of Stoic indifference. Viewing things as changeable, like a flowing river, can help weaken our emotional attachment to them. Sometimes he goes further and reminds himself of his own transience—his *mortality*. We will achieve indifference to painful feelings, he says, if we remember that the demands they place on our attention will only be for a limited time, because life is short and will soon be at an end.[31]

## STOIC ACCEPTANCE

Epictetus also said that we should actively accept sickness and painful feelings if they befall us ("Stoic acceptance"). He said that our feet, if they had minds of their own, would willingly be driven into the mud with each footstep we take, accepting it as a necessary part of their natural function.[32] This recalls the early Stoic metaphor of the dog following the cart. A dog tethered to a moving cart can either pull on his leash and be roughly dragged along or accept his fate and run along smoothly beside the cart. Indeed, one of the earliest Stoic definitions of man's natural goal is that it consists in a "smoothly flowing" life, free from unnecessary struggle. The concept of radically *accepting* unpleasant feelings has likewise become central to modern cognitive-behavioral therapy (CBT). Pain becomes *more painful* when we struggle against it, but the burden is often lightened, paradoxically, if we can accept the sensation and relax into it or even welcome it. Struggling to suppress, control, or eliminate unpleasant feelings adds another layer to our misery and frequently backfires by making the original problem worse.

Marcus actually imagines Nature herself as a physician, like Asclepius, the god of medicine, prescribing hardships to him as if they were painful remedies.[33] To take Nature's medicine properly, we must accept our fate and respond virtuously, with courage and self-discipline, thereby improving our character. So Marcus sees voluntarily *accepting* hardship as a psychotherapy of the passions. We must swallow the bitter pills of Fate and accept painful feelings and other unpleasant symptoms of illness when they befall us.

The Stoics were influenced in this regard by the older Cynic practice of voluntary hardship, as we've seen. They would deliberately expose themselves to discomfort, such as intense heat or cold, in order to develop psychological endurance. The *paradox* of accepting discomfort is that it often leads to less suffering. Diogenes the Cynic reputedly taught that we should treat painful sensations like wild dogs. They will bite and tear at our heels the more we try to flee in panic but will often back down if we have the courage to turn and face them calmly.

> It is like the bite that one can get when one takes hold of a wild beast, says Bion [of Borysthenes]; if you grasp a snake by its middle, you will get bitten, but if you seize it by the head, nothing bad will happen to you. And likewise, he says, the pain that you may suffer as a result of things outside yourself depends on how you apprehend them, and if you apprehend them in the same way as Socrates, you will feel no pain, but if you take them in any other way, you will suffer, not on account of any of the things themselves, but of your own character and false opinions.[34]

However, most ordinary people unwittingly invite the assaults of Fortune by turning their backs in flight rather than confronting her face to face.

Dio Chrysostom, a Sophist who studied under the great Stoic teacher Musonius Rufus, compared the Cynic to a boxer who fares better if he prepares himself to be struck and to accept it with indifference. If, on the other hand, he shrinks anxiously away from his opponent, he will expose himself to a worse beating. Chrysostom also compared enduring pain to trampling out a fire—if we do it gingerly, we're more likely to be burned than if we stamp on it confidently. Children even make a game of quenching flames on their tongues, he says, by doing it quickly and confidently. Today, we speak of "grasping the nettle" to make the point that facing something and accepting it often leads to less injury than approaching it hesitantly and defensively. (If you brush against a nettle, you'll get stung; if you hold the nettle tight in the right way, pressing the sharp spines flat, you'll prevent it from stinging you.) By calmly *grasping the nettle of pain* rather than struggling against it, resenting it, or complaining about it, we can learn to suffer less from it.

The Cynics and Stoics were thousands of years ahead of their time in proposing voluntary *acceptance* as a way of coping with pain and other unpleasant feelings. This acceptance has long been part of modern behavior therapy protocols for pain management, and in recent decades it's become the central focus of many therapists dealing with these issues. Distraction can *sometimes* work for very brief (acute) pain, such as surgical procedures or dentistry, but avoidance strategies tend to backfire when used for coping with *chronic* pain. Like the Stoic dog following the cart, we have no real choice but to face our pain. Nevertheless, you can choose whether to do so roughly, struggling and fighting against it, or smoothly, through calm acceptance. Most people find that accepting pain greatly diminishes the emotional suffering it causes. Struggling with pain, trying to suppress or avoid it, consumes your time and energy, limits your behavior, and stops you from getting on with other things—so acceptance can also improve your quality of life in this respect. Moreover, in some cases, accepting our bodily sensations can allow natural *habituation* to take place, so that we begin to notice our pain less, and painful sensations may even begin to diminish as a result.

It's therefore important to avoid struggling too much against painful or uncomfortable bodily sensations because there's considerable evidence from modern psychology that doing so can be counterproductive. Researchers call this urge to control or avoid unpleasant feelings "experiential avoidance," and it has proven quite toxic to mental health. People who strongly believe that unpleasant feelings are bad and try to suppress them from their minds often become more tense and preoccupied with the very feelings they're trying to avoid, trapping themselves in a vicious cycle. For the Stoics, pain is "indifferent" and not bad. It's therefore accepted as a natural process. In one graphic passage, Marcus tells himself that complaining about events is as futile and unhelpful as the kicks and squeals that piglets make as they struggle to free themselves during a ritual sacrifice.[35] Struggling against things we can't control does us more harm than good.

## CONTEMPLATING VIRTUE

Epictetus actually delivered a discourse titled "In What Manner We Ought to Bear Sickness." In it he argues that pain and sickness are an inevitable part of life, and just as in any other part of life, there are relevant virtues, which are always within our power to exercise.

If you bear a fever well, you have all that belongs to a man in a fever. What is it to bear a fever well? Not to blame God or man; not to be afflicted at that which happens, to expect death well and nobly, to do what must be done: when the physician comes in, not to be frightened at what he says; nor if he says, "you are doing well," to be overjoyed.[36]

Epictetus liked to tell his students that in the face of everything that befalls them, they should get into the habit of asking themselves what capacity, or virtue, they possess for making good use of the event. Similarly, cognitive therapists ask their clients, "What resources do you have that might help you to cope better with pain?" For example, if we're faced with severe pain, then we will find that Nature has equipped us with the potential for endurance, and if we get into the habit of exercising that virtue, then the painful sensations will no longer have mastery over us.[37]

Another useful way to approach pain is to ask ourselves how someone experiencing the same kind of pain or illness we're facing might cope with it more admirably (modeling virtue). What would we praise other people for doing in the same situation? Consider then to what extent we can do the same by emulating those strengths or virtues.

Like Epictetus, Marcus often stresses that many ordinary people show great courage and self-discipline in the service of worldly goals, such as greed or showing off to impress others.

Nothing happens to anyone that he is not fitted by Nature to bear. The same things happen to another, and either because he fails to realize that they have happened to him, or because he wants to display his strength of mind, he stands firm and remains unaffected. Is it not extraordinary that ignorance and self-conceit should prove more powerful than wisdom?[38]

Marcus reminds himself, though, that we can render everything that befalls us in life bearable by suggesting to ourselves either that it is in our interest to do so or that our duty somehow demands it. When we have a *reason* to endure something, it becomes easier. As Nietzsche said, "He who has a why to live for can bear almost any how."[39] It's often easier to endure pain if we are confident that it's doing us no harm or if we're fixated on some goal. Boxers take punches without complaining to win matches. Their ability to do this puts philosophers to shame, even though the latter believe themselves to be motivated by something infinitely more important: the love of wisdom. Nevertheless, we can learn from observing others that anyone can endure great pain and hardship if they are sufficiently motivated to do so.

## STOICISM IN EARLY PSYCHOTHERAPY

You've learned how the Stoic techniques for coping with pain and illness described by Marcus resemble some of those employed in modern CBT. However, at the start of the twentieth century, long before CBT, there was another "rational" or "cognitive" approach to psychotherapy that competed with Freudian psychoanalysis but is now largely forgotten. The Swiss psychiatrist and neuropathologist Paul Dubois, author of *The Psychoneuroses and Their Moral Treatment* (1904), was the main proponent of what became known as "rational psychotherapy." Dubois believed that psychological problems were due mainly to negative thinking, which worked like negative autosuggestion, and he favored a treatment based on the practice of "Socratic dialogue" through which he sought to rationally persuade patients to abandon the unhealthy ideas responsible for various neurotic and psychosomatic conditions. The influence of the ancient Stoics is clear from Dubois's scattered references to them.

> If we eliminate from ancient writings a few allusions that gave them local colour, we shall find the ideas of Socrates, Epictetus, Seneca, and Marcus Aurelius absolutely modern and applicable to our times.[40]

Dubois was particularly interested in the way Stoicism could be used to help psychotherapy patients cope with chronic pain and other physical or psychosomatic symptoms.

> The idea is not new; the stoics have pushed to the last degree this resistance to pain and misfortune. The following lines, written by Seneca, seem to be drawn from a modern treatise on psychotherapy: "Beware of aggravating your troubles yourself and of making your position worse by your complaints. Grief is light when opinion does not exaggerate it; and if one encourages one's self by saying, 'This is nothing,' or, at least, 'This is slight; let us try to endure it, for it will end,' one makes one's grief slight by reason of believing it such." And, further: "One is only unfortunate in proportion as one believes one's self so." One could truly say concerning nervous pains that one only suffers when he thinks he does.[41]

Dubois quoted Seneca's letters to illustrate the role of patience and acceptance, as opposed to worry, in helping us to cope with and avoid exacerbating physical illness. He also quoted Seneca's remarks that the principles of Stoic philosophy consoled him during illness and acted upon him "like medicine," strengthening the body by elevating the soul.

However, one of the most striking and memorable passages in Dubois concerns something that one of his patients said to him about the Stoics:

A young man into whom I tried to instil a few principles of stoicism towards ailments stopped me at the first words, saying, "I understand, doctor; let me show you." And taking a pencil he drew a large black spot on a piece of paper.

"This," said he, "is the disease, in its most general sense, the physical trouble—rheumatism, toothache, what you will—moral trouble, sadness, discouragement, melancholy. If I acknowledge it by fixing my attention upon it, I already trace a circle to the periphery of the black spot, and it has become larger. If I affirm it with acerbity the spot is increased by a new circle. There I am, busied with my pain, hunting for means to get rid of it, and the spot only becomes larger. If I preoccupy myself with it, if I fear the consequences, if I see the future gloomily, I have doubled or trebled the original spot." And, showing me the central point of the circle, the trouble reduced to its simplest expression, he said with a smile, "Should I not have done better to leave it as it was?"

"One exaggerates, imagines, anticipates affliction," wrote Seneca. For a long time, I have told my discouraged patients and have repeated to myself, "Do not let us build a second story to our sorrow by being sorry for our sorrow."[42]

This diagram, added Dubois, illustrates that "he who knows how to suffer suffers less." The burden of physical pain or illness is light when we look at it objectively, without "drawing concentric circles" around it, which multiply our suffering by adding layers of fear and worry.

By the time he wrote *The Meditations*, Marcus had a different relationship with pain than he had when he exchanged complaints with Fronto. According to the Stoics, our initial reaction to pain or illness may be natural and reasonable, but amplifying or perpetuating our suffering by complaining about it over time is unnatural and unreasonable. Animals may cry out in pain and lick their wounds for a while, but they don't ruminate about it for weeks afterward or write letters to their friends complaining about how badly they've been sleeping. Marcus had learned how to suffer properly and thereby to suffer less, as Dubois would have put it. This is how he must have coped with both chronic pain and illness throughout the course of the First Marcomannic War, in which he led Rome to victory.

# 6.

# THE INNER CITADEL AND WAR OF MANY NATIONS

It was an *ambush*! Wave after wave of Sarmatian horsemen crashed out of the forest on the far side of the River Danube to engage the Roman legionaries head on. Some split off in a classic pincer maneuver, outflanking and encircling the men standing helplessly in the killing zone, midway across the frozen river. Marcus looked on quietly with his generals. The barbarians regularly sneaked across the river that marked the front line to raid settlements in the province of Pannonia. The Romans had learned that the enemy horsemen were most vulnerable when encumbered with loot on their return journey, so they would pursue them across the river, hoping to catch them as they slowed their pace to make the crossing back into their own lands. Sometimes, however, the raiders were just leading the Romans into a trap.

As soon as the Romans recognized the enemy ambush was being sprung, the infantry assumed their standard defensive formation, known as a "hollow square." Officers and lightly armored troops were protected on the inside by legionaries facing outward on all four sides, their rectangular shields packed tightly together forming a protective wall. The Sarmatians knew that tactic very well. It worked as long as the Romans could hold formation, but they would be massacred if a cavalry charge managed to break through the square and throw them into disarray. That's why the Sarmatians had lured them onto the river: their horses were trained to charge across the ice. When their lances smashed into the shields of the legionaries forming those defensive walls, the Romans would slip, lose their footing, and tumble like bowling pins.

The Sarmatians were a mysterious, intimidating enemy. They were actually a loose coalition of nomadic tribes led by King Bandaspus, ruler of the Iazyges, the most warlike among the tribes. Sarmatian men were tall and muscular, with fierce blue eyes and long reddish-yellow hair and beards. These exceptional horsemen rode into battle clad in a type of scale mail carved from hooves. Their unusual armor reminded the Romans of a python's skin, perhaps even conjuring images of dragons. It was said that the Iazyges worshiped fire. They wore great helms and fought with huge wooden lances tipped with sharpened bone. However, what shocked the Romans most of all was the discovery, as they removed helmets from the corpses of slain Sarmatians, that many of the warriors were women.

The sight of hundreds, perhaps thousands of Sarmatian horsemen charging across the frozen Danube must have been terrifying. Marcus had learned to gaze calmly on these fearsome warriors and the carnage of the battlefield by recalling the Stoic precepts he'd studied as a young man. He took a slow, deep breath as he watched the first wave of lancers collide against Roman shields. Almost immediately, his general and son-in-law, Claudius Pompeianus, turned toward him and smiled. Their plan was working: this time the Sarmatians were in for a surprise. The legionaries held formation perfectly as the lances struck their shields and glanced off harmlessly. Marcus's infantry had learned a new trick. Men on the interior of the square had laid their shields on the ice, holding them fast in place. The legionaries forming the outer wall then braced their rear foot against their comrades' shields. So far, that was proving good enough to stabilize them against the impact of enemy lances.

As the Sarmatian horsemen reeled from the shock of their failed charge, the Roman counterattack began with deadly efficiency. Skirmishers darted out between the legionaries' shields. The Romans quickly grabbed hold of the horses' bridles and used their own body weight to make the horses slip and fall sideways onto the ice, dismounting their riders. The Roman legionaries thrust spears at the Sarmatians from behind their wall of shields. The ice was soon awash with blood as bodies piled up. The remaining barbarians found themselves struggling to keep their footing. Unable to flee back to the safety of the forest, they were thrown into disarray right where the Romans wanted them. Before long everyone was slipping, caught up in a melee, Romans grappling with Sarmatians on the bloody ice. However, Marcus's legionaries were trained in wrestling. If a Sarmatian knocked a Roman down, the Roman would pull his assailant on top of him while lying prone on the ice, then kick him off with both legs, throwing him onto his back and reversing their positions. The tribesmen had little experience of this kind of disciplined close-combat fighting and, caught off guard by the change of tactics, were eventually routed.

Marcus had successfully turned the ambush around and inflicted a major defeat on King Bandaspus. After several initial setbacks, the tide of war now began to turn in Rome's favor.

The Sarmatians could no longer depend on using the terrain to their advantage. Voluntarily walking into an ambush had obviously been a dangerous strategy for the Romans. It required immense discipline and careful preparation—the troops had trained in secret during the winter months. And it worked. They had kept their nerve in a chaotic situation, facing their most fearsome enemy, and snatched victory from the very jaws of defeat.

## HOW TO RELINQUISH FEAR

Epictetus taught his students to think of Stoic philosophy as being like the *caduceus*, the magic wand of Hermes: every misfortune is transformed into something good by its touch.[1] Marcus had learned to become adept at this sort of thinking. Stoics calmly envisaged different types of misfortune on a daily basis as part of their contemplative training, learning to view them with relative indifference. Indeed, envisaging feared catastrophes as if they were really happening can be viewed as a kind of *emotional battle drill*, a way of preparing for worst-case scenarios. Stoics would mentally rehearse ways of responding to these events with wisdom and virtue, turning obstacles into opportunities where possible. One consequence of embracing our fears is that we're more likely to creatively turn apparent setbacks to our advantage, as the Romans did in their battle on the Danube. These Sarmatian ambushes must have seemed like military catastrophes to the Romans at first. What if they concealed the opportunity to spring a deadly trap, though, that could turn the tide of the war? The obstacle standing in the way becomes the way.

These opportunities came more readily to Stoic leaders because they were trained to be unafraid of seeming misfortunes. After all, Fortune favors the brave, as the Roman poets said. However, for the Stoics, the *supreme* goal was to remain composed and exercise wisdom even in the face of great danger, whatever the outcome. Marcus tells himself to always remember when he starts to feel frustrated with events that "this is not a misfortune, but rather to bear it nobly is good fortune." After Lucius's sudden death in 169 AD, Marcus had been unexpectedly left in sole command of the troops assembling along the Danube for the First Marcomannic War. In his late fifties, with no military experience whatsoever, he'd found himself in command of the largest army ever massed on a Roman frontier. He stood at the head of roughly 140,000 men who awaited his orders, unsure what to expect of him. It must have been incredibly daunting. Yet he embraced his new role completely and turned it into an opportunity to deepen his Stoic resolve.

There should be no question that he risked his own life in stationing himself at the front. At the outbreak of the war, Pannonia had been completely overrun by a huge coalition army led by Ballomar, the young king of the Marcomanni. Ballomar had secretly brought together many smaller tribes, but he was also supported by a huge army of the Marcomanni's powerful neighbors, the Quadi. The Romans had suffered a catastrophic defeat at the Battle of Carnuntum, reputedly losing twenty thousand men in a single day, including the praetorian prefect in command, Furius Victorinus. Nevertheless, Marcus remained very close to the action. In *The Meditations*, he vividly describes the sight of severed hands, feet, and heads lying at unsettling distances from their bodies.[2] Indeed, he makes a point of noting down that he's writing at Carnuntum, the main legionary fortress on the front line, and "on the Granua, among the Quadi," which puts him farther east, presumably later, across the Danube inside enemy territory.

Perhaps surprisingly, given the danger that he faced, Marcus never really mentions anxiety about the terrors of war in *The Meditations*. It does seem as though he was a natural worrier at first, anxiously burning the midnight oil as he worked obsessively on matters of state. By the time he was writing these notes to himself on philosophy, though, he seems to have become a much calmer and more self-assured man. Perhaps he *redoubled* his efforts to assimilate Stoicism following the death of his tutor Junius Rusticus, and that accounts for the transformation. When he arrived in Carnuntum to take command of the legions, he was both physically frail and an absolute novice—an "old woman" of a philosopher, sneered the future usurper, Avidius Cassius. Everyone must have questioned Marcus's competence to lead such a massive campaign. However, both his practice of Stoicism and the long and grueling wars against the Marcomanni, Quadi, and Sarmatians were slowly molding his character. Seven years later we find him a hardened veteran, and the northern legions, having learned to revere their new commander, are now fiercely loyal to Marcus Aurelius.

The soldiers firmly believed that the gods were on their emperor's side, and they even attributed two legendary battlefield miracles to Marcus Aurelius's presence. The first, called the "Thunder Miracle," occurred in 174 AD, when the troops claimed that Marcus's prayers had called down a lightning bolt that destroyed a siege engine being used by the Sarmatians. A month later, in July 174 AD, it was claimed that Marcus brought about a "Rain Miracle." A detachment of men from the Thundering Legion, led by Pertinax, found themselves surrounded, vastly outnumbered, and out of water. According to one account, Marcus raised his hand and prayed: "With this hand which has never taken life, I turn to Thee and worship the Giver of life." (That would surely be the Stoic Zeus, although Christians later implausibly claimed that Marcus was praying to *their* God.) At that moment, a torrential rainstorm ensued, and as they fought on, it's said the Romans gulped down water from their helmets, mixed with the blood running from their wounds. Marcus wasn't superstitious, as we've seen. The legions, however, clearly believed that he was blessed by the gods and acclaimed him their victorious commander. We're told that when he eventually passed away, the soldiers wept loudly.

## THE STOIC RESERVE CLAUSE

So how did Marcus overcome his total lack of experience and become such an accomplished military leader? How did he remain *composed* in the face of uncertain odds against such formidable enemies? One of the most important Stoic techniques that he employed was called acting "with a reserve clause" (*hupexhairesis*), a technical term that he mentions at least five times in *The Meditations*. Although the idea goes back to the early Stoics, Marcus actually learned how to perform every action cautiously and with a "reserve clause" from reading Epictetus's *Discourses*.[3] In essence, it means undertaking any action while calmly accepting that the outcome isn't entirely under your control. We learn from Seneca and others that it could take the form of a caveat, such as "Fate permitting," "God willing," or "If nothing prevents me." It implies that one is taking action while *excluding* something: assumptions regarding the eventual outcome, particularly any *expectations* of success. We say "reserve clause," incidentally, because our expectations are *reserved* for what is within our sphere of control. We're pursuing an external result "with the reservation" that the outcome is not entirely up to us. "Do what you must, let happen what may," as the saying goes.

In Cicero's dialogue *De Finibus*, the Roman Stoic hero Cato of Utica uses the memorable image of an archer or spearman to explain this subtle concept. The Stoic-minded archer's true goal should be to fire his bow skillfully, insofar as doing so is within his power. Paradoxically, though, he's *indifferent* to whether or not his arrow actually hits the target. He controls his aim but not the arrow's flight. So he does the best he can and accepts whatever happens next. The target—perhaps an animal he's hunting—could move *unexpectedly*. Marcus perhaps had this analogy in mind when he was spearing birds and hunting wild boar as a young man. Virtue consists in doing your very best and yet not becoming upset if you come home from the hunt empty-handed—we typically admire people who approach life in this way.

Marcus makes it clear that his *internal* goal is to live with virtue, particularly wisdom and justice, but his *external* aim, his preferred outcome, is the *common welfare of mankind* (not just of his Roman subjects, incidentally). Although the outcome is ultimately indifferent to Stoics, it's precisely the action of pursuing the common good that constitutes the virtue of justice. Indeed, whether you succeed or fail in your attempts to benefit others, you may still be perfectly virtuous as long as your efforts are sincere. It's your *intentions* that count, both morally and psychologically. Nevertheless, you must aim them at an appropriate outcome. For instance, acting in accord with justice means preferring to achieve, Fate willing, an external outcome that is both fair and beneficial for humankind. Marcus refers to this countless times throughout *The Meditations*.

Indeed, whereas other philosophical schools sometimes advised their students to preserve their equanimity by *avoiding* the stress and responsibilities of public life, Chrysippus told the Stoics that "the wise man will take part in politics, *if nothing prevents him.*" The wise man, in other words, desires to act virtuously with wisdom and justice in the social sphere, insofar as he's practically able to do so. He simultaneously accepts, though, that the outcome of his actions is not under his direct control. There's no guarantee that he'll succeed in benefiting his fellow citizens, but he does his best anyway. In a sense, the Stoic gets to have his cake and eat it: to retain his emotional detachment while nevertheless taking action in the world. Like Cato's archer, his goal is to do what's within his sphere of control to the best of his ability while remaining somewhat aloof from the outcome. Likewise, we can imagine that on taking command of the legions in the north, Marcus might have said to himself something along the lines of "I will quell the Marcomanni and protect Rome, *Fate permitting.*"

Later, Christians would take to adding D.V. (*Deo volente*, "God willing") to the end of their letters, and Muslims likewise say *inshallah* to this day. There's a wonderfully clear description of this sentiment in the New Testament:

> Now listen, you who say, "Today or tomorrow we will go to this or that city, spend a year there, carry on business and make money." Why, you do not even know what will happen tomorrow. What is your life? You are a mist that appears for a little while and then vanishes. Instead, you ought to say, "If it is the Lord's will, we will live and do this or that."[4]

Marcus Aurelius could easily have said those words in reference to the Stoic Zeus. They remind us that nothing is certain in

life. Nothing is entirely under your control, except your own volition. Always accepting this and preparing yourself in advance
to meet both success and failure with equanimity can help you
avoid feeling angry, surprised, or frustrated when events don't turn
out as you might have wished. It can also stop you from worrying
about things in anticipation of them going wrong. We naturally
focus our attention on what's most important to us. Stoics treat
their own judgments and actions as the only thing truly good or
bad. That inevitably shifts focus to the present and lessens emotional investment in the past and future. The worried mind is
always getting too far ahead of itself; it is always in suspense over
the future. The Stoic Sage, by contrast, is grounded in the here
and now.

Marcus uses the analogy of a blazing fire to describe the wise
man acting with the reserve clause. Imagine a fire so intense that
its flames naturally consume everything cast upon them. Likewise,
the mind of the Sage, acting with the reserve clause, adapts itself,
without hesitation, to whatever befalls him. Whether he meets
with success or failure, he makes good use of his experience. Stoics can only be obstructed externally, not internally, as long as
they attach the caveat "Fate permitting" to their desires. For instance, when people disagreed with Marcus, he first tried to persuade them to see things from his perspective. However, if they
persisted in obstructing what he believed to be a just course of action, he remained calm and transformed the obstacle into an opportunity to exercise some other virtue, such as patience, restraint,
or understanding. His equanimity remained intact as long as he
never desired what was beyond his grasp, which constitutes one
of the foundations of the Stoic remedy for worry and anxiety.[5]

Indeed, Marcus goes so far as to say that if you *don't* act with the reserve clause in mind, then any failure immediately becomes an evil to you or a potential source of distress. By contrast, if you accept that the outcome couldn't have been other than it was and wasn't under your direct control, then you should suffer no harm or frustration. In this way, the mind is saved from anxiety and preserved in its natural equanimity, like the sacred sphere described by the pre-Socratic philosopher Empedocles, "round and true," touched by neither fire nor steel, tyrant nor public censure.[6] The poet Horace also employed this image of the pure sphere when describing the Stoic ideal of a wise man who is master of himself, undaunted by poverty, chains, or death, defying his passions and looking down on positions of power. A man "complete in himself, smooth and round, who prevents extraneous elements clinging to his polished surface, who is such that when Fortune attacks him she maims only herself."[7] Misfortune gains no foothold in his mind because he remains detached from external events, refusing to invest them with any intrinsic value. We could also simply describe this as "adopting a philosophical attitude" toward the outcome of our actions: being resigned to whatever happens and remaining unperturbed come what may.

## THE PREMEDITATION OF ADVERSITY

If every action is to be undertaken with the reserve clause, an acceptance that we may fail, then it follows that we should anticipate a whole range of setbacks that can potentially befall us. Indeed, the Stoics broaden this strategy, preparing themselves to cope with adversity by patiently visualizing every major type of misfortune, one at a time, as if it were *already* happening to them. They might picture themselves already in exile, in poverty, bereaved, or suffering from a terrible illness. As we'll see, going one step further and anticipating your own death plays a very special role in Stoicism. The technique of exposing yourself to stressful situations repeatedly in small doses so that you build up a more general resistance to emotional disturbance is known in behavioral psychology as "stress inoculation." It's like inoculating yourself against a virus, and it's similar to what we've come to think of as resilience building.

Seneca calls this *praemeditatio malorum*, or the "premeditation of adversity." The clearest example of this *prospective* meditation strategy in *The Meditations* comes when Marcus describes part of his morning routine—preparing himself for the day ahead by anticipating various obstacles. Whereas other Stoics focus on the threat of disease, poverty, exile, and so on, Marcus is clearly more concerned with facing *interpersonal* problems, such as dishonesty, ingratitude, or betrayal. He imagines himself encountering a variety of difficult people in order to accustom himself to coping with them.

> Begin the morning by saying to yourself, I shall meet with the busy-body, the ungrateful, arrogant, deceitful, envious, unsocial.[8]

It's easy to see how this passage might relate to his life as emperor. Marcus certainly had enemies in the Senate, a faction opposing his military policy, and he later faced a full-scale civil war. He says that he was surrounded at court by individuals who didn't share his values and who were hostile toward him; some even wished him dead. However, the Marcomannic Wars were themselves about treachery and deceit. King Ballomar of the Marcomanni was a Roman client and ally. Yet he secretly conspired for years to launch his surprise attack deep into Italy, bringing war to the very doorstep of Rome itself. He seized his chance at the height of the Antonine Plague, when the Romans were weak and troops normally garrisoned along the Danube were still returning from the Parthian War. It was a huge betrayal. So when we read this famous passage from *The Meditations*, we should bear in mind that Marcus was using Stoicism to prepare himself to deal calmly not only with petty nuisances but also with major political and military crises that changed the shape of European history. All of Rome was thrown into a panic by the news that a massive horde of barbarian warriors was plundering its way through Italy. Marcus responded calmly and with self-assurance. He used Stoic exercises like the premeditation of adversity to ready himself for sudden crises that would have left other men reeling.

Premeditation of adversity can be useful in confronting anger and other negative emotions, but its techniques are particularly suited to treat fear and anxiety. The Stoics defined fear as the expectation that *something bad is going to happen*, which is virtually identical to the definition originally proposed by Aaron T. Beck, the founder of modern cognitive therapy. Fear is essentially a future-focused emotion, so it's natural that we should counter it by addressing our thoughts concerning the future. Inoculating ourselves against stress and anxiety through the Stoic premeditation of adversity is one of the most useful techniques for building general *emotional resilience*, which is what psychologists call the long-term ability to endure stressful situations without becoming overwhelmed by them.

Aesop's fable "The Boar and the Fox" is all about building resilience. One day a fox was walking through the woods when he spotted a wild boar sharpening his tusks against the stump of a tree. The fox found this hilarious and made fun of the boar for worrying about nothing. When he finally stopped laughing, he asked, "Why are you being so fretful, you fool? There's nobody here for you to fight!" The boar smiled and said, "True, but when one day I do hear the huntsmen coming, it will be too late then to prepare for battle." The moral is that in times of peace, we should prepare for war if we want to be ready to defend ourselves. The Stoics likewise used moments of leisure to prepare themselves to remain calm in the face of adversity.

## EMOTIONAL HABITUATION

Of course, we don't always know what specific challenges we're about to face in life. However, your *general* emotional resilience can be developed by training yourself in advance to cope with a broad enough range of situations. That's precisely what the Stoics did through the premeditation of adversity strategy. One of the most robustly established findings in the entire field of modern psychotherapy research is the fact that anxiety tends to abate *naturally* during prolonged exposure to feared situations, under normal conditions. That's been the basis of evidence-based phobia treatments since the 1950s, and it's also an integral part of modern treatment protocols for other, more complex forms of anxiety, such as post-traumatic stress disorder (PTSD) and obsessive-compulsive disorder (OCD).

Take a person with a severe cat phobia, for instance, and place them in a room with some cats. Their heart rate will go up, probably almost doubling within a few seconds. But what happens next? Well, what goes up must come down . . . If they remain in the room and do nothing but wait, their anxiety will typically diminish over time. That may take as little as five minutes or maybe as long as half an hour or more. Nevertheless, in most cases, their heart rate will eventually go back down to something approaching its normal resting level. If you bring them back the next day and put them in the room with the cats once again, you'll typically notice that their heart rate will go back up but not as high as before, and it will tend to lower more quickly. If you repeat this exercise for several days, then they will become emotionally "habituated" to the cats, their anxiety having *permanently* reduced to a normal or negligible level.

That this basic truth was understood long ago is nicely illustrated by another of Aesop's fables, called "The Fox and the Lion." One day a fox strolling through the woods spotted a lion—a creature she'd never seen before. She froze with terror but stopped to watch from a distance before slowly creeping away. The next day she went back to the same spot and saw the lion again, but she was able to get closer than before, hiding behind a bush for a while before making her escape. On the third day, the fox returned, but this time she found the courage to walk right up to the lion and say hello, and somehow the two became friends. The moral of the story is that familiarity breeds not contempt but *indifference*. We can expect anxiety to abate naturally with repeated exposure, under normal conditions.

What the Stoic literature doesn't make clear, though, is that the feared situation must be experienced for considerably *longer* than normal for anxiety to properly habituate. In fact, if exposure is terminated too soon, the technique may actually backfire and *increase* anxiety and sensitization to the feared situation. So it's important to compare what the Stoics recommend to what we know from clinical research using similar techniques.

Exposure therapy works best when the anxiety-provoking trigger is physically present, like the cats in our example above. Therapists call this *in vivo*, or "real-world," exposure. However, anxiety *also* habituates almost as reliably, in most cases, when the threat is merely imagined, something known as *in vitro*, or "imaginal," exposure. The Stoics realized that exposure to imagined events can lead to emotional habituation in this way, allowing anxiety to abate naturally. Their recommendation to regularly picture catastrophic events, which we've called the premeditation of adversity, is essentially a form of imaginal exposure therapy. Aesop's fable "The Fox and the Lion" shows that people have long grasped this phenomenon, but it's still quite remarkable to discover a philosophical therapy employing it over two thousand years before it was rediscovered by modern behavior therapists.

However, in the case of *imaginal* exposure, maintaining the image for long enough requires considerable patience and concentration, especially when practiced as a form of self-help without the aid of a therapist. Many people find that it helps to imagine the anxiety-provoking situation as if it were a short movie clip, or sequence of events, with a beginning, middle, and end, lasting roughly a minute or so. They can then replay the same scene repeatedly, in their mind's eye, for five to fifteen minutes or even longer. For example, someone who is anxious about losing their job might visualize being called into their boss's office, told that they're being sacked or made redundant, and later clearing their desk and leaving, etc. They'd picture this as a short movie, perhaps repeatedly on a loop. As noted, the actual amount of time required varies, but anxiety should have reduced to at least half its initial level before ending the exercise. The most common reason for failure is that people terminate these sorts of exposure exercises before their emotions have had enough time to habituate. It takes patience, in other words.

Therapists will often ask their clients to rate their discomfort or anxiety level while picturing a scene on a scale from zero to ten, or as a percentage. Clients then re-rate their anxiety every few minutes during repeated imaginal exposure until it has sufficiently reduced. For example, the cat phobic might patiently visualize stroking a cat over and over, until their anxiety reduces from 80 percent to at least 40 percent or even lower if possible (where 100 percent would be the most severe anxiety they could imagine feeling and 0 percent would be no anxiety at all). *Nota bene*: It's important to emphasize that any technique that involves imagining upsetting scenes should be *approached with caution* by individuals who suffer from mental health problems or those vulnerable to being emotionally overwhelmed, such as sufferers of panic attacks. When doing this alone, don't pick an image that's going to be too much for you to handle, such as a traumatic memory of sexual assault, for instance—that's where the support of a qualified psychotherapist may be necessary. Nevertheless, most people are capable of safely confronting ordinary fears and worries in their imagination.

## SPONTANEOUS PSYCHOLOGICAL CHANGE

Emotional habituation is the most important process to take place during imaginal exposure, such as the premeditation of adversity. However, we can activate a surprising number of other beneficial psychological processes when we patiently and repeatedly picture stressful events. Therapy clients who are asked to mentally review emotional situations in this way may exhibit one or more of the following changes:

1. *Emotional habituation*, as described above, where anxiety or other feelings naturally wear off over time and become blunted through exposure to the feared situation.

2. *Emotional acceptance*, where we gradually reduce our struggle *against* unpleasant feelings such as pain or anxiety, come to view them with greater indifference, and learn to live *with* them—something that, paradoxically, often greatly alleviates emotional distress.

3. *Cognitive distancing*, where we increasingly view thoughts and beliefs with detachment: we begin to notice that it's not things themselves that upset us but our judgments about them.

4. *Decatastrophizing*, where we gradually reappraise our judgments about the severity of a situation, of how *awful* it seems, downgrading it by going from "*What if* this happens? How will I cope?" to "*So what* if this happens? It's not the end of the world."

5. *Reality testing*, where we reappraise our assumptions about a situation to make them progressively more realistic and objective; for example, reevaluating the probability of the worst-case scenario or that something bad will even happen at all.

6. *Problem-solving*, where repeatedly reviewing an event leads us to creatively figure out a solution to some problem facing us—perhaps like Marcus and his generals' paradoxical idea of deliberately marching their legion-

aries into a Sarmatian ambush in order to spring a trap on the enemy.

7. *Behavioral rehearsal*, where our perception of our ability to cope improves as we practice, in our mind's eye, employing skills and coping strategies in an increasingly refined manner—for example, mentally rehearsing assertive ways to deal with unfair criticism until we're more confident about doing so in reality. This can take the form of modeling the behavior of others whose way of coping we admire and want to emulate—we imagine how they would act and then picture ourselves doing something similar.

I've found that informing patients that other people often experience these sorts of changes is helpful because it can make the same processes more noticeable in their own mind and more likely to happen *spontaneously*. Of course, it's also possible to *deliberately* utilize these psychological mechanisms by employing various psychological techniques. For instance, in addition to the premeditation of adversity, Marcus refers to the repeated use of two particularly important Stoic exercises that resemble cognitive distancing and decatastrophizing in modern psychotherapy. We've mentioned these already, and now we're ready to consider their use in relation to worry and anxiety.

## THE INNER CITADEL

Although Marcus says little about *anxiety* explicitly, he often talks about the kind of *peace* that Stoicism offers, and his words obviously have implications for the Stoic therapy of anxiety. During his early reign, after the death of Antoninus, he took trips to his holiday villas in Italy to get a break from the worries of the Parthian War and running the empire. We can see from his letters to Fronto that he was wrestling with the whole idea of taking time away from work, feeling instead that it was his duty to attend to state business even though his friends advised him that retreats were necessary for his health.

By the time he wrote *The Meditations*, during the Marcomannic Wars, pleasant retreats were a thing of the past, and his life was spent far from Rome. Marcus still found himself pining after his beautiful holiday villas, such as Antoninus's family home at Lorium on the Italian coast, where Marcus spent much of his youth. He says that at times, like many other people, he feels a strong desire to get away from things and retreat to the peace of the countryside, seashore, or mountains.[9] However, he tells himself that feeling the need to escape from life's stresses in this way is a sign of weakness. It might be what the Stoics called a "preferred indifferent," but escape is not something we should demand from life or feel we really need as a coping tool—that sort of *dependence* on being able to escape from stressful situations just creates its own problems. Marcus tells himself that he doesn't literally *need* to get away from it all because true inner peace comes from the nature of our thoughts rather than pleasant natural surroundings. He tells himself that resilience comes from his ability to regain his composure wherever he finds himself. This is the "inner citadel" to which he can retreat, even on the frigid battlefields of the northern campaign.

Marcus returns, in particular, to the analogy of a mountain retreat several times. He reminds himself that it makes no difference where he is or what he's doing; the time left for him in life is short, and he should therefore learn to "live as though on a mountaintop," regardless of his circumstances. In fact, everything that troubles us here is just as it would be on a hilltop, by the seashore, or anywhere else—what matters is how we choose to view it.[10] The Stoic can live with contentment and joy in his heart this way, even if men are against him and his physical environment is torturous. Wherever we find ourselves, our judgments are still free, and they are the seat of our passions.

In order to achieve this sense of inner peace, Marcus tells himself to frequently retreat not to the hilltops but to his own faculty of reason, thereby rising above external events and purifying his mind of attachment to them. He believes that to do this effectively he must reflect, in particular, on two concise but fundamental Stoic principles:[11]

1. Everything that we see is changing and will soon be gone, and we should bear in mind how many things have already changed over time, like the waters of streams flowing ceaselessly past—an idea that we can call the contemplation of impermanence.

2. External things cannot touch the soul, but our disturbances all arise from within. Marcus means that things don't upset us, but our value judgments about them do. However, we can regain our composure by separating our values from external events using the strategy we've called cognitive distancing.

In other words, peace of mind can be achieved even in the chaos of the battlefield—as Socrates reputedly showed—or in the clamor of the Senate, as long as we keep our mind in good order. Marcus concludes by condensing this into six Greek words, perhaps quoted from a previous author, which we might translate as *The universe is change: life is opinion.*

## COGNITIVE DISTANCING FOR ANXIETY

The second of these two fundamental techniques for securing peace is familiar to us as cognitive distancing. We can employ it in response to *real-world* situations or during the sort of premeditation, or *imaginal* exposure technique, described earlier. Although we know that anxiety habituates naturally through repeated exposure and the Stoics presumably must have observed this during their use of regular premeditation, their real goal was to change our *opinions* about external events, not just our feelings.

Gaining cognitive distance is, in a sense, the most important aspect of Stoic anxiety management. This is what Marcus meant by "life is opinion": that the quality of our life is determined by our value judgments, because those shape our emotions. When we deliberately remind ourselves that we project our values onto external events and that how we judge those events is what upsets us, we gain cognitive distance and recover our mental composure.

## DECATASTROPHIZING AND THE CONTEMPLATION OF IMPERMANENCE

The first basic technique for attaining peace, described by Marcus above, is related to decatastrophizing, or learning to downgrade the perceived severity of a threat from "total catastrophe" to a more realistic level. Again, decatastrophizing can be applied in real situations or in imagined ones, during the premeditation of adversity. For example, suppose you're worried that you'll fail an important exam and you become very anxious, feeling that failure would be the end of the world, a total disaster. Decatastrophizing would entail reevaluating the situation in a more balanced manner so that it seems less overwhelming and you're more able to identify potential ways of coping. Viewing things in a more moderate and realistic way like this tends to reduce anxiety. You might experience setbacks, but it's an exaggeration to talk as though they're the end of the world.

As it happens, most people find it easier to visualize a scene if they write down a description of it first and perhaps review it later. Staying with the example above, you might write a page or so about losing your job: how it begins, being told the bad news, the immediate aftermath, etc. People often find that reading their description aloud several times before attempting to visualize it helps them to clarify the details and picture the scene more vividly. As always, it's important to leave out emotive language ("They just treated me like trash and threw me out on my backside.") or value judgments ("This is totally unfair!"). Just stick to the facts as accurately and objectively as possible.

Asking yourself "What next?" a few times can move your focus past the most distressing part of the scene and take away its catastrophic appearance. For example, what would happen *after* losing your job? It might be tough for a while, but eventually you'd find something else and your life would move on. Another simple and powerful technique is to ask yourself how you would feel about the situation that worries you in ten or twenty years' time, looking back on it from the future. It's an example of a more general strategy known as "time projection." In other words, you can help yourself develop a philosophical attitude toward adversity by asking, "If this will seem trivial to me twenty years from now, then why shouldn't I view it as trivial *today* instead of worrying about it as if it's a catastrophe?" You'll often find that shifting your perspective in terms of time can change how you feel about a setback by making it seem less catastrophic.

## WORRY POSTPONEMENT

In recent decades, researchers and clinicians have gained a better understanding of the ways in which excessive worrying can perpetuate anxiety. By "worry" they mean something quite specific: an anxious *process* exhibiting a particular *style* of thinking. Worried thinking is perseverative—it goes on and on. It tends to involve "What if?" thoughts about feared catastrophes: "What if they get so angry they fire me? What if I can't get another job? How will I pay for my kids' college?" These questions often feel as if they're unanswerable. One just leads to another, in a chain reaction, which goes on and on, fueling anxiety. Severe worrying can often *feel* out of control, but, perhaps surprisingly, it's actually a relatively conscious and voluntary type of thinking. People sometimes don't even realize that what they're doing is worrying. They may confuse it with problem-solving, believing that they're trying to "figure out a solution" when in fact they're just going in circles making their anxiety worse and worse.

There's a tendency, ironically, for people struggling with anxiety to try too hard to control *involuntary* aspects of the emotion while neglecting to take control of the *voluntary* aspects. We've already discussed how the Stoics acknowledged that our initial emotional reactions are often automatic. We should accept these as natural, view them with indifference, and accept them without a struggle rather than try to suppress them. On the other hand, we should learn to suspend the voluntary thoughts we have in response to these initial feelings and the situation that triggered them. In the case of worrying, perhaps surprisingly, that's usually just a matter of noticing we're doing it and stopping.

One of the leading researchers on the psychology of worry, Thomas D. Borkovec, carried out a groundbreaking study on "worry postponement." He asked a group of college students to spot the times during a four-week period when they began to worry about something and to respond by postponing thinking about it any further until a specified "worry time" later in the day. Using this simple technique, the subjects were able to reduce the time spent worrying by almost half, and other symptoms of anxiety were also reduced. Worry postponement is now a central component of most CBT protocols for generalized anxiety disorder (GAD), a psychiatric condition characterized by severe, pathological worrying.[12] However, we can apply the same approach to ordinary, everyday worries like those of the students in the research study.

The steps to follow in worry postponement build upon the general framework that should be familiar to you by now:

1. Self-monitoring: Be constantly on the lookout for early warning signs of worry, such as frowning or fidgeting in certain ways—this awareness alone will often derail the habit of worrying.
2. If you are unable to address your anxiety immediately using Stoic techniques, postpone thinking about it until your feelings have abated naturally, returning to the problem at a specified "worry time" of your choosing.
3. Let go of the thoughts *without* trying to actively suppress them—instead, just tell yourself you're setting

them aside temporarily to come back to them later at a specified time and place. Cognitive distancing techniques can be helpful in this regard. You can also write down a word or two on a piece of paper to remind yourself of the thing you're worried about, then fold it up and put it in your pocket to address later.

4. Return your attention to the here and now, expanding your awareness through your body and your surroundings, and try to notice small details you'd overlooked before. Worry goes chasing after future catastrophes and therefore requires *inattention* to the present moment. Become grounded in the here and now instead: "Lose your mind and come to your senses!"

5. Later, when you return to the worry, if it no longer seems important, you might just leave it alone. Otherwise, visualize the worst-case scenario or feared outcome that's making you anxious, using the technique of imaginal exposure or premeditation of adversity.

6. Use cognitive distancing by telling yourself "It's not things that upset me but my judgments about them." You can also decatastrophize by describing the feared event in objective terms, without emotive language or value judgments. Remind yourself of its temporary nature by asking "What next?" and considering how things will move on over time.

Stoics tell us to be constantly mindful of our actions and look out for disturbing impressions, automatic thoughts, or images that pop into our stream of consciousness. Instead of giving our assent to them and allowing ourselves to be swept along by them into worry, we should tell ourselves that they are just impressions and not the things they claim to represent. In this way we gain cognitive distance from them and can postpone evaluating them until we're in a better frame of mind to deal with them. Chrysippus reputedly said that with the passage of time, "emotional inflammation abates" and as reason returns, finding room to function properly, it can then expose the irrational nature of our passions.

In this chapter, we've looked at ways Stoics cope with worry and anxiety, with a focus on the Stoic reserve clause and premeditation of adversity. Many of the other techniques we mentioned in previous chapters are useful for coping with anxiety, but Marcus mentions two in particular that allow us to focus on the transience of upsetting events: cognitive distancing and decatastrophizing. We also looked at how the modern evidence-based technique of worry postponement resembles coping strategies described by the ancient Stoics.

Indeed, Stoicism provides some very powerful ways of overcoming fear and anxiety, which often resemble those supported by research on modern CBT. Remaining grounded in the present, spotting worry when it begins, and gaining cognitive distance from worry are healthy and effective ways of coping. We can also take advantage of the natural process of emotional habituation by patiently facing our fears in our imagination long enough for our anxiety to abate. This is an inevitable benefit of the Stoic technique called "premeditation of adversity," but we can also help ourselves do this by employing verbal decatastrophizing and describing the feared event in very calm and objective language, suspending the value judgments responsible for our distress.

After decades of training in these and other Stoic techniques, Marcus was able to go calmly and confidently to the defense of the empire. The majority of people in Rome were thrown into total panic, fearing an impending catastrophe at the hands of the barbarian hordes invading Italy from the north. As emperor, Marcus faced one setback after another, and he must have felt out of his depth at times. However, he calmly persevered in the face of great adversity. Slowly, with his trusted generals Pompeianus and Pertinax by his side, Marcus began to gain the upper hand over the northern tribes.

The more warlike Zanticus replaced King Bandaspus of the Iazyges, but as the war turned against him, he finally surrendered and sued for peace in June 175 AD. Marcus was shortly afterward acclaimed emperor for the eighth time and granted the title *Sarmaticus*, conqueror of the Sarmatians. It's reported that 100,000 Roman prisoners were freed as a result of the victory. Marcus resettled many thousands of the Germanic tribesmen and women in Italy rather than kill or enslave them, albeit with mixed success. This wasn't an option with the nomadic and warlike Sarmatians, though. Instead, Marcus conscripted eight thousand of their horsemen into the Roman army, forming an elite auxiliary cavalry unit, most of whom were sent to garrison the Roman forts in Britain. He wrote in his notes that men who take pride in capturing Sarmatians as though they were fish in a net are no better than thieves or robbers.[13]

However, Marcus had to rush the final stages of the First Marcomannic War and the ensuing peace negotiations with the Sarmatians because an even greater threat suddenly loomed on the horizon. The Stoic precepts and practices that Marcus had honed during the First Marcomannic War were about to be put to the test once again. Far away in the east, a rival had staked his claim to the imperial throne, and that could mean only one thing: Romans were about to be divided by civil war, which threatened to tear the empire apart.

# 7.

# TEMPORARY MADNESS

May 175 AD. A nervous courier hands over a letter to Gaius Avidius Cassius, commander of the Syrian legions and governor general of the eastern provinces. It contains only a single Greek word, which to his consternation reads *emanes* ("You're mad"—you've lost your mind).

Cassius is furious and tears it to pieces. He's not someone to be trifled with. In fact, his brutality has become notorious. One of his favorite punishments is to chain men together in groups of ten and let them drown in the middle of a river. Rumors circulated that he once had dozens of the enemy bound to a pole nearly two hundred feet high and set it ablaze so that for miles around their countrymen could watch them burn alive. Even by the brutal standards of the Roman army, that was considered horrifically cruel. He was renowned among his own troops as a strict disciplinarian, sometimes to the point of savagery. He cut off the hands of deserters or broke their legs and hips, leaving them crippled. Letting them live on in misery was his way of warning others against disobeying his orders. However, Cassius was also a distinguished military hero. Next to the emperor, he was the second most important commander in the Roman army, perhaps even the second most powerful man in the whole empire.

Cassius's iron grip on his troops was legendary, and it made him indispensable to Rome. Marcus and Cassius had long been family friends, although Cassius was rumored to criticize the emperor behind his back. Marcus would tell his courtiers, "It is impossible to make men exactly as one would wish them to be; we must use them such as they are." His reputation for clemency and forgiveness stood in total contrast to Cassius's severity. Nevertheless, despite their opposing characters, Marcus placed his trust in Cassius as a general. During the Parthian War, while Lucius Verus indulged his vices at a safe distance from any actual fighting, Cassius achieved one stunning victory after another, relentlessly pursuing King Vologases deep into Parthian territory. He quickly rose to become Lucius's second in command. Near the end of the war, however, he allowed his men to sack the twin cities of Ctesiphon and Seleucia, on the River Tigris, where, it was claimed, they contracted the plague. The returning troops brought it home to their legionary bases throughout the provinces, and from there it ravaged the empire. Cassius was rewarded, however, for driving the Parthians out of Syria by being appointed imperial legate (a governor with supreme command) of the province, answerable directly to the emperors. A few years later, in 169 AD, the Emperor Lucius's untimely demise left a power vacuum waiting to be filled.

In 172 AD, while Marcus was occupied with the First Marcomannic War, on the northern frontier, a tribe called the Bucoli, or "Herdsmen," who came from the northwest region of the Nile

Delta near Alexandria, instigated a revolt against the Roman authorities. This was a major emergency requiring Cassius to enter Egypt with his two Syrian legions, which meant he had to be granted *imperium*, supreme military authority equal to that of the emperor in his absence. Native Egyptians had borne the brunt of tax increases required to fund Marcus's war in the north. As a result, more and more of them had turned to banditry, and eventually, out of desperation, they formed a rebel army, led by a charismatic young warrior-priest called Isidorus. The story goes that a handful of these men disguised themselves in women's clothing and approached a Roman centurion, pretending that they were going to pay him a ransom of gold for their captured husbands. They ambushed him, however, and then captured and sacrificed another officer, reputedly swearing an oath over his bloody entrails before ritually devouring them. News of this reputed act of terrorism quickly spread across Egypt, and a general uprising ensued.

The Bucoli rapidly gained enough support from other tribes to surround and attack Alexandria. When the Egyptian legion confronted the tribesmen in a pitched battle, the vastly outnumbered Romans suffered a humiliating defeat. The Bucoli and their allies continued to besiege Alexandria for months while plague and famine devastated the city. They would have sacked Alexandria had Cassius and his troops not been sent from Syria to relieve the Alexandrian garrison and put down the uprising. He faced so many tribal warriors, though, that he dared not launch a direct counterattack even with three legions under his command. Instead, he chose to bide his time, sowing dissent and instigating quarrels among the enemy tribes until he was finally able to divide and conquer them. Cassius's reward was to retain *imperium* throughout the eastern provinces, granting him a unique status and set of powers, dangerously close to those of an emperor.

At the age of forty-five, Cassius had become a hero to his countrymen as a result of his dramatic military victories. His authority was further enhanced by his noble lineage: his mother, Julia Cassia Alexandra, was one of the *Cassii*, an ancient Roman family famous for their old-fashioned toughness. She was a princess, descended on her father's side from King Herod the Great of Judea and on her mother's from Augustus, the first Roman emperor. She also claimed descent from another Roman client-king, Antiochus IV Epiphanes of Commagene, making Cassius a member of the Seleucid imperial dynasty.

In short, Cassius was born to rule. Given his noble pedigree and celebrated military victories, he doubtless viewed himself as a natural successor to the Emperor Lucius Verus. However, far to the north, Marcus had promoted Claudius Pompeianus, another Syrian general, and one from much humbler stock. Pompeianus had already distinguished himself during the Parthian War and subsequently married Marcus's daughter Lucilla, the widow of Lucius Verus. He served as the most senior general on the northern frontier during the Marcomannic Wars and became the emperor's right-hand man. It was even rumored that Marcus had invited Pompeianus to become Caesar, although for some reason he declined. It seems likely that Cassius found the idea intolerable that a *commoner* from his own country might be promoted above him.

Cassius has steadily climbed the ladder of power since the day the Emperor Lucius died. Now, in 175 AD, Cassius has been holding the authority of an emperor in the east for three years; he has one rung left to climb, and Marcus Aurelius is the only person standing in his way. The single word he holds in his hands, *emanes*, comes from Herodes Atticus, the Sophist who tutored Marcus in Greek rhetoric as a youth. Herodes was known for his eloquence in delivering elaborate speeches, but this letter had the sort of laconic punch more typical of Stoics than Sophists. Only one word was necessary to make his point. Driven by his lust for absolute power, Cassius has rashly instigated a civil war that threatens to tear the whole empire apart and engulf the lives of millions in bloodshed.

At the far side of the empire, over fifteen hundred miles away, an exhausted dispatch rider arrives at the army camp at Sirmium, the capital of Lower Pannonia (in modern-day Serbia). The soldiers who meet him rush him straight to the emperor's residence in the middle of the camp. It has taken over ten days, using the emergency relay system, to get the news from the east via Rome to the northern frontier. He hesitates before speaking. His news is so astonishing that he can scarcely believe it himself: "My lord Caesar, General Avidius Cassius has betrayed you . . . *the Egyptian legion have acclaimed him emperor!*"

The courier has with him a letter from the Senate confirming the news: on May 3, 175 AD, Avidius Cassius had been acclaimed emperor of Rome by the Egyptian legion in Alexandria. "My lord, they're telling everyone that you're dead," the messenger explains. The news came from Publius Martius Verus, governor of the Roman province of Cappadocia (in modern-day Turkey). He had served with great distinction as a general along with Cassius and Pompeianus in the Parthian War. Crucially, Martius Verus's alarming news comes with the reassurance that he and the three legions under his command have declared their unwavering loyalty to Marcus. However, Cassius reputedly has garnered support for his rebellion throughout the region lying south of the Taurus mountain range, roughly half the eastern empire. A number of senators at Rome who had opposed the Marcomannic campaign have seized the opportunity to petition in favor of Cassius. So far, though, the Senate as a whole remains loyal to Marcus. Nevertheless, Cassius is a highly accomplished general with seven legions under his command. He also controls Egypt, the breadbasket of the empire and by far the wealthiest province in the east. Its capital, Alexandria, is the second largest city and has the largest port in the empire. If exports from Egypt are cut off, Rome will eventually run out of bread, leading to rioting and looting. The fate of the empire therefore hangs in the balance.

Marcus, in fact, has recently been very sick, perhaps even close to death. Aged fifty-four and widely perceived as frail and in poor health, he has long been the subject of gossip at Rome. His wife, Faustina, had traveled back to Rome several months earlier. Rumors say that she was frightened by the possibility of Marcus's imminent demise and urged Cassius to stake his claim to the throne. Marcus's only surviving son, Commodus, is thirteen years old and acutely aware that if his father dies or the throne is usurped before he reaches adulthood, his own life will be in grave peril. Faustina had allegedly schemed that by preempting Marcus's death, Cassius can outmaneuver other pretenders to the throne and perhaps even safeguard the succession of Commodus by marrying her. Others say that Cassius acted on his own initiative, deliberately circulating bogus rumors of Marcus's death to seize power. Or perhaps he simply acted prematurely, not treasonously, genuinely deceived by false intelligence that declared the emperor dead or dying. The Senate was alarmed, though, and immediately declared Cassius *hostis publicus*, a public enemy, seizing his assets and those of his family. That has only served to escalate the conflict. Cassius must feel the situation spiraling out of control. He can't back down; civil war has become inevitable.

Whatever Cassius's motives, Marcus now finds himself confronting one of the most serious crises of his reign. The emperor has recovered from his latest bout of illness and wastes no time in responding to the sedition. He looks over the faces of his generals. They already know that he must prepare to leave the northern frontier and lead an army to the east with great haste. Cassius's legions may march against Rome itself in an effort to secure his claim on the imperial throne. This looming threat has cast the city into a state of total panic and emboldened Marcus's critics in the Senate. However, Marcus's reputation with the mighty legions serving him on the Danube is now unassailable.

The following morning, Marcus sends the dispatch rider on his way with letters for the Senate in Rome, his ally Martius Verus in Cappadocia, and, most importantly, Cassius in Egypt. His message is clear: *the emperor confirms that he is alive, in good health, and will soon return.* Now he must make rapid arrangements for peace in the north so that he will be free to march southeast, reinforce the loyalists in Cappadocia, and quell unrest by appearing in person. However, it would be premature to address his troops about the incident until he knows that a civil war is unavoidable. They're still fighting pockets of resistance among the northern tribes, and he doesn't want the barbarians along the Danube getting wind of the crisis back home while negotiations for peace are still underway.

In private, he continues to meditate on his reaction to the news. The hardest thing to deal with is the *uncertainty* of the situation. Marcus assumes that at some level Cassius believes he is doing the right thing: he acts out of ignorance of what is genuinely right and wrong, for, as Socrates and the Stoics taught, *no man does wrong knowingly.* Of course, it's precisely this philosophical attitude that Cassius resents in Marcus, because to him forgiveness is merely a sign of weakness. It leads to a contest between their personalities, two ways of ruling, and two philosophies of life: one harsh, the other forgiving.

Several weeks have now passed since Marcus received the Senate's dispatch notifying him of events in Egypt. His first action on receiving news of the rebellion was to summon his thirteen-year-old son, Commodus, to Sirmium, where he took the *toga virilis*, officially making him an adult Roman citizen in preparation for being acclaimed emperor. He is being commended to the legions as Marcus's natural heir in order to help quash Cassius's claim on the throne. The news must have reached Cassius that the emperor was still alive, but there has been no word of him standing down. However, the failure of Cassius's rebellion to spread across the Taurus mountain range into Cappadocia means he doesn't have enough troops to be confident of holding Syria against a major offensive by the loyalist army. Nevertheless, rumor and unrest are growing in Marcus's camp. The time has come for the emperor to address his men and announce that they will be marching southeast to join forces with Martius Verus in Cappadocia before engaging Cassius's main army in Syria.

Marcus prepares himself for the day ahead, contemplating the actions of Cassius and the senators who are working against him. Marcus tells himself, as always, that he must be ready to accept meddling, ingratitude, violence, treachery, and envy.[1] According to the Stoics, individuals are bound to make moral errors, because the majority do not have a firm grasp on the true nature of good and evil. Nobody is born wise, but rather we must become so through education and training. Marcus believes that philosophy has taught him right from wrong and the ability to understand the nature of men like Cassius, who appear to act unjustly. He reminds himself that even those who oppose him are his kin, not necessarily through blood but because they are his fellow citizens in the universal community, sharing the potential for wisdom and virtue. Even though they may act unjustly, they cannot truly harm him because their actions cannot tarnish his character. As long as Marcus understands this, he cannot be angry with them or hate them. Those who oppose him have come into being, he says, to work together with him, just as the upper and lower rows of our teeth work together to grind our food. To turn against men like Cassius in anger, or even to turn his back on them, would be contrary to reason and against the law of Nature. Marcus reminds himself not to regard the rebel faction as enemies but to view them as benignly as a physician does his patients. He takes his time, in quiet contemplation, knowing how important it is to preserve a rational frame of mind in the face of adversity, especially given the tremendous power invested in him by the Roman people. As soon as Marcus has finished these meditations, he dons the military cape. Pompeianus and several other advisors meet him outside his room. It is time for him to address the ranks of legionaries assembled in the center of the camp.

Marcus greets them as his fellow soldiers. He says there's no point complaining or feeling bitter about the rebellion in the east. He accepts whatever ensues as the will of Zeus. He asks them not to be angry with the heavens, and assures them of his heartfelt regret that they must be engaged in war after war in his service. He wishes that Cassius had come to him first and argued his case before the army and the Senate. Astoundingly, Marcus promises them that he would even have stepped down and relinquished the empire without a struggle if he had been persuaded that it was for the common good. However, it's too late for that now, as war is already upon them.

He reminds his troops that their reputation far surpasses that of the eastern legions, and so they have reason to be optimistic. Although Cassius is one of his most esteemed generals, he says, they have nothing to fear from "an eagle at the head of jackdaws"—a comment that draws a few somber laughs. It wasn't really Cassius who won those famous victories, after all, but the very soldiers who now stand before him. Moreover, loyal Martius Verus will be by their side, a general no less accomplished than Avidius Cassius. Marcus tells them of his hope that Cassius may still repent now that he knows the emperor lives. He must assume that it was only through mistakenly believing him to be dead that his once-loyal general would have betrayed him in this manner. If not, and Cassius persists in his rebellion, he will be forced to think again when he learns that Marcus Aurelius is marching against him at the head of such a formidable army of seasoned veterans from the north. (The Roman historian Cassius Dio presents what he claims to be the original text of this remarkable speech.)

The legionaries gathered before Marcus know well enough that their beloved sovereign and commander is a philosopher of the Stoic sect. Nevertheless, what happens next must have left them stunned. Marcus assures them that his greatest desire is to show clemency.

> To forgive a man who has done wrong, to be still a friend to one who has trodden friendship underfoot, to continue being faithful to one who has broken faith. What I say may perhaps seem incredible to you, but you must not doubt it. For surely all goodness has not yet entirely perished from among men, but there is

still in us a remnant of the ancient virtue. However, if anyone should disbelieve it, that merely strengthens my desire, in order that men may see accomplished with their own eyes what no one would believe could come to pass. For this would be the one profit I could gain from my present troubles, if I were able to bring the matter to an honorable conclusion, and show all the world that there is a right way to deal even with civil war.

This is not misfortune, in other words, but to bear it nobly is good fortune. That was something Rusticus and the other Stoics had taught him as a boy. There isn't a trace of anger in Marcus's words, although the news of Cassius's rebellion has turned Rome upside down and left the whole empire in turmoil. The men serving under Marcus's command know him well enough to expect that he would respond with dignity and calm, even to such a shocking betrayal as this. Even so, it must seem remarkable to the average legionary, standing there in the mud that day, to hear the Emperor Marcus Aurelius summarily pardon not only this usurper but also the rest of those ranged against him.

Upon finishing his speech to the troops, Marcus instructs his secretary to forward a copy to the Senate. He retires to his residence once again, closes his eyes, and continues to meditate on how best to cope with the emerging crisis, turning to his philosophy for guidance.

## HOW TO CONQUER ANGER

Marcus did not have a completely placid disposition by nature—he had to work on overcoming his temper. In the very first sentence of *The Meditations*, he praises his grandfather for being so calm and mild mannered, and throughout the rest of his notes, he keeps returning to the problem of mastering one's anger.[2] We know that Marcus struggled with his own feelings of anger and worked to become a more calm and reasonable man because he says so. He concludes the first book of *The Meditations* by thanking the gods that he never lapsed into offending his friends, family, or teachers, even though he felt inclined to lose his temper at times. People who suffer from fatigue and chronic pain, as Marcus did, can often be prone to irritability and anger. It shouldn't surprise us if a frail man who slept poorly and was bothered by severe chest and stomach pains sometimes felt irritated with the countless people who were trying to manipulate or deceive him.

For Stoics, full-blown anger is an irrational and unhealthy passion that we should never indulge. As we've seen, though, it's human nature to have some *automatic* feelings of irritation in response to life's problems. The Stoics consider these "proto-passions" inevitable and accept their occurrence with an attitude of indifference. A Stoic might reasonably prefer that someone behave differently. They might even take determined action to stop them, as Marcus did when he mobilized his army to march against Avidius Cassius. Being a Stoic clearly doesn't mean being a passive doormat. However, the wise man will not get upset about things that lie beyond his direct control, such as other people's actions. The Stoics therefore have a variety of psychological techniques that they employ to help them counteract feelings of anger and replace them with a more even-tempered, but equally determined, attitude.

Dealing with feelings of anger by cultivating greater empathy and understanding toward others is one of the major recurring themes of *The Meditations*. Whereas modern psychotherapy typically focuses on anxiety and depression, the Stoics concerned themselves more with the problem of anger. Indeed, an entire book by Seneca titled *On Anger*, which survives today, describes the Stoic theory and treatment of this passion in great detail.

As in most aspects of life, Marcus's supreme role model here was his adoptive father. From the Emperor Antoninus he learned "gentleness" first and foremost, and mildness of temperament. Antoninus exhibited "patient tolerance" of those who harshly criticized his cautious handling of the empire's resources. Marcus specifically reminds himself of how gracefully his adoptive father accepted the apology of a customs officer at Tusculum on one occasion, and that this was typical of his gentle character. Unlike his predecessor Hadrian, Antoninus was never rude, overbearing, or violent to people, and he never lost his temper. He considered every situation on a case-by-case basis, calmly, methodically, and consistently, as if doing so at his leisure. Elsewhere we hear again of Antoninus's gentle disposition and "how he put up with those who found fault with him unfairly, finding no fault with them in return" and "his forbearance towards those who openly opposed his views, and his pleasure when somebody pointed out something better."[3] The patience and gentleness Antoninus showed as a ruler were among the most important virtues Marcus learned. Indeed, Marcus was famous for remaining calm in the face of provocation. Nevertheless, he had to *practice* and train himself to overcome his feelings of anger.

So what therapy did the Stoics prescribe? They believed that anger is a form of *desire*: "a desire for revenge on one who seems to have done an injustice inappropriately," according to Diogenes Laertius. Speaking less formally, we might say that anger typically consists in the desire to harm someone because we think they've done wrong and deserve to be punished. (Occasionally it might be more of a desire for someone *else* to harm them, as in, "I hope someone teaches her a lesson!") This is not unlike modern cognitive theories of anger, which typically define it as based upon the belief that a rule that is personally important to you has somehow been violated. Anger stems from the idea that an injustice has been committed, or someone has done something they *shouldn't* have done. It's often associated with the impression that you've somehow been threatened or harmed by the other person, making anger a close companion of fear: "He did something *to me* that he shouldn't have done—that was *wrong*!" Not surprisingly, the Stoic antidote for anger resembles the general therapy applied to desire we described earlier. So it's worth briefly reviewing the typical steps in this approach and considering how they would apply to this passion:

1. **Self-monitoring.** Spot early warning signs of anger, to nip it in the bud before it escalates. For example, you might notice that your voice begins to change, or that you frown or your muscles tense, when you're beginning to grow angry, or you may think of someone's actions as unjust or in violation of a personal rule. ("How dare she say that to me!")

2. **Cognitive distancing.** Remind yourself that the events themselves don't make you angry, but rather your judgments about them cause the passion. ("I notice that I am telling myself 'How dare she say that,' and it's that way of looking at things that's causing me to feel angry.")

3. **Postponement.** Wait until your feelings of anger have naturally abated before you decide how to respond to the situation. Take a breath, walk away, and come back to it a few hours later. If you still feel like you need to do

something, then calmly decide upon the best response; otherwise, just let it go and forget about it.

4. **Modeling virtue.** Ask yourself what a wise person such as Socrates or Zeno would do. What virtues might help you to respond wisely? In your case, it might be easier to think of a role model you're more familiar with, like Marcus Aurelius or someone you've encountered in your own life. ("A wiser person would try to empathize, put themselves in her shoes, and then exercise patience when they're responding . . .")

5. **Functional analysis.** Picture the consequences of following anger versus following reason and exercising virtues such as moderation. ("If I let my anger guide me then I'll probably just yell at her and get into another argument, and things will get a lot worse over time until we're not speaking anymore. If I wait until I've calmed down and then try to listen patiently, though, it might be difficult at first but it will probably start to work better with practice, and once she's calmed down maybe she'll begin listening to my perspective.")

The Stoics probably learned the ancient concept of postponing their actions until anger has abated from the Pythagoreans, whose school was nearly seven centuries old by Marcus's time. They were known for never speaking in anger but withdrawing for a while until their feelings had died down. They would only give their response when they could do so calmly and rationally. Today therapists sometimes call that taking a "time-out" from anger in order to regain your composure.

In addition to these basic strategies, Marcus also describes a whole repertoire of Stoic *cognitive* techniques, which focus on addressing the underlying beliefs that cause our anger in the first place. These are different ways of thinking about the situation: *alternative perspectives*. They could be used at any time. However, it's difficult to change your point of view while you're still in the grip of anger. In fact, one of the most common mistakes we make is trying to challenge our angry thoughts when we're not in the best frame of mind to do so. Instead, use these thinking strategies *beforehand*, in advance of facing situations that might provoke anger, or *after* you've taken time to regain your composure. Marcus reminded himself to contemplate some of these ideas first thing in the morning while preparing to encounter difficult people during the day ahead.

In one of the most striking passages of *The Meditations*, Marcus introduces a list of ten thinking strategies to use when "guarding against being angry with others."[4] He describes these anger-management techniques as *ten gifts from Apollo* and his nine Muses. Apollo is the god of medicine and healing—the god of therapy, we might say—and these are Stoic psychotherapeutic prescriptions. *The Meditations* contains numerous additional references to the same methods, which help clarify what Marcus had in mind.

## 1. WE ARE NATURALLY SOCIAL ANIMALS, DESIGNED TO HELP ONE ANOTHER

The first strategy Marcus describes using in response to anger involves reminding himself of the Stoic doctrine that rational beings are inherently *social*, designed to live in communities and to help one another in a spirit of goodwill. As such, we have a duty to live wisely and harmoniously with our fellow humans in order to fulfill our natural potential and to flourish.

In one of the most famous quotes from *The Meditations*, the opening passage of book 2 mentioned earlier, Marcus describes mentally preparing himself each morning to deal with troublesome people. He adds, "Nor can I be angry with my kinsman nor hate him for we have come into being for co-operation," and that to obstruct one another by feeling resentment or turning our back on others goes against our rational and social nature. Indeed, he says that the good for a rational creature lies, partly, in having an attitude of fellowship toward others. Marcus also goes so far as to claim that ignoring our fellowship with others is a form of injustice, a vice, and an impiety because it goes against Nature.[5]

The Stoic goal of living in concord, or harmony, with the rest of mankind doesn't mean that we should expect everyone to act like our friend. On the contrary, we should be prepared to meet many foolish and vicious people in life and to accept this as inevitable. We should not meet disagreeable people and enemies with anger, but treat this as an opportunity to exercise our own wisdom and virtue. Stoics think of troublesome people as if they are a prescription from a physician, or a training partner we've been assigned by a wrestling coach. We exist for one another, says Marcus, and if we can't educate those who oppose us, we have to learn at least to tolerate them.[6]

These challenges will help us grow in virtue and become more resilient. If no one ever tested your patience, then you'd lack an opportunity to exhibit virtue in your relationships. In the *Eulogium on Marcus Aurelius*, an eighteenth-century work of historical fiction closely based on the Roman histories, the Stoic teacher

Apollonius is portrayed saying, "There are wicked men—they are useful to thee; without them, what need would there be for virtues?"

## 2. CONSIDER A PERSON'S CHARACTER AS A WHOLE

The next strategy involves picturing the person you're angry with in a more rounded and complete manner—don't just focus on the aspects of their character or behavior you find most annoying. Marcus tells himself to consider carefully the sort of people who typically offend him. He then patiently imagines them in their daily lives: eating at their dinner tables, sleeping in their beds, having sex, relieving themselves, and so on. He considers how they can be arrogant, overbearing, and angry, but he also contemplates times when they've been enslaved by other desires.[7] The idea is that we should broaden our awareness, not only thinking of the person's actions that offend us but of the other person as a whole, remembering that nobody is perfect. As we widen our perspective, we're likely to dilute our anger toward them. Doing so can be seen as a variation of the depreciation by analysis technique.

Indeed, Marcus says that when others hate, blame, or slander you, you should imagine looking into their souls and understanding what kind of people they really are. The more you understand them, the more their hostility toward you will seem misguided and powerless to offend you. He seems to have viewed Cassius in this way, which probably helped Marcus respond calmly to the sudden crisis of the civil war, whereas the Senate offered a knee-jerk reaction.

Marcus says that in addition to putting yourself in the other person's shoes, you should analyze their character in a manner that gets straight to the core questions: what kind of people do they want to please, for what purpose, and through what kind of actions? What are their guiding principles in life, what do they busy themselves doing, how do they spend their time? You should imagine their souls laid bare before you, with all their errors exposed. If you can picture this, eventually it will seem absurd to you that their blame or praise ever carried any real authority.[8] Indeed, the wise man only really pays attention to the opinions of those "living in agreement with Nature," and so he is continually mindful of what sort of men he's dealing with. He understands who they are "at home and abroad, by night and in the day, in what vices they wallow and with whom."[9]

The Stoics believed that vicious people fundamentally lack self-love and are alienated from themselves. We must learn to empathize with them and see them as the victims of misguided beliefs or errors of judgment, not as malicious. Marcus says that you should contemplate how they are blinded by their own mistaken opinions and compelled by them to act as they do—they don't know any better. If you realize that, it will be easier to ignore their censure, forgive them, and yet oppose their actions when necessary. To understand all is to forgive all, as the saying goes.

## 3. NOBODY DOES WRONG WILLINGLY

This follows on from the previous point. It's a statement of one of the central paradoxes of Socrates's philosophy and was embraced by the Stoics: no man does evil *knowingly*, which also entails that no man does it *willingly*. Marcus gave Cassius the benefit of the doubt by assuming that at some level the usurper believed he was doing the right thing and was simply mistaken. In *The Meditations*, he says you should view others' actions in terms of a simple di-chotomy: either they are doing what is right or doing what is wrong. If they are doing what is right, then you should accept it and cease to be annoyed with them. Let go of your anger and learn from them. However, if they are doing what is wrong, then you should assume it's because they don't know any better. As Socrates pointed out, nobody wants to make mistakes or be deceived; all reasoning creatures inherently desire the truth. So if someone is genuinely mistaken about what is right, you should, if anything, feel sorry for them.

Everyone resents being called vicious or dishonorable. In some sense, they believe that what they're doing is right, or at least acceptable. No matter how perverse that conclusion may seem, it's justified in their own mind. If we constantly think of others as being mistaken rather than simply malicious, as deprived of wisdom against their wishes, we will inevitably deal more gently with them. Marcus therefore says that whenever you believe someone has wronged you, you should first consider what under-lying opinions they hold about what's right and wrong. Once you really understand their thinking, you'll have no excuse for being *surprised* at their actions, which should naturally weaken your feelings of anger.[10] Errors of judgment compel people just as much as illness or insanity, and we learn to make allowances for such people and forgive them on that basis. In the same way, we don't judge children harshly when they make mistakes because they don't know better. However, adults still make the same moral errors as children. They don't want to be ignorant, but they act as such unwittingly and unintentionally.

Marcus thinks the rest of humanity deserves our love insofar as they are our kin. Yet they also deserve our compassion, he says, insofar as they are ignorant of good and evil, a handicap as severe as visual blindness. Our moral errors lead us into passions such as anger that easily spiral out of control. We should tell ourselves that other people are compelled by their ignorance to act as they do, and let go of our anger. When faced with someone whose behavior appears objectionable, Epictetus therefore advised his students simply to repeat this maxim to themselves: "It seemed right to him."[11]

## 4. NOBODY IS PERFECT, YOURSELF INCLUDED

Remembering that other people are human, and flawed, can help you to receive criticism (or praise) from them in a more balanced and less emotional way. In a similar manner, reminding yourself that you're not perfect either—none of us are—can help you to moderate your feelings of anger. It's a double standard to criticize other people without acknowledging our own imperfections. Marcus therefore reminds himself that he too does many things that are wrong, and he is just like others in that regard. He actually recommends that whenever we're offended by the faults of another, we should treat it as a signal to pause and immediately turn our attention to our own character, reflecting on the similar ways in which we go wrong.[12] He makes the very honest psychological observation that he often refrains from wrongdoing himself only because he's afraid of the consequences or worried about his reputation. Often all that holds us back from committing one vice is another vice, he says (another idea that goes back at least to Socrates). Many people refrain from crime, for instance, because they're afraid of being caught, not because they're virtuous. So even if we do not engage in the same wrongdoing as others, the inclination may still be there. Marcus was willing to hear Cassius out because, despite being emperor, he didn't consider himself beyond reproach.

There are no gurus in Stoicism. Even the founders of the school—Zeno, Cleanthes, and Chrysippus—don't claim that they were perfectly wise. They believe we're all foolish, vicious, and to some extent enslaved to our passions. The ideal Sage is perfect by definition, but he's a *hypothetical* ideal, like the notion of a Utopian society. Ironically, the very anger we feel toward those who offend us can *itself* be seen as evidence of fallibility on our part. Our anger proves that we too are capable of doing the wrong thing under the influence of strong emotions. Remembering that fallibility is the common lot of mankind—including you—can help diminish feelings of anger. When you point your finger in anger at someone else, remember that three fingers on the same hand point back in your own direction.

## 5. YOU CAN NEVER BE CERTAIN OF OTHER PEOPLE'S MOTIVES

We can't read other people's minds, so we shouldn't jump to conclusions about what their intentions are. However, without knowing someone's intentions, we can never really be sure they're doing wrong. People can do things that appear bad for what they believe are good reasons. Marcus was actually an experienced judge in the Roman court of law as well as a good judge of character. He reminds himself that it's necessary to learn a great many things about another person before we can deliver a firm opinion concerning their personality and motives—and even then we're basing our conclusions on probability. In the same way, when it came to the civil war, Marcus took it for granted that he could never really know for *certain* what was in Cassius's heart.

By contrast, anger assumes an unwarranted *certainty* about the motives of other people. Cognitive therapists call this the fallacy of "mind-reading"—leaping to conclusions about other people's motives although they are always somewhat veiled from us. You should always remain open to the *possibility* that the other person's intentions are not in the wrong.[13] Consider that other plausible interpretations of their actions exist. Keeping an open mind will help you dilute your feelings of anger.

## 6. REMEMBER WE ALL WILL DIE

Marcus tells himself to focus on the transience of the events in the grand scheme of things. He suggests contemplating the fact that both he and the person with whom he's angry will eventually be dead and forgotten. When viewed from this perspective, it doesn't seem worth getting flustered by people's behavior. Nothing lasts forever. If events will seem trivial in the future when we look back on them, then why should we care strongly about them now? This doesn't mean that we should do nothing. Indeed, by remaining calm, we can plan our response better and take action. Marcus didn't sit on his hands when Cassius instigated the civil war; he rapidly mobilized a huge army against him. He didn't allow fear or anger to cloud his judgment in doing so, however.

*The Meditations* was likely written before the civil war, but when it occurred Marcus probably adopted the same philosophical attitude toward Cassius's rebellion. Remember that this moment will soon pass, he says, and things inevitably change.

As we'll see, the civil war turned out to be very short-lived. There are no surviving statues of Avidius Cassius. Few people today would even recognize his name, although he was *technically* an emperor of Rome, albeit for just a few months. One day, however, Marcus Aurelius will also be forgotten. He always kept that in mind when making decisions. He reminded himself not to worry about how future generations would judge him but to do only what reason commended as the right course of action. When we remember that nothing lasts forever, it no longer seems worthwhile getting angry with other people.

## 7. IT'S OUR OWN JUDGMENT THAT UPSETS US

It should come as no surprise that Marcus includes perhaps the best-known Stoic technique of all, which we've called cognitive distancing. When you're angry, remind yourself that it's not things or other people that make you angry but your judgments about them. If you can let go of your value judgments and stop calling other people's actions "awful," then your anger will diminish. Of course, as Seneca pointed out, there are initial feelings of anger that we can't control, which the Stoics call the proto-passions (*propatheiai*). We share these emotional reactions to some extent with other animals, and so they're natural and inevitable, like the anxiety of the Stoic teacher whom Gellius described being caught in a storm. Marcus says that it's up to you, though, whether you persist in your anger. We don't control our initial reaction, perhaps, but we do control how we respond to it: *it's not what happens first that matters but what you do next.*

How can you learn to pause and gain cognitive distance from your initial feelings of anger rather than being swept along by them? By realizing that another person's actions can't harm your character, Marcus says. All that really matters in life is whether you're a good person or a bad person, and that's down to you alone. Other people can harm your property or even your body, but they can't harm your character unless you allow them to do so. As Marcus puts it, if you let go of the opinion "I am harmed," the feeling of being harmed will disappear, and when the feeling is gone, so is any real harm.[14] Often, though, just reminding yourself that it's not events that are making you angry but your judgments about them will be enough to weaken the hold anger has on you.

## 8. ANGER DOES US MORE HARM THAN GOOD

Marcus often links gaining cognitive distance with the next technique, which we've called functional analysis. Think about the consequences of responding with anger and compare them to those of responding rationally, calmly, and perhaps with empathy and kindness. Alternatively, just remind yourself that anger actually does you more harm than good. The Stoics liked to consider how ugly and unnatural anger looks—a scowling face, grimacing, turning puce with rage, like someone in the throes of a horrible disease.[15] Marcus views the profound ugliness of anger as a sign that it is unnatural and against reason.

Also, where does anger get us? It's often totally *impotent*. Bear in mind, says Marcus, that men will carry on doing the same things anyway, even if they cause you to burst with rage.[16] Worse, though, our anger is not only futile but also *counterproductive*. He notes that it often requires more effort to deal with the consequences of losing our temper than it does just to tolerate the very acts with which we're angry. The Stoics believe that we take offense because we assume other people's actions threaten our interests in some way. However, once you consider that your own anger is a *bigger* threat to you than the thing you're angry about, then you inevitably start to weaken its grip.

Anger about perceived slights does us more harm than the slights themselves in an even more fundamental sense, though. The actions of others are external to us and cannot touch our character, but our own anger transforms us into a different sort of person, almost like an animal, and for Stoics that's the greater harm. Marcus therefore reminds himself that the vice of another man cannot penetrate your character unless you allow it to do so. Ironically, anger does the most harm to the person experiencing it, although he has the power to stop it.[17] Your first priority in most cases should therefore be doing something about your own anger before attempting to do anything about the events that triggered it.

Throughout *The Meditations*, Marcus frequently expresses this in another way, by reminding himself to leave the wrong with the wrongdoer: "Does another do me wrong? That's his business, not mine." He who does wrong does wrong against himself; he who acts unjustly acts unjustly to himself, because he harms only himself, he says. The wrongdoer damages his own character; you shouldn't join him in his misery by making the value judgment that he has offended and harmed you too.[18]

It's tempting, once again, to imagine that Marcus may have been thinking of adversaries like Cassius when he warns himself not to feel toward his enemies as they feel toward him. Likewise, you shouldn't start to harbor the sort of opinions the wicked hold or those they wish you to hold. In short, the best form of revenge is not to sink to their level by allowing yourself to become angry with them.[19] If someone hates you, Marcus says, that's their problem. Your only concern is to avoid doing anything to *deserve* being hated.

## 9. NATURE GAVE US THE VIRTUES TO DEAL WITH ANGER

Marcus also recommends applying another familiar Stoic technique to anger, the one we've called contemplation of virtue. You should ask yourself what virtue or capacity Nature has given you to cope with the situation you're facing. There are several closely related questions you might also ask: How do other people cope with anger? What would your role models do? What do you *admire* certain people for doing when faced with situations that would make others lose their temper? Marcus says that you should accept that wrongdoing inevitably exists in the world and then ask, "What virtue has Nature given man as a response to the wrongdoing in question?" He explains this by comparing virtues to medicines prescribed by Nature as the "antidotes" to vice.[20]

The main antidote to anger for Marcus is the Stoic virtue of *kindness*, which along with *fairness* makes up the cardinal social virtue of *justice*. Whereas the Stoics viewed anger as the desire to *harm* others, kindness is essentially the opposite: goodwill toward others and the desire to *help* them. However, what other people do is not strictly up to us, so we should exercise kindness and goodwill toward others with the reserve clause in mind, by adding the caveat "Fate permitting." Like Cato's archer, a Stoic should aim at the target (of benefiting others) but be satisfied if he has acted with kindness, and willing to accept both success and failure with equanimity.

Marcus actually gives a specific example of what he means, by describing an imaginary encounter with someone who was testing his patience with their hostility. He imagines gently encouraging the person in the right direction by responding along the lines of "No, my son, we have been made for other things; I shall be in no way harmed, but you are harming yourself." Marcus says we should speak to them delicately, reminding them that human beings are meant to live together in society, like bees and other communal animals, and not to be at odds with each other. We should not speak sarcastically or include harsh rebukes but rather reply with affectionate kindness in our hearts. We should be simple and honest and not lecture them as though from a schoolmaster's chair or as though trying to impress bystanders. It's tempting again to wonder if Marcus was thinking how he should talk to men like Cassius, or even his own son Commodus.

For Stoics, kindness first and foremost means educating others or wishing they would become wise, free from vice and passion. It's a desire to turn enemies into friends, Fate permitting. Marcus's example of acting with kindness actually entails educating the other person in two of the most important strategies he mentioned earlier:

1. Anger does more harm to us than to the person with whom we're angry.
2. Humans are essentially social creatures; Nature didn't intend us to fight but to help each other.

He views this as another dichotomy: either we can educate the other person and change their opinions or we can't. If we can teach them a better way, then we should do so; if not, we should accept that fact, without anger. Marcus therefore shows great consideration for the person with whom he's angry, and he thinks about tactful ways in which they might be reconciled. Did he learn this from the way Rusticus and others spoke to him, correcting his own behavior, when he was a young man?

## 10. IT'S MADNESS TO EXPECT OTHERS TO BE PERFECT

Marcus describes these first nine strategies as gifts from Apollo's Muses, which he says we should take to heart. He adds one more piece of advice from the Leader of the Muses himself: *to expect bad people not to do bad things is madness because that is wishing for the impossible*. Moreover, to accept their wrongdoing toward others while expecting them never to wrong you is both inconsiderate and foolish.

This final strategy is about Stoic determinism: the wise man who views the world rationally is never surprised by anything in life. It's another standard type of Stoic argument. We already know that there are both good men and bad men in the world. Bad men are bound to do bad things. Therefore, it would be irrational to expect otherwise. "To crave impossibilities is insanity, but it is impossible for the wicked to act otherwise." Wishing bad men never to do wrong is as foolish as wishing that babies would never cry and becoming angry with them when they do.[21] We can easily imagine that Marcus had prepared for Cassius's betrayal in this way. The Senate was shocked and caught off guard, and their hasty reaction just made full civil war more likely. Marcus, by contrast, responded calmly and confidently, as if he expected these things to happen in life.

People say "I can't believe this!" when they're upset, but usually they're describing things that are very common in life, such as betrayal, deceit, or insults. The Stoics realized that in this sense surprise is not entirely authentic and needlessly exaggerates our emotional reaction. By contrast, someone with a more philosophical attitude might say, "That's no surprise, these things are bound to happen—*c'est la vie*." Marcus tells himself, "Everything that happens is as usual and familiar as the rose in spring and the fruit in summer," including slander and treachery. When we're surprised that a bad person acts badly, then we're to blame for expecting the impossible.[22] We can easily anticipate the sort of wrongs people do, at least in general terms, but when they actually happen, we behave as if it's shocking. You should learn to immediately ask yourself this rhetorical question when you're offended by someone's shameless behavior: "Could it be that no obnoxious people exist in the world?" Of course not. So remember not to demand the impossible, and apply this technique to all forms of wrongdoing. Marcus believes that you will be able to show kindness toward others if you set aside feigned shock and surprise and adopt a more philosophical attitude to vice.

Marcus used these ten gifts from Apollo to cope with anger. Throughout *The Meditations* he returns again and again to selections from the list:

> It is peculiar to man to love even those who do wrong. And this happens, if when they do wrong it occurs to you that they are kinsmen, and that they do wrong through ignorance and unintentionally, and that soon both of you will die; and above all, that the wrongdoer has done you no harm, for he has not made [the character of your mind] worse than it was before.[23]

Those are clearly tactics derived from the ten gifts of Apollo, as are the following:

> With what are you discontented? The wickedness of men? Take this conclusion to heart, that rational creatures have been

made for one another; that forbearance is part of justice; that wrongdoing is involuntary; and think how many before now, after passing their lives in implacable enmity, suspicion, hatred, and at daggers drawn with one another, have been laid out and burnt to ashes—think of this, I say, and at last stop your fretting.[24]

However, the strategy Marcus leans on most heavily when coping with anger is the first gift from Apollo and his Muses: he reminds himself to view others as his kinsmen, brothers, or sisters, and that Nature meant for people to work together. We should view even our enemies as part of our family. It's our duty to learn how to live in harmony with them so that our life can go smoothly, even if they try to oppose us.

After listing the ten Gifts from Apollo, though, Marcus also reminds himself to have this precept at hand when he senses he might lose his temper: "To be angry is not manly but rather a mild and gentle disposition is more manly because it is more human." This is striking because, as we've seen, Cassius reputedly insulted him by calling him a "philosophical old woman." He meant to insinuate that Marcus was weak. However, Marcus believed that in reality someone who is capable of exercising gentleness and kindness in the face of provocation is stronger and more courageous than one who gives way to their anger, as Cassius was prone to do. Whereas people like Cassius often mistake this passionate anger for strength, the Stoics viewed it as very much a sign of *weakness*. This brings us back to our story: *What was the outcome of the civil war between Cassius the hawk and Marcus the dove?*

# THE MARCH SOUTHEAST
# AND CASSIUS'S DEATH

By means of daily meditations such as these, Marcus has maintained his famous composure in the face of Cassius's rebellion. Philosophy has taught him to calmly anticipate events such as the appearance of a would-be usurper. Now, as a Stoic, it is time for him to *reconcile* acceptance with action as he marches toward another war far from home. The troops have gradually come to view him as blessed and divine. They're genuinely humbled by the calm demeanor with which he faces adversity—even this, the greatest in a series of betrayals.

Rome is in a state of hysteria following the news of Cassius's sedition, made worse by the Senate's knee-jerk response. The people are terrified that Cassius will invade in Marcus's absence and sack the whole city in revenge. One of Marcus's senior officers on the northern frontier, Marcus Valerius Maximianus, has already been sent racing ahead to engage Cassius's legions in Syria with a cavalry regiment twenty thousand strong. Marcus has also sent the distinguished military commander Vettius Sabinianus with a detachment from Pannonia to protect the city of Rome in case the enemy legions advance through Italy.

Cassius seems to be in a strong position at first. With the Syrian legions under his command and Egypt, the breadbasket of the empire, joining his cause, others have started to rally behind him. However, support for his rebellion fails to spread north of Syria. The legions of Cappadocia and Bithynia both remain fiercely loyal to Marcus Aurelius. Marcus has also retained the overall support of the Roman Senate. Cassius is left commanding seven legions: three in Syria, two in Roman Judaea, one in Arabia, and one in Egypt. However, they amount to less than a third of the troops still under Marcus's command throughout the rest of the empire. Moreover, Marcus's northern legions are formidable and highly disciplined veterans, whereas the legions under Cassius are still notoriously weak despite his draconian attempts to enforce discipline.

Now, precisely three months and six days after Cassius was acclaimed emperor, as Marcus's main army marches toward Syria, another messenger arrives with startling news: While walking through his camp, Cassius was attacked by a centurion called Antonius, who charged him on horseback and thrust a blade into his neck as he rode past. Cassius was badly wounded, but nearly escaped. However, a junior cavalry officer joined the ambush, and together these two officers hacked off their newly acclaimed emperor's head and are on their way to deliver it to Marcus in a bag.

Cassius's revolt came to this sudden end after his legions discovered that Marcus was alive and marching against them. Now, several days have passed, and Antonius and his companion have arrived with the grisly evidence of the usurper's demise. Marcus turns them away, refusing to look at the severed head of a man who was once his friend and ally. He instructs them to bury it. Although his troops are euphoric, Marcus does not celebrate. By forgiving the rebel legions, he had inadvertently signed Cassius's death warrant. Cassius's men simply had no more reason to fight the superior army approaching them from the north. The only thing between them and their pardon was Cassius, who refused to stand down, and so his fate was sealed.

Marcus was recognized as sole emperor again throughout the empire by July 175 AD. Cassius had earned a reputation for being cruel, changeable, and untrustworthy—and in the end his own men gave him the same callous treatment that he had shown them over the years. History proved that his authoritarian approach ultimately backfired. By contrast, Marcus was known for his constancy and sincerity, and when his legions in Cappadocia repaid him in kind with their steadfast loyalty, his victory was secured. Marcus rewarded the Twelfth, known as the Thunderbolt Legion, with the title *Certa Constans* ("Surely Constant") and the Fifteenth, Apollo's Legion, with the title *Pia Fidelis* ("Faithful and Loyal"). Cassius, by contrast, had tried to frighten and coerce his own men into risking their lives for him. At the first sign of danger they were bound to turn against him.

After the civil war in Syria had ended, Marcus did not take severe measures against Cassius's family or allies. He only had a handful of men involved in the plot executed, those who had committed additional crimes. As agreed, he did not punish the legionaries under Cassius's command but sent them back to their usual stations. He also pardoned the cities that had sided with Cassius. Indeed, Marcus wrote a letter to the "Conscript Fathers" of the Senate, pleading with them to act with clemency toward those involved in Cassius's rebellion. He asked that no senator be punished, that no man of noble birth be executed, that the exiled should be allowed to come home, and that goods be returned to those from whom they had been seized. Accomplices of Cassius were to be protected from any type of punishment or harm. "Would that I could recall the condemned also from the grave," he said. The children of Cassius were to be pardoned, along with Cassius's son-in-law and wife, because they had done no wrong. Marcus went even further and ordered that they were to live under his protection, free to travel as they pleased, with Cassius's wealth divided fairly among them. He wished to be able to say that only those slain *during* the rebellion had died as a result of it: there were to be no witch hunts or acts of revenge afterward. Commodus now accompanied him to Syria and Egypt, and Marcus commended him to the legions as his official heir before they finally made their way back to Rome.

Marcus doubtless wanted to restore peace quickly in Rome so that he could return to the northern frontier, where there was still much work to be done, so he wisely showed mercy toward those senators who had supported Cassius. First, though, he found it necessary to tour the eastern provinces to restore order there. Indeed, his popularity in the east grew considerably as a result, and we're even told that the people were inspired to adopt aspects of his Stoic philosophy.

The Empress Faustina died in spring 176 AD, within half a year of the revolt's suppression. There were rumors that she committed suicide because of her association with Avidius Cassius. She was held in high regard by Marcus, however, who had her deified after her death. She remained an immensely popular figure, despite all the loose talk about her alleged conspiracies. Not long after Faustina's death, Commodus was appointed consul, and then in 177 AD, co-emperor with Marcus. Shortly after Marcus's death, ignoring his father's orders for clemency, Commodus would have the descendants of Cassius hunted down and burned alive as traitors.

# 8.

# DEATH AND THE VIEW
# FROM ABOVE

Vindobona, March 17, 180 AD. The emperor beckons his guard to come close and whispers: *Go to the rising sun, for I am already setting.* He barely has enough strength to pronounce these words. Marcus glimpses fear in the young officer's eyes. The guard hesitates for a moment before nodding awkwardly and returning to his post at the entrance to the imperial quarters. Marcus pulls the sheet above his head and rolls over uncomfortably, as if to go to sleep for the last time. He can feel death beckoning him on all sides. How easy it would be to slip into oblivion and be free from the pain and discomfort once and for all. The pestilence is devouring his frail old body from within. He hasn't eaten for days, weakening himself by fasting. Now, as the sun goes down, everything is very quiet. His eyelids flutter, although the pain keeps him awake. The emperor slips in and out of consciousness. But he doesn't die.

He thinks to himself, "Your eyes feel so heavy now—it's time to let them close." The sweet sensation of consciousness dissolving begins to creep over him . . .

I must have fallen asleep, or lost consciousness again. I can't tell if my eyes are open or closed. Everything is dark. Soon it will be daybreak and the sparrows will sing their morning song. Spring has broken and the streams have thawed. Their waters flow into the mighty river passing by the camp outside.

The soldiers picture the spirit of the Danube as an ancient river god. He silently offers us all a lesson if only we pause to listen: *all things change, and before long they are gone.* You cannot step into the same river twice, Heraclitus once said, because new waters are constantly flowing through it. Nature herself is a rushing torrent, just like the Danube, sweeping along all things in her stream. No sooner has something come into existence than the great river of time washes it away again, only to carry something else into view. The long-forgotten past lies upstream from me now, and downstream waits the immeasurable darkness of the future, vanishing from sight.

I won't be needing my medicines or physicians again. I'm relieved the fuss is over. The time has come to let the river wash me away too. Change is both life and death. We can try to stall the inevitable, but we never escape it. It's a fool's game,

> With meats and drinks and magic spells
> To turn aside the stream and hold death at bay.[1]

Looking back, it seems more obvious to me now than ever before that the lives of most men are tragedies of their own making. Men let themselves either get puffed up with pride or tormented by grievances. Everything they concern themselves with is fragile, trivial, and fleeting. We're left with nowhere to stand firm. Amid the torrent of things rushing past, there's nothing secure in which we can invest our hopes.

You may as well lose your heart to one of the little sparrows who nest by the riverbank—that's what I used to say. As soon as it's charmed you, it will flit away, vanishing from sight. I once set my heart on my own little sparrows. I called them my chicks in their nest: thirteen boys and girls, given to me by Faustina. Now only Commodus and four of the girls are left, wearing grave faces and weeping for me. The rest were taken before their time, long ago now. At first I grieved terribly, but the Stoics taught me how to both love my children and endure when Nature reclaimed them. When I was mourning my little twin boys, Apollonius patiently consoled me and helped me slowly regain my composure. It's natural to mourn—even some animals grieve the loss of their young. But there are those who go beyond the natural bounds of grief and let themselves be swept away entirely by melancholy thoughts and passions. The wise man accepts his pain, endures it, but does not add to it.

Nature also reclaimed my beloved son Marcus Annius Verus, not long before my brother Lucius died. I gave him the name I bore myself as a child, passed down through generations in my family. My little Marcus bled to death on the doctor's table while they were removing a tumor from beneath his ear. I could only mourn him five days before I had to leave Rome for the war in Pannonia. Later, gentle Apollonius would remind me of a saying from Epictetus: "Only a madman seeks figs in winter." Such is one who pines for his child when his loan has been returned to Nature. I loved them, by all means, but learned also to accept that they were mortal.

Leaves that the wind scatters to the ground,
Such are the generations of men.[2]

And what were my children but such leaves? They arrived
with the spring and were brought down by the winter blast; then
others grew to take their place. I wanted to keep them forever,
although I always knew that they were mortal. Yet the heart that
cries "Oh let my child be safe!" is like an eye wanting only to
gaze on pleasant sights, refusing to accept that all things change,
whether we like it or not.

The wise man sees life and death as two sides of the same
coin. When Xenophon, one of Socrates's noblest students, received
word that his son had fallen in battle, what did he say? "I knew
my son was mortal." He grasped so firmly the precept that what
is born must surely also perish. I had evidence of this from an
early age, having lost my father, Annius Verus, when I was just
a child. I barely knew him, except through his reputation as a
good and humble man. My mother, Lucilla, buried him, and in
due course it fell to me to bury her. The Emperor Antoninus,
my adoptive father, buried his empress, and then the time came
for Lucius and me, his sons, to place him in his tomb and mourn
for him. Then my brother the Emperor Lucius died quite unexpectedly, and I buried him too. Finally, I laid to rest my own
beloved empress, Faustina. Soon I shall be reunited with her
when Commodus lays my remains in Hadrian's great mausoleum
on the banks of the Tiber. My friends will deliver eulogies for me
in Rome and remind the people that Marcus Aurelius has not
been lost but only returned to Nature. The sun sets this evening
and takes me down with it; tomorrow it will be another who
rises to take my place.

So now you're finally here, Death, my old friend, for assuredly

I can call you a friend. You've been my guest many times, after all, welcomed through the gates of my imagination. How often have you accompanied me as I pictured the reigns of emperors from long ago while deep in my meditations? Everything is different, but underneath it's all the same: anonymous individuals marrying, raising children, falling sick, and dying. Some fight wars, feast, work the land, and trade their wares. Some flatter others or seek to be flattered, suspect their fellows of plotting against them, or hatch their own plots. Countless among them engage in intrigues, pray for the death of others, grumble at their lot, fall in love, pile up fortunes, or dream of high office or even a crown. How many individuals whose names we'll never know, their lives extinguished, lie forgotten, as if they had never been born at all? Yet turn your thoughts to the mighty, and what difference does it make? Death comes knocking at the king's palace and the beggar's shack alike. Augustus, the founder of the empire, his family, ancestors, priests, advisors, and his whole entourage—*where are they now*? Nowhere to be seen. Alexander the Great and his mule driver both reduced to dust, made equals at last by death.

And what of great dynasties, now utterly extinct? Think of the efforts their ancestors took to leave behind an heir, only to have their whole lineage end abruptly with the epitaph "Last of his line" engraved upon some tomb. And how many cities have, as it were, also died? Entire nations wiped out from history. Asked why he wasn't rejoicing at the annihilation of Carthage, great Scipio wept and prophesied that one day even Rome herself will fall. Every era of history teaches us the same lesson: *nothing lasts forever*. From the court of Alexander, long gone, to those of Hadrian and Antoninus, among whom I once walked, known today through monuments and stories only. The very names "Hadrian" and "Antoninus" have acquired an archaic ring, like the names of Scipio Africanus and Cato of Utica inscribed in history books. Tomorrow my own name will sound old to others, describing a bygone era: "the reign of Marcus Aurelius."

I will be joining them: Augustus, Vespasian, Trajan, and the rest. Yet it is a thing indifferent to me how or even whether I shall be remembered. How many of those whose praises were once sung have long since been forgotten? And those who sang their praises too. It's vanity to worry about how history will record your actions. Even now, I'm surrounded by people who are overly concerned with what future generations will think of them. They might as well lament the fact that centuries ago, before their birth, their names were utterly unknown. The lips of mankind can grant you neither fame nor glory worth seeking. What matters is how I face this moment, which shall soon be gone, for I can already feel my very self evaporating, slipping gradually into extinction as if into a dream.

Death, when I rode in triumph through the streets of Rome alongside Lucius, were you with me then? The slaves stood with us in the chariots, holding golden wreaths above our heads, whispering at our backs "remember you must die." Even as Lucius paraded his haul of gold and treasures and shackled lines of captured Parthians, his legionaries were bringing back something far more sinister from the east: the pestilence that followed them to Rome. It's taken fourteen years, but the disease that saw Roman dead piled high on carts has finally claimed another Caesar. The Stoics taught me to look death square in the eye, to tell myself with merciless honesty each day "I am a mortal," all the while remaining in good cheer. They say that when Zeno, the founder of our school, was elderly, he once tripped and fell. He banged on the ground and quipped: "I come of my own accord;

why then do you call me?" Now I too am an old man, and, though you call me, I come readily to meet you, Death.

Yet there are still many afraid even to utter your name aloud. The Stoics taught me that there are no such words of ill omen. Socrates was the first to call the idea that death is terrible a mask to frighten small children. He said, "Friends, if a childish part of you is still afraid of death, you should sing a charm over him every day until he's cured." If I consider death for what it is, analyzing it rationally, stripping away all the assumptions encrusted round it, it's revealed to be nothing but a process of Nature. Look at what is behind the mask, study it, and you will see it does not bite. Yet this childish fear of death is perhaps our greatest bane in life. Fear of death does us more harm than death itself because it turns us into cowards, whereas death merely returns us to Nature. The wise and good enjoy life, without a doubt, but nevertheless are unafraid of dying. Surely we are never fully alive as long as we fear the end? Indeed, to learn how to die is to unlearn how to be a slave.

I must die, but must I die groaning? For it's not death that upsets us but our judgments about it. Socrates did not fear death; he saw that it was neither good nor bad. On the morning of his execution, he casually informed his friends that philosophy is a lifelong meditation on our own mortality. True philosophers, he said, fear their own demise least of all men. For those who love wisdom above everything else are continually in training for the end. To practice death in advance is to practice freedom and to prepare oneself to let go of life gracefully.

Indeed, I have been traveling along the road to death since the very day I came into this world. From a green grape to a ripened cluster to a shriveled raisin, everything in Nature has a beginning, a middle, and an end. Each stage of man has its own ending or demise—childhood, adolescence, prime, and old age. Assuredly, this body is not the one to which my mother gave birth. Indeed, I've been changing, dying, every day since I was born. If there is nothing to fear in that, then why should I fear the final step? And if death is a loss of awareness, then why should I fret? For only that which is something can be good or evil, but death is nothing, the mere absence of experience. It's no worse than sleep. Moreover, death is a release from all pain, a boundary beyond which our sufferings cannot go. It returns us to that state of peacefulness in which we lay before we were even born. I was dead for countless eons before my birth, and it did not vex me then. *I was not; I was; I am not; I do not care*—as the Epicureans say.

For if it troubles me not at all that my body only occupies a small portion of space, then why should I be afraid that it only occupies a small span of time? In any case, from another point of view, we don't disappear into nothingness but are dispersed back into Nature. I shall be returned to the earth from which my father drew his seed, my mother her blood, my nurse her milk, and from which I have taken my daily food and drink. For everything comes ultimately from one source and returns there taking another form. It is as though from softened wax you might shape a little horse, then a little tree, then a human form. Nothing is ever really destroyed, just sent back into Nature's arms and turned into something else, over and over—one thing becomes another.

Today a drop of semen, tomorrow a pile of ash or bones. Not eternal, but mortal; a part of the whole, as an hour is of the day. Like an hour I must come and like an hour pass away. The more our minds comprehend that we are parts of the whole in this way, the more we realize our own body's frailty. I always reminded myself that I wasn't meant to live a thousand years and that death would be here for me soon enough. I lived each day as if it were to be my last, preparing myself for this very moment. Now that it's finally upon me, I realize it's just the same as every other moment. I have the choice to die well or die badly. Philosophy has prepared me well enough. Do you suppose that human life can seem any great matter, said Socrates, to a great-souled individual who has embraced the whole of time and the whole of reality in his thoughts? No. To such a person not even death will seem terrible.

My soul disperses for a while, in drowsy reveries, teetering on the brink of insensibility. What a miraculous power thought has to travel swiftly across the world, or to consume grand vistas, enveloping more and more within its scope. Roaming dreamily over the whole wide world and bidding it farewell, I realize that I have taken flight above it. Like Homer's Zeus, looking down on earth from Mount Olympus, observing now the lands of the horse-loving Thracians, now Greece, Persia, India, and surrounding everything the wine-dark sea. Or like our Scipio Aemilianus, who, slumbering in Numidia, dreamt that he was transported aloft, allowed to gaze down briefly on the world of men from among the stars.

I have long prepared my mind to embrace the most comprehensive outlook through the daily practice of philosophy. Plato said anyone seeking to understand human affairs should gaze down upon all earthly things this way, as though from a high watchtower. Each day I would rehearse, just as my teachers did, imagining myself suddenly raised aloft and looking down on the complex tapestry of human life from high above. Now, as the life keeps fading from my body, my daydreams turn into visions, real enough to touch. How insignificant the countless things men squabble over seem from this high vantage point. Like children, though, who think only of what baubles belong to their play, men, their minds captivated by narrow fears and desires, are alienated from Nature as a whole.

I can see them now below me, the great herds of human animals: numerous workers toiling in the fields, far-traveled merchants of all nations, and huge armies massed for battle—all of them like ants scuttling over the earth. Always busy at something, an anonymous, swarming mass, wandering astray down the countless labyrinthine paths that stretch before them. Men, women, and children, slaves and nobles, those being born and those dying, marrying and separating, celebrating festivals and mourning their losses; the tiresome clapping of tongues in courts of law—I see a hundred thousand faces of friends and strangers pass me by. I see great cities growing from humble settlements, thriving for a spell, then one day crumbling into deserted ruins. Races barbarous in their infancy, struggling toward civilization, then falling into barbarism again; after darkness and ignorance come arts and sciences, then the inevitable descent once again into darkness and ignorance. I see exotic and undiscovered races hidden in the far corners of the world. The many different rituals, languages, and stories of men. The countless lives of others long ago and the lives that will be lived many years from now after my own demise. And even though I was fated to be acclaimed the emperor of Rome, how few there are in the vast world who have even heard my name, let alone known me for who I really am. Those who do will soon be gone themselves and forgotten.

I find myself marveling once more at the soul's capacity to rid

itself of myriad unnecessary troubles in this way. Enlarging itself, embracing the whole universe, and reflecting on the finitude
and transience of all individual things, the brevity of our entire
life, and the lives of others, when compared to the eternity of time.
We become *magnanimous*, great-souled, by expanding our minds
and rising above trivial things, which belong far beneath us. The
soul flies free when it's not weighed down by earthly fears and
desires and returns to its homeland, a citizen of the entire cosmos, making its abode the immeasurable vastness of universal
Nature.

Thanks be to the gods that I was encouraged to make a habit
of picturing the whole cosmos thus, and contemplating the im-
mensity of both time and space. I learned to set each particular
thing in life against the whole substance of the universe in my
mind's eye and see it as far less than a fig seed, and measure it
against the whole of time as nothing more than the turn of a
screw. For what is impossible to see with mortal eyes is nevertheless possible to grasp with the intellect.

Before me now a mental image forms: the representation of a
shining sphere enclosing all creation, each part distinct but nevertheless one, gathered into a single vision. All the stars of the
heavens, the sun, the moon, our earth, both land and sea, and all
living creatures, just as though seen within a transparent globe,
which I can almost imagine holding in the palm of my hand.
From this cosmic perspective, in truth, to rail against the universe
in fury over all the troubles in history would be like weeping over
a cut on my smallest finger.

My life all but over, nothing remains—no fears and no desires to separate me from the rest of Nature. I see before me the
whole of the cosmos, its vast design, and the mighty revolutions

performed by the celestial orbs. And I find myself plunged deep in this imagination, traversing the heavens above, as strength leaves my limbs.

In this vast ocean of being, what a minute dot our whole earth seems. Asia and Europe in their entirety are merely specks of dirt, the great oceans nothing but a raindrop, and the highest mountain merely a grain of sand.

I can only admire the grace and majesty of the stars as my mind is blessed to accompany them, and I marvel further still at the vision of the whole cosmos before me. May I be transformed through the proximity of death into something worthy of Nature and the cosmos, an alien in my motherland no more. Traveling through the breadth of Nature, my mind expands to a vastness that envelops individual events, swallowing them up and making them appear like a pinpoint by comparison. Where is the tragedy in such negligible incidents? Where is the surprise or astonishment?

What I spent my life learning I now see everywhere—as I turn my attention from one thing to another, all sides grant me the same vision. The universe is a single living being, with a single body and a single consciousness. Every individual mind a tiny particle of one great mind. Each living creature like a limb or organ of one great body, working together, whether they realize it or not, to bring about events in accord with one great impulse. Everything in the universe so intricately woven together, forming a single fabric and chain of events. Whereas I once saw each fragmentary part and with some effort imagined the whole, my sight is now transformed. Having let go of fear and desire forever, I can see only the whole to which every part belongs, and this appears more real to me than anything else. What I knew before, my life and opinions, seem like smoke through which I glimpsed Nature darkly.

Rejoicing in this comprehensive vision, my self is dilated until it becomes one with infinite universal Nature. How minuscule the fraction of cosmic time that has been assigned to each of our lives. How small this clod of earth over which we creep. The more confidently I grasp this vision, the more clearly I understand that nothing is of any great moment in life except that we should do two simple things: First we must follow the guidance of our own higher nature, submitting ourselves to reason's dictates. Second, we must deal wisely and dispassionately with whatever universal Nature sends to be our fate, whether pleasure or pain, praise or censure, life or death.

My soul ascends higher as the remaining life now ebbs from my limbs. The difference between knowing and seeing has somehow given way. Before my very gaze, the constellations surround me, like those adorning the walls in the temples of Mithras. I glide effortlessly alongside them like a ship sailing over the smoothest waters. Around me are the multitude of stars, a host of beings composed of pure light. Naked and flawless, they gracefully follow their course through the heavens without deviation. How they differ from men below on earth. We possess the same divine spark, yet it lies buried deep within us, and we live as though imprisoned, anchored down in the mud by our own folly and greed.

The mind of the Sage is like a star or our own sun, from which purity and simplicity shine forth. I've been fortunate enough to observe these characteristics in others. Men like Apollonius, Junius Rusticus, and Claudius Maximus by their own example showed me how to live wisely, virtuously, and in accord with Nature. Released now from earthly attachments, I feel my soul being transformed and cleansed, unveiling within me some glimmer of the deep wisdom that I once glimpsed in the words and actions of my beloved teachers. As I let life slip away, content to part from it, my mind is finally liberated to follow its own true nature without obstruction. I see things more clearly than ever before. The sun does not do the work of the rain or of the wind.

The sun himself and every star in heaven are telling me, "I was born to do what I am doing." And I too was born to follow my own nature by striving for wisdom. Countless stars punctuate the night sky. Each one is distinct from the others, yet they all work together, forming the whole panoply of heaven. Man was meant to be like this: striving his whole life with patient endurance to cultivate the pure light of wisdom within himself and allowing it to shine forth for the benefit of others. Alone and yet at one with the community of fellow men around him, living wisely and in concord with them. The ancient Pythagoreans were right. To contemplate the unwavering purity and simplicity of the stars in this way is to cleanse our mind of earthly dross and set it free.

The rays of Apollo pour down in every direction but are not exhausted. Extending itself, sunlight touches objects and illuminates them without being weakened or defiled. It rests where it falls, caressing objects and exposing their features, neither deflected like the wind nor absorbed like the rain. Indeed, the mind of the wise man is itself like a heavenly sphere radiating the purest sunlight. It falls gracefully upon things, illuminating them without becoming entangled or degraded by them. For what does not welcome the light condemns itself to darkness. In the mind of one who has been purified, though, nothing is veiled or hidden.

Pure wisdom like the blazing fire of a sun consumes anything cast into it and burns brighter still. Reason adapts itself to any obstacle if it's allowed to, finding the right virtue with which to respond. We have been given a duty of sorts to take care of this paltry body with its unruly feelings, but only our intellect is genuinely our own. We let go of our attachment to everything external, purifying and separating ourselves from things, when we firmly grasp the realization that they are transient and ultimately indifferent. When we cut our ties to the past and the future and center ourselves in the present moment, we set our soul free from external things, leaving it to invest itself wholly in fulfilling its own nature.

Things external to our own character such as health, wealth, and reputation are neither good nor bad. They present us with opportunities, which the wise man uses well and the fool badly. Though men desire wealth and other such things, these no more improve a man's soul than a golden bridle improves a horse. We contaminate ourselves with these externals, blending and merging into things when we confuse them with our soul's natural good. Rising above indifferent things, the mind of the wise becomes a well-rounded sphere, as Empedocles used to say. It neither overreaches itself, mingling with external things, nor shrinks away from them. Its light spreads evenly over the world around it. Complete in itself, smooth and round, bright and shining. Nothing clings to its surface and no harm can touch it.

I can still feel the pain over there in my body. That part of me that still lies bleeding and shuddering beneath the bedsheet. It seems very far away now. It doesn't bother me in the slightest.

Soon another lapse into unconsciousness will come. I think it will be the last one. And so I bid farewell to myself, in good cheer, not begrudging the loss. I take one last step forward to meet Death, not as an enemy but as an old friend and sparring partner. Clenching my fists gently and bracing myself against the unknown and unforeseen, I arm myself once more with the precepts of my philosophy:

> The duration of a man's life is merely a small point in time; the substance of it ever flowing away, the sense obscure; and the whole composition of the body tending to decay.
>
> His soul is a restless vortex, good fortune is uncertain and fame is unreliable; in a word, as a rushing stream so are all things belonging to the body; as a dream, or as vapor, are all those that belong to the soul.
>
> Life is warfare and a sojourn in a foreign land. Our reputation after life is nothing but oblivion. What is it then that will guide man? One thing alone: philosophy, the love of wisdom.
>
> And philosophy consists in this: for a man to preserve that inner genius or divine spark within him from violence and injuries, and above all from harmful pains or pleasures; never to do anything either without purpose, or falsely, or hypocritically, regardless of the actions or inaction of others; to contentedly embrace all things that happen to him, as coming from the same source from whom he came himself, and above all things, with humility and calm cheerfulness, to anticipate death as being nothing else but the dissolution of those elements of which every living being is composed.
>
> And if the elements themselves suffer nothing by this, their perpetual conversion of one into another, that dissolution, and alteration, which is so common to them all, why should it be

feared by any man? Is this not according to Nature? But nothing that is according to Nature can be evil.[3]

It must be nearing dawn outside but I can no longer tell. My eyes have grown so feeble, surrounded by darkness on every side. I won't live to see another sunrise. It doesn't matter.

# ACKNOWLEDGMENTS

I would like to thank Stephen Hanselman and Tim Bartlett for their support and advice with regard to this book. I'd also like to thank my colleagues in the Modern Stoicism organization for sharing their ideas with me over the years and for helping me to arrive at my interpretation of Stoicism.

# NOTES

I've normally used quotes from Robin Hard's translation of *The Meditations*, but in some cases I've replaced these with my own translations from the Greek or modified them.

## INTRODUCTION

1. Spinoza, *On the Improvement of the Understanding*, 4–5.
2. Plato, *Apology*, trans. G. M. A. Grube, in *Plato: Collected Works*, ed. John M. Cooper (Indianapolis: Hackett, 1997), 30b.
3. Beck, Rush, Shaw, and Emery, *Cognitive Therapy of Depression*, 8.
4. *Meditations*, 10.16.

## 1: THE DEAD EMPEROR

1. Watson, *Marcus Aurelius Antoninus*, 96.
2. *Meditations*, 10.31.
3. *Historia Augusta*, 28.5.
4. *Meditations*, 10.36.
5. Cassius Dio, 72.34.
6. Diogenes Laertius, 7.1.4.

## 2: THE MOST TRUTHFUL CHILD IN ROME

1. *Historia Augusta*, 4.1.
2. *Historia Augusta*, 15.13.
3. *Discourses*, 3.23.
4. *Meditations*, 1.3.
5. *Meditations*, 8.9; 6.12; 5.16.
6. *Meditations*, 1.7.
7. *Meditations*, 5.33.
8. *Meditations*, 1.5.

9. *Meditations*, 1.6.

10. *Meditations*, 7.19.

11. *Meditations*, 1.17; 6.30.

12. Fronto, Letters, in *Meditations* (trans. Hard).

13. Fronto, Letters, in *Meditations* (trans. Hard).

14. *Historia Augusta*, 10.4.

15. *Meditations*, 1.8.

16. Fronto, Letters, in *Meditations* (trans. Hard).

17. *On Anger*, 2.3–4.

18. *Letters*, 53.

19. *On the Constancy of the Sage*, 10.4.

20. *Meditations*, 7.17.

21. *Meditations*, 5.26.

22. *Meditations*, 9.29; 4.51.

23. *Meditations*, 9.1.

24. *Meditations*, 3.5; 3.11.

25. *Discourses*, 3.8.

26. *Discourses*, 3.8.

27. *Handbook*, 45.

28. *Meditations*, 8.49.

29. Hadot, *Philosophy as a Way of Life*, 187–88.

30. *Discourses*, 3.8.

31. *Handbook*, 45.

32. Beck, *Cognitive Therapy and the Emotional Disorders*.

33. Epictetus, Fragment 21 in *Discourses*, books 3–4: *Fragments, Handbook*.

34. *Handbook*, 5.

35. Alford and Beck, *Integrative Power of Cognitive Therapy*, 142.

## 3: CONTEMPLATING THE SAGE

1. Galen, *Diagnosis and Cure of the Soul's Passions*.

2. *Meditations*, 6.12.

3. Themistius, "In Reply to Those Who Found Fault with Him for Accepting Public Office," Oration 34, in Robert J. Penella, *The Private Orations of Themistius* (Berkeley: University of California Press, 2000).

4. *Meditations*, 11.29.

5. *Handbook*, 46.

6. Fronto, Letters, in *Meditations* (trans. Hard).

7. *Meditations*, 6.14.

8. *Meditations*, 1.13.

9. *Meditations*, 1.10.

10. *Meditations*, 8.30.

11. *Meditations*, 1.9; 5.28; *Discourses*, 2.12.

12. *Meditations*, 8.61.

13. *Meditations*, 6.21.

14. Galen, *Diagnosis and Cure of the Soul's Passions*.

15. *Meditations*, 12.4; 3.4; 10.1; 3.7.

16. Galen, *Diagnosis and Cure of the Soul's Passions*.

17. *Handbook*, 38.

18. *Meditations*, 8.32.

19. *Meditations*, 7.7.

20. *Meditations*, 11.26; 4.38.

21. *Meditations*, 6.48.

22. *Meditations*, 1.16; 6.30.

23. *Meditations*, 6.30.

24. *Meditations*, 3.4.

25. *Meditations*, 3.8.

26. *Meditations*, 11.27; 5.1; 2.1.

27. *Discourses*, 3.10.

28. *Meditations*, 4.46.

29. *Meditations*, 5.11.

30. Simon, Howe, and Kirschenbaum, *Values Clarification*, 1972.

## 4: THE CHOICE OF HERCULES

1. *Historia Augusta*.

2. *Meditations*, 1.17.

3. Lucian, *Philosophies for Sale*.

4. *Discourses*, 1.16 (slightly modified).

5. *Meditations*, 7.3.

6. Fronto, Letters, in *Meditations* (trans. Hard), 16.

7. *Meditations*, 11.22.

8. *Meditations*, 3.16; 7.68.

9. *Meditations*, 10.12.

10. *Meditations*, 9.16.

11. *Meditations*, 6.7.

12. *Meditations*, 7.28; 6.48; 7.27.

13. *Meditations*, 3.16.

14. *Meditations*, 10.33.

15. *Meditations*, 8.2.

16. Baudouin and Lestchinsky, *The Inner Discipline*, 48.

17. *Meditations*, 10.29.

18. *Meditations*, 11.2.

19. *Meditations*, 6.13.

20. *Meditations*, 6.13.

21. *Meditations*, 1.17.

22. *Meditations*, 6.13.

23. *Meditations*, 8.39.

## 5: GRASPING THE NETTLE

1. Cassius Dio, *Roman History*, 72.34.
2. *Meditations*, 1.17.
3. Fronto to Marcus, *Letter* 9.
4. Fronto to Marcus, *Letter* 22.
5. Marcus to Fronto, *Letter* 8.
6. *Meditations*, 1.17.
7. *Meditations*, 3.7; 1.9.
8. *Meditations*, 1.15.
9. *Meditations*, 1.16; 6.30.
10. Epicurus, quoted in *Meditations*, 9.41.
11. *Meditations*, 9.41.
12. *Meditations*, 7.33.
13. *Meditations*, 7.64 (my italics).
14. *Meditations*, 7.64.
15. *Handbook*, 9.
16. *Meditations*, 7.43.
17. *Handbook*, 5.
18. *Meditations*, 4.39.
19. *Meditations*, 11.16.
20. *Meditations*, 5.26.
21. *Meditations*, 4.7.
22. *Discourses*, 2.1.
23. *Meditations*, 7.17.
24. *Meditations*, 10.24.
25. *Discourses*, 2.1.
26. *Meditations*, 6.13.
27. *Meditations*, 8.36.
28. *Meditations*, 11.16.
29. *Meditations*, 7.16; 7.14.
30. *Meditations*, 7.33.
31. *Meditations*, 11.16.
32. *Discourses*, 2.6.
33. *Meditations*, 5.8.
34. Teles of Megara, *On Self-Sufficiency*, in *Diogenes the Cynic: Sayings and Anecdotes with Other Popular Moralists* (2012), trans. Robin Hard (Oxford: Oxford University Press, 2012).
35. *Meditations*, 10.28.
36. *Discourses*, 3.10.
37. *Handbook*, 10.
38. *Meditations*, 5.18.
39. *Meditations*, 10.3; well-known quote from Victor Frankl's *Man's Search for*

*Meaning*, attributed to Friedrich Nietzsche, *Twilight of the Idols*, Maxims and Arrows, 12.

40. P. Dubois, *Self-Control and How to Secure It*, trans. H. Boyd (New York: Funk & Wagnalls, 1909), 108–9.

41. P. Dubois, *The Psychic Treatment of Nervous Disorders: The Psychoneuroses and Their Moral Treatment* (New York: Funk & Wagnalls, 1904), 394–95.

42. Dubois, *Self-Control*, 235–36.

## 6: THE INNER CITADEL AND WAR OF MANY NATIONS

1. *Discourses*, 3.20.

2. *Meditations*, 8.34.

3. *Meditations*, 11.37.

4. James 4:13–15.

5. *Meditations*, 4.1; 5.20; 6.50.

6. *Meditations*, 8.41.

7. Satire 2.7 in *The Satires of Horace and Persius*, trans. Niall Rudd (London: Penguin, 2005).

8. *Meditations*, 2.1.

9. *Meditations*, 4.3.

10. *Meditations*, 10.15; 10.23.

11. *Meditations*, 4.3.

12. T. Borkovec and B. Sharpless, "Generalized Anxiety Disorder: Bringing Cognitive-Behavioral Therapy into the Valued Present," in *Mindfulness and Acceptance: Expanding the Cognitive-Behavioral Tradition*, ed. S. C. Hayes, V. M. Follette, and M. M. Linehan (New York: Guilford Press, 2004), 209–42.

13. *Meditations*, 10.10.

## 7: TEMPORARY MADNESS

1. *Meditations*, 2.1.

2. *Meditations*, 1.1.

3. *Meditations*, 1.16; 6.30.

4. *Meditations*, 11.18.

5. *Meditations*, 2.1; 5.16; 9.1.

6. *Meditations*, 8.59.

7. *Meditations*, 10.19.

8. *Meditations*, 9.27; 7.62; 6.59; 9.34.

9. *Meditations*, 3.4.

10. *Meditations*, 7.63; 7.26.

11. *Meditations*, 2.13; 10.30; *Handbook*, 42.

12. *Meditations*, 10.30.

13. *Meditations*, 9.33.

14. *Meditations*, 4.7.

15. *Meditations*, 7.24.
16. *Meditations*, 8.4.
17. *Meditations*, 8.55; 7.71.
18. *Meditations*, 5.25; 9.4; 9.20.
19. *Meditations*, 7.65; 4.11; 6.6.
20. *Meditations*, 9.42.
21. *Meditations*, 5.15; 12.16.
22. *Meditations*, 4.44; 9.42.
23. *Meditations*, 7.22.
24. *Meditations*, 4.3.

## 8: DEATH AND THE VIEW FROM ABOVE

1. Euripides, *The Suppliants*.
2. Homer, *The Iliad*.
3. *Meditations*, 2.17.

# BIBLIOGRAPHY

Adams, G. W. (2013). *Marcus Aurelius in the Historia Augusta and Beyond*. New York: Lexington Books.

Alford, B. A., and A. T. Beck. (1997). *The Integrative Power of Cognitive Therapy*. New York: Guilford.

Baudouin, C., and A. Lestchinsky. (1924). *The Inner Discipline*. London: Allen & Unwin.

Beck, A. T. (1976). *Cognitive Therapy and the Emotional Disorders*. Middlesex: Penguin.

Beck, A. T., J. A. Rush, B. F. Shaw, and G. Emery. (1979). *Cognitive Therapy of Depression*. New York: Guilford.

Birley, A. R. (2002). *Marcus Aurelius: A Biography*. London: Routledge.

Borkovec, T., and B. Sharpless. (2004). "Generalized Anxiety Disorder: Bringing Cognitive-Behavioral Therapy into the Valued Present." In *Mindfulness and Acceptance: Expanding the Cognitive-Behavioral Tradition*. Edited by S. C. Hayes, V. M. Follette, and M. M. Linehan, 209–42. New York: Guilford Press.

Brunt, P. (2013). *Studies in Stoicism*. Oxford: Oxford University Press.

Dubois, P. (1904). *The Psychic Treatment of Nervous Disorders: The Psychoneuroses and Their Moral Treatment*. New York: Funk & Wagnalls.

———. (1909). *Self-Control and How to Secure It*. Translated by H. Boyd. New York: Funk & Wagnalls.

Epictetus. (1925). *Discourses*, books 1–2. Translated by W. A. Oldfather. Loeb Classical Library 131. Cambridge, MA: Harvard University Press.

———. (1928). *Discourses*, books 3–4: Fragments, Handbook. Translated by W. A. Oldfather. Loeb Classical Library 218. Cambridge, MA: Harvard University Press.

Farquharson, A. (1952). *Marcus Aurelius: His Life and His World*. Oxford: Blackwell.

Gill, C. (2010). *Naturalistic Psychology in Galen and Stoicism*. Oxford: Oxford University Press.

———. (2013). *Marcus Aurelius: Meditations, Books 1–6.* Oxford: Oxford University Press.

Grant, M. (1996). *The Antonines: The Roman Empire in Transition.* New York: Routledge.

Guthrie, K., T. Taylor, D. Fideler, A. Fairbanks, and J. Godwin. (1988). *The Pythagorean Sourcebook and Library.* Grand Rapids, MI: Phanes Press.

Hadot, P. (1995). *Philosophy as a Way of Life.* Edited by A. I. Davidson. Malden, MA: Blackwell.

———. (2001). *The Inner Citadel: The Meditations of Marcus Aurelius.* Translated by M. Chase. Cambridge, MA: Harvard University Press.

———. (2004). *What Is Ancient Philosophy?* Translated by M. Chase. Cambridge, MA: Belknap Press.

Holiday, R. (2015). *The Obstacle Is the Way.* London: Profile Books.

Holiday, R., and S. Hanselman. (2016). *The Daily Stoic: 366 Meditations on Wisdom, Perseverance, and the Art of Living.* London: Profile Books.

Long, A. A. (2002). *Epictetus: A Stoic and Socratic Guide to Life.* Oxford: Oxford University Press.

Marcus Aurelius. (1916). *Marcus Aurelius.* Translated by C. Haines. Loeb Classical Library 58. Cambridge, MA: Harvard University Press.

———. (2003). *Meditations: A New Translation.* Translated by G. Hays. New York: Random House.

———. (2011). *Meditations: Selected Correspondence.* Translated by R. Hard. Oxford: Oxford University Press.

McLynn, F. (2010). *Marcus Aurelius: A Life.* London: Vintage Books.

Rand, B. (2005). *The Life, Unpublished Letters, and Philosophical Regimen of Antony, Earl of Shaftesbury.* Adamant Media.

Robertson, D. J. (July 2005). "Stoicism: A Lurking Presence." *Counselling & Psychotherapy Journal.*

———. (2010). *The Philosophy of Cognitive-Behavioural Therapy: Stoic Philosophy as Rational and Cognitive Psychotherapy.* London: Karnac.

———. (2013). *Stoicism and the Art of Happiness.* London: Hodder & Stoughton.

———. (2016). "The Stoic Influence on Modern Psychotherapy." In *The Routledge Handbook of the Stoic Tradition.* Edited by J. Sellar, 374–88. New York: Routledge.

———. (2012). *Build Your Resilience.* London: Hodder & Stoughton.

Sedgwick, H. D. (1921). *Marcus Aurelius: A Biography Told as Much as May Be by Letters.* New Haven, CT: Yale University Press.

Sellars, J. (2003). *The Art of Living: The Stoics on the Nature and Function of Philosophy.*

———. (2014). *Stoicism.* Hoboken, NJ: Taylor & Francis.

———. (2016). *The Routledge Handbook of the Stoic Tradition.* New York: Routledge.

Seneca. (1928). *Moral Essays*, volume I. Translated by J. W. Basore. Loeb Classical Library 214. Cambridge, MA: Harvard University Press.

Seneca. (1928). "On Anger." In *Moral Essays*, volume I. Translated by J. W. Basore. Loeb Classical Library 214. Cambridge, MA: Harvard University Press.

Seneca. (1928). "On Constancy." In *Moral Essays*, volume I. Translated by J. W. Basore. Loeb Classical Library 214. Cambridge, MA: Harvard University Press.

Simon, S. B., L. W. Howe, and H. Kirschenbaum. (1972). *Values Clarification: A Practical, Action Directed Workbook*. New York: Warner.

Spinoza, B. (1955). *On the Improvement of the Understanding; The Ethics; Correspondence*. Translated by R. Elwes. New York: Dover.

Stephens, W. O. (2012). *Marcus Aurelius: A Guide for the Perplexed*. London: Continuum.

Thomas, A. L. (1808). *Eulogium on Marcus Aurelius*. New York: Bernard Dornin.

Ussher, P. (ed.). (2014). *Stoicism Today: Selected Writings*. Modern Stoicism.

———. (2016). *Stoicism Today: Selected Writings*. Vol. 2. Modern Stoicism.

Watson, P. B. (1884). *Marcus Aurelius Antoninus*. New York: Harper & Brothers.

Yourcenar, M. (1974). *Memoirs of Hadrian*. New York: Farrar, Straus, and Giroux.

# INDEX

Academic school of philosophy, 31–32, 35

Aesop's fables
    *The Boar and the Fox*, 199–200
    fable of two bags, 89
    *The Fox and the Lion*, 201–202
    *The Town Mouse and the Country Mouse*, 129

affection, 18, 41, 116, 130, 157, 244

*agoge* (Greek training), 53

*agora*, 11, 32

Agrippinus, Paconius, 76

alcohol, 43, 90, 117, 126–127, 135

Alexander of Cotiaeum, 59–60, 92

Alexander the Great, 20, 91, 93, 257

*amor fati* (love of one's fate), 133

anger
    cognitive distancing for, 230
    cognitive distancing from our own judgment for, 240–241
    contemplation of death for, 239–240
    as desire, 229–231
    example of Marcus's response to Cassius's rebellion, 217–227, 248–251
    functional analysis for, 231, 241–242
    human imperfection and, 237–238
    modeling virtue technique for, 231
    nobody does wrong willingly technique for, 235–237
    postponement technique for, 230–231
    self-monitoring technique for, 230
    social nature of human beings and, 232–234
    Stoic cognitive techniques for, 231–232
    Stoic determinism and, 245–247
    as temporary madness, 84
    ten gifts from Apollo and, 232, 245–247
    virtues and, 243–244
    uncertainty of others' motives technique for, 238–239
    whole character of the other person technique for, 234–235

Antiochus IV Epiphanes of Commagene, 220

antirhetoric, 71, 80–81

Antonine Plague, 17–19, 23–26, 59, 86, 113, 128, 156–160, 199, 218–219

Antoninus Pius
    adoption of Marcus, 18, 55–57, 59
    death of, 22, 101, 205, 256
    as emperor, 57–58, 85–86, 100–102
    family home of, 206
    gentleness and patience of, 58–59, 83, 229
    Hadrian compared with, 57–58, 83–84
    influence on Marcus, 20–21, 85, 100–102, 149–150, 161, 229
    Marcus on, 20, 57, 161, 229, 256, 257
    Marcus's education under, 18, 59–61
    named official heir to Hadrian, 55
    *Pius* cognomen earned by, 57

Antoninus Pius (*continued*)
  Roman cultural shift to philosophy
    under, 58–61
anxiety and worry
  cognitive-behavioral therapy for,
    9, 14
  cognitive distancing for, 208
  contemplation of impermanence for,
    208
  coping plans for, 75
  decatastrophizing for, 73–75, 208
  emotional habituation and, 200–205
  existential, 3
  generalized anxiety disorder (GAD),
    211
  inner citadel and, 205–206
  lack of mention of in *The
    Meditations*, 192
  of Lucius Verus, 126–127
  premeditation of adversity for, 199
  reserve clause for, 196–197
  responses to, 63–66
  social anxiety disorder, 7–8
  Stoicism's theory of emotions and,
    63–67
  values and, 7–8
  worry postponement for, 210–213
  *See also* fear
*apatheia* (freedom from harmful
    desires and passions), 62, 145
Apollo, 30, 232, 245–247, 266
Apollonius of Chalcedon, 54, 60–63,
    84, 87, 93, 118, 160–161, 234, 255,
    265
apostrophizing, 79, 142, 173
*apotheosis* (elevation to status of a god),
    119–120
*arete* (excellence of character), 38
Arete, 119
Aristo of Chios, 88
aristocrats, 30, 46
Aristotelianism, 18
Aristotle, 80
Arrian, 37, 48, 55, 85–86
Asclepius, 179

*ataraxia* (freedom from pain and
    suffering), 162
Augustus, 20, 36, 220, 257–258

Ballomar, 191, 198–199
Bandaspus, 188, 189–190, 214
Battle of Carnuntum, 155–156, 165,
    191–192
Baudouin, Charles, 144
Beck, Aaron T., 9, 73–74, 77, 80, 199
Bion of Borysthenes, 179
Borkovec, Thomas D., 211
brotherhood of man, 41
Brown, Derren, 10
Bucoli, 218–219

*caduceus* (magic wand of Hermes), 190
cardinal virtues, 4, 21, 38, 109, 243
  *See also* courage; justice;
    moderation; virtue; wisdom
Cassius Dio, 13, 114–115, 155–156, 226
Cassius, Avidius, 116, 192
  in Parthian War, 126, 127–128
  rebellion of, 24, 217–228, 234–235,
    238–240, 242, 244–245, 247, 251
catastrophizing, 73, 164. *See also*
    decatastrophizing
Cato of Utica, 36, 194–195, 243, 258
Catulus, Cinna, 91
Cerberus, 119
*chara* (inner joy), 131, 133
*charis* (gratitude), 133
*Choice of Hercules, The* (moral fable),
    118–122, 129, 138–139, 149
Chrysippus, 34–35, 55, 63, 89, 99, 110,
    195, 213, 238
Chrysostom, Dio, 180
Cicero, 35–37, 194
Claudius Maximus, 160–161, 265–266
Cleanthes, 34–35, 60, 238
cognitive-behavioral therapy (CBT),
    7–9, 43, 77–78
  for changing desires, 136–150
  divide-and-conquer techniques, 144,
    176

for pain management, 178, 183
Stoicism as inspiration for, 9, 14
worry postponement, 210–213
cognitive distancing
anger and, 230, 240–242
anxiety and, 205, 207–208, 212–213
definition of, 14
desire and, 136, 142–147, 153, 171
Dichotomy of Control (Stoic Fork), 79
*katharsis* (purification) and, 80–81, 171
language (wise speaking) and, 77–81
pain management and, 166,
    168–171, 174
cognitive therapy
decatastrophizing, 73–77, 81, 102,
    204, 205, 208–209, 212–214
definition of fear and, 199
mindfulness and acceptance-based,
    78, 172
mind-reading fallacy, 239
objective representation and, 146
pain tolerance and, 168, 182
philosophical origins of, 9, 73–74,
    144, 146, 168, 172, 182, 199
*See also* cognitive-behavioral
    therapy; cognitive distancing
College of the Salii, 46
Commodus (Marcus's son), 18, 23–29,
    55, 114, 222, 255, 256
appointed official heir and title of
    Caesar, 23–24
Cassius's rebellion and, 24, 224, 251
as emperor, 27–28, 251
Marcus's clemency for Cassius
    ignored by, 251
fear of death by, 26
murder of, 28
*toga virilis* assumed by, 24, 224
cosmopolitanism, 41
cost-benefit analysis, 137
counterrhetoric, 71, 80–81
courage (fortitude), 8, 14, 38–39, 42–43,
    65–66, 120, 133, 138
in Aesop's *The Fox and the Lion*, 201
anger and, 247

as cardinal virtue, 4, 21, 38, 109
*The Choice of Hercules* and, 120
core values compared with, 109
definition of, 39
Freemasonry and, 4
pain tolerance and, 170
in role models, 102
Seneca on, 42, 65
Socratic philosophy and, 8, 30, 38
Stoic acceptance and, 179
Stoic language and, 68
worldly goals and, 182–183
Crates of Thebes, 31
cynicism, 31
Cynicism
Aristo of Chios and, 88
*The Choice of Hercules* and, 120–121
clothing of, 53–54, 56
cold/heat tolerance and, 165
courage and, 93
exposed shoulders and, 54, 56
in history of Stoicism, 31–34
Marcus's mentors, 50–54
plain speaking of, 91, 93
Plato's Academy compared with,
    31–32
Stoicism compared with, 33–34,
    50–54, 93
transparency and, 95
virtue as only true good in, 33–34, 39
voluntary acceptance in, 179–180
voluntary hardship in, 53, 56,
    179–180
*See also* Diogenes the Cynic

D.V. (*Deo volente*, "God willing"),
    195–196
death, meditation on, 253–269
decatastrophizing scripts, 73–77
decatastrophizing, 81, 102, 164
of Agrippinus, 76
for anxiety, 73–77, 208–209
definition of, 73, 204
for fear, 204, 205, 208–209, 212–214
techniques, 73–77

depression, 1, 7, 9, 14, 88, 109–110, 136, 228

desire
  Aesop's *The Town Mouse and the Country Mouse*, 129
  cognitive distancing for, 142–147, 171
  conquering, 129–134
  doing something else technique for, 147–150
  Epicureanism and, 162–164, 168–169, 177
  evaluating consequences for, 137–139
  gratitude and, 133, 136, 151–152
  spotting early warning signs of, 139–142
  steps for change, 135–150
  therapy of the passions, 62, 71, 89, 110, 179
  *See also* pleasure

Dichotomy of Control (Stoic Fork), 79

Dickens, Charles, 108

Diogenes the Cynic, 31–32, 75, 91, 93, 99, 120, 149, 179

Diognetus, 52–54

divide-and-conquer cognitive therapy techniques, 144, 176

double standard, 108, 150, 237

drug use and abuse, 43, 90, 135

Dubois, Paul, 183–186

*elenchus* (Socratic method of questioning), 107–108, 150

Ellis, Albert, 9

*emanes* (you've lost your mind), 217, 221

emotions, Stoicism's theory of, 9, 41–43, 62–68. *See also* anger; anxiety and worry; depression; fear

Empedocles, 197, 267

Epaphroditus, 166

Epictetus, 36–37, 84, 237, 255
  beard of, 126
  cognitive distancing and, 76–81
  on desire, 138, 142–143

*Discourses*, 37, 48, 55, 63, 71, 85, 97, 166, 168–169, 193
  on emotions, 63–64, 66
  *The Golden Verses of Pythagoras* and, 104–106, 110
  on gratitude, 152
  *Handbook* (*Enchiridion*), 37, 48, 79, 85
  "In What Manner We Ought to Bear Sickness," 181–182
  on language, 87, 93
  Marcus's admiration for, 54–55, 85, 99
  on myth of Hercules, 120
  on objective representation, 71–73, 175
  on pain of philosophical training, 48
  on pain tolerance, 166–170, 173–175, 178
  on reserve clause, 193
  on self-awareness, 96
  on Socrates, 93
  Socratic questioning used by, 150
  on Stoic acceptance, 178
  on Stoic philosophy as like the *caduceus*, 190
  Stoicism of, 37, 50–51

Epicureanism, 33, 162–164, 260

Epicurus, 33, 162–164, 168–169, 177

ethical cosmopolitanism, 41

Euclid of Megara, 4, 31

*eudaimonia* (fulfillment), 117–119, 131

Eudaimonia (in *The Choice of Hercules*), 118–119

*eupatheiai* (good passion), 41–42

fairness, 41, 43, 243

Fate, 15, 97, 101, 193–196, 243–244

Faustina (Marcus's wife), 18, 222, 251, 255–256

Favorinus of Arelate, 47

fear
  cognitive distancing for, 208
  decatastrophizing for, 208–210

emotional habituation for, 200–203

example of Marcus's defeat of
  Sarmatian ambush, 187–190,
  204–205, 214–215

inner citadel technique for, 205–208

premeditation of adversity for,
  198–200, 202–205, 208–209,
  212–213

spontaneous psychological change
  and, 203–205

Stoic reserve clause for, 193–197, 213

worry postponement for, 210–213

*See also* anxiety and worry

fortitude, 4, 21. *See also* courage

Freemasonry, 3–6

Fronto, Marcus Cornelius (Marcus's
  rhetoric tutor), 59–60, 67–69,
  84–85, 88, 92, 123, 127, 157–158,
  160–162, 186, 206

functional analysis
  for anger, 231, 241
  for changing desire, 137–139
  definition of, 14
  for pain management, 169, 174

Furius Victorinus, 191

Galen, 19, 89–95, 98–99, 104–105, 110,
  159
  *On the Diagnosis and Cure of the
    Soul's Passions*, 89

Gellius, Aulus, 62–63, 66–67, 240

generalized anxiety disorder (GAD), 211

Gnaeus Claudius Severus, 23

Gnosticism, 4

Hadot, Pierre, 8–10, 53, 72

Hadrian, 18, 20, 22, 45–51, 54–60, 69,
  83–86, 114, 145, 256–257

*Hamlet* (Shakespeare), 71–72

Hanselman, Stephen, 10

happiness, 2, 152
  *The Choice of Hercules* and, 117–119
  desire and, 136
  Marcus and, 130–131

*See also* desire; joy; pleasure

*hedone* (pleasure), 131, 162. *See also*
  pleasure

*hegemonikon* (ruling faculty), 40.
  *See also* reason

Heraclitus, 99, 106, 149, 254

Hercules. See *Choice of Hercules, The*

Hermes, 190

Herodes Atticus, 59, 69, 88, 160, 221

Herodian, 13, 29

*Historia Augusta*, 13, 47, 50, 52–53,
  60–61, 116, 125, 130

Holiday, Ryan, 10

Homer, 98, 261

*hostis publicus* (public enemy), 222

*hupexhairesis* (with a reserve clause), 193

Iazyges, 188, 214

*imperium* (supreme military authority
  equal to that of the emperor in
  his absence), 219–220

*in vitro* (imaginal), 202. *See also*
  modeling strategies

*in vivo* (real world), 202. *See also*
  modeling strategies

injustice, 229–230, 233

*inshallah* (God willing), 195

internet, 10–12, 47, 164
  social media, 117, 135, 142, 144

Isidorus, 219

Jarrett, Thomas, 10

joy, 42, 100–101, 130–134, 151–154, 207

judgment. *See* value judgments

Julia Cassia Alexandra, 220

Julian, 159

Julius Caesar, 36

justice, 38–41, 43, 101, 194–195
  anger and, 243
  as cardinal virtue, 4, 21, 38, 109, 243
  *The Choice of Hercules* and, 119
  core values compared with, 109
  definition of, 38–39
  intrinsic value of, 194

justice (*continued*)
  joy and, 132
  of Marcus, 194
  in role models, 102
  in social sphere, 102, 195, 243, 247
  Socratic philosophy and, 30
  Stoic Sage and, 101
  *See also* injustice

Kakia, 118–119
*katharsis* (purification), 80–81, 171
  *See also* cognitive distancing
kindness, 41–43, 57, 241, 243–244,
    246–247
"know thyself," 3, 89

Laelius the Wise, 35
Laertius, Diogenes, 70, 229
language of Stoicism
  conciseness, 69–70, 78, 108
  counterrhetoric, 71, 80–81
  emotion and, 70–71
  objective representation (*phantasia
    kataleptike*), 71–73, 76, 80–81,
    145–146, 168–169, 175, 204, 209,
    212–214
  objectivity and, 69
  traditional rhetoric compared with, 70
  truth as goal of, 69–70
  value judgments and, 69–73
  virtues of, 70
  wisdom and, 72
Lazarus, Richard, 74–75
learning cycle, 103–111
  evening meditation, 104, 105–106
  morning meditation, 103–105
logic (discipline), 31, 32, 34, 88. *See also*
    reason
Lombardi, Michael, 10
Lucius Aelius, 55, 145
Lucius Verus, 113–117, 121, 124–130,
    134–135
  adopted by Antoninus, 55–56
  Cassius Dio on, 114–115

*The Choice of Hercules* and, 121
co-emperor with Marcus, 56,
    114–115
death of, 128, 191, 220, 256
excesses of, 113–117
in First Marcomannic War, 128
*Historia Augusta* on, 116
Marcus on in *The Meditations*, 116
in Parthian War, 124–127, 218, 258
wife of (Lucilla), 220

Mai, Angelo, 157
Marcomannic Wars, 22–24, 124, 160,
    198–199, 220, 222
  Battle of Carnuntum, 155–156, 165,
    191–192
  First Marcomannic War, 24, 49, 128,
    155, 186, 191, 214, 215, 218
Marcus Aurelius
  adopted by Hadrian as grandson,
    55–57
  anger and, 217–227, 248–251
  assumption of title Caesar, 22
  birth of, 45
  commitment to Stoicism under
    Junius Rusticus, 67–68
  daughter (Lucilla), 113, 126, 220
  death of, 26–27, 29
  death of children, 18
  death of father, 2, 17–18, 45
  death of wife, 18
  defeat of Sarmatian ambush,
    187–190, 204–205, 214–215
  early childhood, 45–46
  early training in philosophy, 50–51
  final days of, 17–29
  as final famous Ancient Stoic, 29
  final words of, 29
  formal study of philosophy from
    Diognetus, 52–54
  generosity of, 49–50
  inner citadel and, 205–208
  many "deaths" of, 22
  military skills of, 187–193, 214

mother (Domitia Lucilla), 18, 45,
   49–50, 53, 56, 59, 256
premeditation of adversity and,
   198–199
resilience of, 20, 21, 23, 56, 155, 206
response to Cassius's rebellion,
   217–227, 248–251
Stoic reserve clause and, 193–197
"Thunderbolt Miracle" of, 192
"The universe is change; life is
   opinion," 208
wife of (Faustina), 18, 222, 251,
   255–256
*See also Meditations, The* (Marcus
   Aurelius)
Marcus Valerius Maximianus, 248
McGeehan, Pat, 10
meditation, 3, 4, 19–21, 225, 248,
   253–269
meditation scripts, 10
Stoicism's morning and evening,
   104–106, 109–110, 154
*Meditations, The* (Marcus Aurelius),
   13–14, 28–29
on Alexander of Cotiaeum (Greek
   grammarian tutor), 59–60
on anger, 227–228, 232–233, 236,
   239, 242, 246
on Antonius, 83, 100
on Apollonius (philosopher), 60–62
catalogue of virtues, 13
on court life, 49
details in, 52
on distaste for pretense, 49
on emotions, 67
on Epictetus, 51, 55, 63, 85
Epictetus as most quoted author in, 37
on Fronto (rhetoric tutor), 59–60
Hadrian's absence from, 57, 83
on inner citadel, 206–207
on language, 87–88, 92
on Lucius, 116
on most-admired philosophers, 99
on pain, 156–161, 163–164, 166, 186

praise for unnamed household tutor,
   51–52
on premeditation of adversity, 198
safeguarding of, 29
on sexual innocence, 146
on social dimension of Stoicism, 41
on Stoic reserve clause, 193–194
on ten gifts of Apollo, 245–246
on virtue, 132, 148–149
on war, 191–192
writing of, 28–29, 96–98
Megarian school of philosophy, 28, 31
mentors and mentoring, 90–98
for attitudes, 103, 110
for behaviors, 102–103, 110
desire and, 141, 153
finding one's, 93
Galen on, 90
honesty and, 94
of Marcus, 50, 81, 84, 90–91, 96, 110
mentoring oneself, 97–98, 106–107
mindfulness and, 95–96, 104–106
models compared with, 87
origin of the term, 98
process of Stoic mentoring, 88–89
*See also* modeling strategies; role
   models
metacognition, 77
mindfulness
mentoring and, 95–96, 106, 110
modern, 172
*prosoche* (paying attention to
   oneself), 104
Stoic, 53, 95–96, 104, 106, 110, 140,
   153, 212, 235
mindfulness and acceptance-based
   cognitive therapy, 78, 172
modeling strategies, 98–110
contemplating role models and ideal
   Sage, 100–103
desired versus admired lists,
   108–109
*elenchus* (Socratic questioning), 107
imagining, 100

modeling strategies (*continued*)
　learning cycle, 103–111
　mental rehearsal of behavior change,
　　103–104
　morning and evening meditation,
　　104–106, 109–110
　values clarification, 108
　writing, 99–100, 102
　*See also* role models
moderation (temperance)
　attachment and, 133
　as cardinal virtue, 4, 21, 38, 109
　definition of, 39
　desire and, 133–134, 137–138
　in eating, 53
　Freemasonry and, 4
　functional analysis and, 231
　of Marcus, 101, 134
　in others, 149
　reason for exercising, 149
　in role models, 102, 149
　Seneca on, 42
　Socratic philosophy and, 30
　Stoicism and, 53, 66, 101, 127, 134
Modern Stoicism, 79
moral wisdom, 30–31, 90. *See also*
　wisdom
Musonius Rufus, 48, 53, 180

natural affection, 41. *See also* affection
Nero, 23, 36, 76, 166
Nietzsche, Friedrich, 133, 183

objective representation (*phantasia
　kataleptike*), 71–73, 76, 204, 209
　for anxiety, 212–214
　for desire, 145–146
　exercises for, 76
　for fear, 175
　for pain tolerance, 168–169
obsessive-compulsive disorder (OCD),
　200
Octavian (Augustus), 20, 36, 220,
　257–258
*Odyssey* (Homer), 98–99

Oracle of Delphi, 3, 30–31, 89
Origen, 166

pain tolerance, 167–183
　cognitive distancing for, 170–174
　contemplating finitude and
　　impermanence for, 176–178
　contemplating virtue for, 181–183
　depreciation by analysis technique
　　for, 175–176
　functional analysis for, 174
　objective representation for, 175
　Stoic acceptance and, 178–181
　Stoic studied indifference and,
　　169–170
Panaetius of Rhodes, 35
*pankration* (ancient sport), 145
*parrhesia* (plain speaking), 52
　*See* language of Stoicism
Parthian War, 124–127, 199, 206, 218,
　220–221, 258
passions. *See* desire
Pertinax, 192, 214
*phantasia kataleptike* (objective
　representation), 72, 145, 169
　*See also* objective representation
*phantasiai* (initial impressions), 63
Philopater, 89
philosophy (ancient world)
　academic philosophy compared
　　with, 53–54
　love of wisdom, 6, 26, 48, 62, 183,
　　259, 266–268
　Marcus's preference for, 48–49, 54,
　　59–61, 67–68, 71, 80–81, 88
　modern applicability of, 1–11
　*See also* Cynicism; Socrates; Stoicism
physicalizing, 177
Pigliucci, Massimo, 10
plague, 17–19, 23–26, 59, 86, 113, 128,
　156–160, 199, 218–219
Plato, 4–5, 18, 60, 89, 261
　Academy of, 31–32, 36
　*Apology*, 5
pleasure

action and, 123, 132
*The Choice of Hercules* and, 117–118, 121
cognitive distancing and, 171
Epicureanism and, 162–164
indifferent nature of, 133, 152, 167
Lucius compared with Marcus regarding, 116–117, 122–130
moderation and, 127, 133–134
pain tolerance and, 167, 171, 176
sensation and, 171, 176
Stoic joy compared with, 131–133
Stoicism's theory of emotion, 42–43
values and, 117, 123–124, 126, 133–139, 142–145, 149–150
virtue and, 127, 130, 132, 134, 150
Pompeianus (Marcus's son-in-law and right-hand man), 23–24, 27, 123, 188, 214, 220–221, 225
*ponos* (voluntary hardship), 51
post-traumatic stress disorder (PTSD), 200
*praemeditatio malorum* (premeditation of adversity), 198–200, 202, 203–205, 208–209, 212–213
Praesens, Bruttius, 23
premeditation of adversity. *See praemeditatio malorum*
problem-solving, 75, 210
Prodicus of Ceos, 118, 129
*propatheiai* (proto-passions), 65, 228, 240
*prosoche* (paying attention to oneself), 104
proto-passions. *See propatheiai*
prudence, 4, 25, 94. *See also* wisdom
psychotherapy, 4, 7–10, 89–90, 142, 144, 179, 200, 203, 205, 228, 232
stoicism in early, 183–186
*See also* cognitive-behavioral therapy; rational emotive behavior therapy
Pythagoras, 4, 99
*The Golden Verses of Pythagoras*, 104–106, 110
Pythagoreans, 105, 231, 266

Quadi, 191–192

rational emotive behavior therapy (REBT), 9, 43
reason
anger and, 225, 231, 241
cognitive-behavioral therapy and, 7
courage and, 42–43
death and, 240, 267
emotions and, 43, 64
enduring hardship and, 183
functional analysis and, 231
inner citadel and, 207
joy and, 153
king metaphor of, 40
of Marcus, 21, 58, 61, 94, 100–101, 105, 109, 207, 225, 240
as ruling faculty (*hegemonikon*), 40, 61
self-control and, 42–43
in Socratic philosophy, 5
in Stoicism, 38, 40–43, 70, 94, 100–101, 105, 109, 138
truth and, 70, 94
value judgments and, 64, 70, 94
wisdom and, 41–43
worry postponement and, 213
reserve clause, 61, 193–197, 213, 243
resilience, 8, 43
in Aesop's *The Boar and the Fox*, 199–200
of Apollonius of Chalcedon, 160
cognitive behavioral therapy and, 14
emotional habituation and, 200–203
learning cycles and, 111
love of wisdom and, 62
of Marcus, 20, 21, 23, 56, 155, 206
objective representation and, 77
social relationships and, 233–234
stress inoculation and, 165–166, 198
Warrior Resilience Training, 10
rhetoric, 46–48
catastrophizing and, 73
desire and, 145
emotion and, 73

rhetoric (*continued*)
hyperbole, 73
Marcus's education in, 18, 51, 54–56, 59–60, 67–68, 88, 92, 116, 157, 160, 162, 221
Marcus's preference for philosophy, 48–49, 54, 59–61, 67–68, 71, 80–81, 88
Second Sophistic, 46, 54, 80
Stoicism's plain speaking compared with formal rhetoric, 48, 69–73
truth and, 127
*See also* Sophistry
rhetoric of pain, 168, 169
rhetoricians, 80
role models
anger and, 229, 231
cognitive distancing and, 143
desire and, 143
fear and, 75
finding one's, 12–13, 99, 101–104, 143
Galen on, 98
for Marcus, 57, 60, 75, 83–87, 99, 149–150, 299
Marcus on, 99
modeling strategies, 99–111
morning meditation on, 104, 153
ourselves as, 149
for youth, 98
*See also* mentors and mentoring; modeling strategies
Rusticus, Arulenus, 84
Rusticus, Junius (Marcus's main Stoic tutor), 81, 84–99
death of, 28, 96–97, 98–99, 192
Epictetus's lecture notes given to Marcus by, 37, 85, 97
influence on Marcus of, 50, 67–68, 81, 84–91, 93–99, 227, 265
mentor for Marcus, 87, 96
role model for Marcus, 87, 149
Stoic plain speaking and, 50
Stoic therapy and, 87, 89, 101–102

Sage, Stoic, 63–64, 101–103, 133, 153–154, 196, 238, 265
Sarmatians, 25, 27
Iazyges, 188, 214
Marcus's defeat of Sarmatian ambush, 187–192, 204–205, 214–215
scholarchs, 34, 35
Scipio Africanus the Younger (Scipio Aemilianus), 35, 257–258, 261
Scipionic Circle, 35
Second Sophistic, 46, 54, 80
self-help, 9–10, 97, 202
Seneca
on cold baths, 53
on emotion, 42, 64–66, 240
execution of, 36
influence of *The Golden Verses of Pythagoras* on, 104, 110
on mentoring, 90
modern applicability of, 184–185
*On Anger*, 64–65, 229
on premeditation of adversity, 198
on reserve clause, 193
rhetoric tutor to Nero, 36
on role toward his students, 32–33
texts of, 37, 64–65, 76, 184–185, 229
Sextus of Chaeronea, 87, 93
Shakespeare, William, 71–72
Skepticism, 5, 35, 47
social anxiety disorder, 7–8
social media, 117, 135, 142, 144
Socrates, 4–8, 11–12, 261
acceptance of death by, 14, 80, 130–131, 259
*Apology* (Plato), 5
barefooted walking of, 54
battlefield peace of mind of, 207
calmness of, 93
*The Choice of Hercules* and, 118
"citizens of the universe" attributed to, 41
on death as prankster, 19
execution of, 5, 30
on external goods, 33–34, 39

history of philosophy and, 8, 30–32, 38

inconclusiveness of, 5

Marcus's admiration for, 55, 99, 100–101

*Memorabilia* (Xenophon), 30–31, 118

as model of virtue, 75, 102–103, 143, 149–150, 153, 231

moderation of, 143

on moderation and self-control, 134

modern applicability of, 4–9, 11–12, 184

on pain, 179

on paradox that nobody does wrong willingly, 223–224, 235–236

on philosophers, 5–6

on Sophists, 46–47

students of, 6, 28, 31

on the unexamined life, 111

on vice and human imperfection, 237

on virtue, 30

Socratic irony, 5

Socratic questioning, 6, 107–108, 150

sophistication, 46, 54

Sophistry, 46–49

Marcus's education and, 54–55, 59–61, 67–71, 80, 87, 88, 221

Second Sophistic, 46, 54, 80

Socrates on, 46–47

Stoicism compared with, 48–49, 51, 54–56, 59–61, 67–71, 87, 162

*See also* rhetoric

Spinoza, 3

Stilpo, 28

*Stoa Poikile* ("Painted Porch"), 32

stoicism, 43

Stoicism

beliefs, 37–44

cardinal virtues and, 38–39

*The Choice of Hercules* and, 120–121

cosmopolitanism (citizens of the universe) and, 41

counterrhetoric of, 71, 80–81

Cynicism compared with, 33–34, 50–54, 93

death and, 26–27, 253–269

emotions and, 41–43, 62–68

good, bad, and indifferent external things, 39–40

history of, 29–37

language and, 69–81

learning cycle of, 103–111

philosophy (love of wisdom) and, 38

sociability of human nature and, 41

Sophistry compared with, 48–49, 51, 54–56, 59–61, 67–71, 87, 162

Stoic acceptance, 170, 178–181

Stoic Fork (Dichotomy of Control), 79

Stoic mindfulness, 104, 140, 153

Stoic Opposition, 36, 84

Stoic Sage, 63–64, 101–103, 133, 153–154, 196, 238, 265

therapy of the passions, 62, 71, 89, 110, 179

virtue as only true good, 33–34, 39

stress

post-traumatic stress disorder, 200

public life and, 195

transactional model of, 74–75

workplace, 140

stress inoculation, 165–166, 198–199

*sunkatatheseis* (assent), 64

Telemachus, 98

temperance, 4, 21, 30, 66. *See also* moderation

ten gifts from Apollo, 232, 245–247

Tertullian, 163

*tetrapharmacum* (fourfold remedy), 145–146

Themistius, 86

*therapeia* (psychological therapy), 62, 87, 110

Thrasea, 36, 85

time projection, 209–210

Titus Aurelius Antoninus, 55

*toga virilis* (toga marking passage to adulthood), 24, 59, 224

*tribôn* (single-garment cloak or shawl), 53–54
truth, 46, 48, 51, 68, 70, 91–93, 95, 236
Twelve Labors of Hercules, 119

value judgments
  anger and, 212, 214, 240, 242
  cognitive distancing and, 73, 80–81, 166
  decatastrophizing and, 73
  emotions and, 43, 64–65
  fear and, 207–209
  language and, 69–73
  objective representation and, 72–73, 145
  pain tolerance and, 170–171, 174
  reason and, 64, 70, 94
  Stoic self-awareness and, 104
  wisdom and, 39
values clarification, 108–110, 148
  desired vs. admired list, 108–109
Verus, Publius Martius, 221
Vettius Sabinianus, 248
Victorinus, Aufidius, 23
Victorinus, Furius, 191
View from above (Stoic technique), 9–10, 13, 176
virtue
  cardinal virtues, 4, 21, 38, 109, 243
  Greek aristocratic view of, 30
  as its own reward, 28, 149
  Socratic philosophy on, 30–31
  *See also* courage; justice; moderation; wisdom
Vologases IV, 124, 218

Warrior Resilience Training, 10
wisdom (prudence)
  appearance of, 47
  as cardinal virtue, 4, 21, 38, 109
  *The Choice of Hercules* and, 119
  cleverness compared with, 48
  cognitive distancing and, 172

core values compared with, 109
death and, 21, 80
decatastrophizing and, 76
definition of, 38–39
emotional resilience and, 62
forms of, 38–39
Freemasonry and, 4
intrinsic value of, 134, 194
joy and, 131–132
language and, 70, 72, 92, 94
love of, 6, 26, 48, 62, 183, 259, 266–268
of Marcus, 18, 21, 60, 130–131, 160, 191, 194
morning meditation and, 105
reason and, 38, 40
reason for exercising, 149–151
of role models, 87, 90, 98–99, 102
social sphere and, 94, 195, 225, 233, 236
Socratic philosophy and, 6, 12, 30, 32
Sophists and, 47–48, 61
Stoicism and, 21, 33–34, 37–43, 48, 66, 130–131, 145, 149–151, 190–191, 225, 233, 236
Zeno on, 33–34, 37
worry. *See* anxiety and worry
worry postponement, 210–213

Xenophon, 5, 11, 256
  *Memorabilia*, 30–31, 118

Zeno of Citium, 29–35, 238
  *The Choice of Hercules* and, 118
  on external goods, 39
  Galen on, 95
  *Handbook of Rhetoric*, 69–70
  history of Stoicism and, 29–35
  as model of virtue, 75, 102–103, 153, 231
  *phantasia kataleptike* (objective representation), 72
  scholarchs, 34, 35
  on wisdom, 33–34, 37